Get Real Website: www.getreal.net.au
Get Real Safety Blog: www.getreal.net.au/safety-blog
Theo Venter's Website: https://www.TheoVenter.com.au
Contact Enquiries: getreal@email.com
Social Media: https://www.facebook.com/KenAndTheo

Book cover and design by Ken Roberts

"Start with Why" and the "Golden Circle" courtesy of https://simonsinek.com

ISBN: 978-0-6485086-0-1

First Edition 1st May 2019
Revised 25th May 2021

10 9 8 7 6 5 4 3 2 1

A Safety Creed

We promote trust and openness as our highest values.

We achieve safety by focusing on our "Safety Mission". The overall Vision and Purpose we have for our work day.

We establish agreements before carrying out any work task. Where the consequences for not keeping them are established in advance.

We hold our own feet to the fire. Supporting each other's accountabilities. No blame or shame if things go wrong. Just voluntary operational discipline.

We underpin our work goals with a mindset and attitude that we can control. Avoiding quantitative numerical targets... those things we cannot.

We speak our minds. There is no status quo. Ownership and autonomy gives meaning to our work.

We strive for continuous improvement in the pursuit of job fulfilment. Job satisfaction allows safety to emerge—in and of itself.

We feel safe; so we act safe. A fair day's work for a fair day's "play".

We should do a risk assessment on our safety procedures.
People are getting a headache just reading them.

The superior man, when resting in safety, does not forget that danger may come. When in a state of security, does not forget the possibility of ruin. When all is orderly, does not forget that disorder may come.

—Confucius (Chinese philosopher & reformer 551 BC—479 BC)

What People Are Saying...

Ken and Theo delivered "Extreme Ownership" to our leadership team and guided work crews to develop a "Safety Mission," which incorporates personal value systems. The result was stronger relationships and higher engagement. I highly recommend you adopt the philosophies in this book. The results being a safer and more productive workplace.
—Sam Francou (General Manager Production - BHP Olympic Dam, SA)

Get Real is a people focused approach and a handbook for business owners who want cultural change. The core philosophy being trusting relationships, which equates to greater safety and efficiency.
—James Robinson (Director, Metrowest Group, WA)

We developed "Safety Missions" across our Rock Drill Maintenance crews underground. Morale improved overnight. The Get Real accountability model creates a better understanding of our expectations. It really works.
—Ben Adams ("Drills" Supervisor - BHP Olympic Dam, SA)

Ken's use of Theo's story to teach an accountability model is a proactive "safety program" that work crews believe in and enthusiastically embrace. My own leadership style has been completely transformed.
—Kenneth Manyumwa (Production Supt. - BHP Olympic Dam, SA)

I was very impressed not only with the approach, but also with the impressive way in which this book was written. Get Real is a deeply intuitive and people focused approach to safety, which from my personal experience, develops an ingrained safety culture and delivers long-term results.
—Peter Leaman (Regional Exploration Manager - Panaust Ltd, SE Asia)

'Ken articulates his ideas and experiences on communicating safety more openly, using Theo's tragic story with craft. It bridges the gap between how work is planned and how work gets done in the field. We did the safety mission process and uncovered "real" values. It has changed the way we approach and deliver safety as managers.
—John Pica (HSE Manager - AusGroup Ltd AGC, WA)

Ken and Theo's Get Real model changed everything for us. Even at the most basic level, ownership and accountability have transformed our perception of safety forever. We use OAR BED to stay focused daily.
—Michelle Ali (Supervisor COVID Sanitisation Team, BHP Olympic Dam, SA)

GET REAL

STAYING ALIVE FOR A LIVING

FEATURING

Just Another Day

The Theo Venter Story

KEN ROBERTS   **THEO VENTER**

CONTENTS

FOREWORD

By Theo Venter

As I reflect on what this book achieves, I can't help but think destiny has played such a huge role. When I first met Ken, he'd been in mining and construction for over forty years. But his involvement in personal development and human sciences meant the pieces of the puzzle had finally fallen into place. I knew one day that someone would be able to put into words what lay *beneath* my story. Those things I couldn't say myself because I thought they were too revealing or controversial. That it might rustle too many feathers. Then it occurred to me. After everything I'd been through, I was still being constrained by old workplace habits. It's time I stopped doing that. Time to speak up and finally Get Real.

For many years after my accident, I had this underlying feeling that I must have somehow been chosen for this. Surely I, and those around me, didn't go through hell and back for nothing. Being a man of faith, I do not say these words lightly. I first spoke about my experience in a room no bigger than my kitchen. Urging small work groups that if they took short-cuts, they'd end up like me. Not very flattering I know. But such was my resolve to make a difference. I had no idea where it would lead. I began visiting factories and mine sites, board rooms and training facilities, taking me all over Australia. Next thing I'm standing in front of packed seminars and conferences around the world. After a while however, I started to feel like I was a spokesperson for industry's failures. A conduit for companies to vent their frustration. I was approached by managers, directors, business owners, HSE people of all sorts. They wanted me to basically communicate the same thing. The consequences of not following procedures.

I was fairly naive when I started out. I used to think not following procedures was why I had my accident too. But the more I spoke, the more I sensed this was the superficial cause. A low-hanging-fruit explanation. There was a much deeper, subtler reason I couldn't put my finger on. Worse still, I wasn't creating the formidable everlasting change that I was looking for. Nothing I said was transforming the way companies went about their business. Sure, I was inspiring them for a while. Except my message would fade. I wanted people to never forget what I went through. There had to be another way.

I decided to start from the ground up, as a Health and Safety advisor. To create change where it mattered most. In the field. Except, I struggled to promote the material I'd lost faith in. The rhetoric from before my accident sounded hollow to me: *zero harm, safety first, all accidents are preventable,* for example. I needed to approach things differently to feel more real. To be more believable. I began to relate my own experience instead. Coaching work crews on a deeper personal level. I told them to forget about safety jargon and catchphrases, and just be more committed to their own sense of values. To be open and willing to share their truth—no matter what. Even if it was confronting to management and leaders. Slowly but surely, they began to reveal work practices that might cause serious injury—or even death. This was "real safety". Heart to heart. And they loved it. We were finally breaking down the barriers to non-disclosure. If only I had benefitted from this kind of coaching before my accident. My life would be so different today.

Eventually, the company I was contracted to said I wasn't following protocol. I had to stop... well, being *real*. Authentic safety was more than they had bargained for. A little too close to the bone. Right there and then, I knew I had uncovered one of the biggest problems facing our industry today. How do you get people to speak up about safety, if they can't say how they really feel? Had our current safety model become its own worst enemy?

As I approach the sixteen-year anniversary of my accident, the day that changed my life forever, I have vowed to offer all of myself to make sure no one goes through the suffering I've endured. I used to think reliving my nightmare to crowds of people would be enough. That somehow, if I reveal enough horror, I'd scare everyone into never taking a risk at work again. But there was an element still missing. I had the 'What' and the 'How'—but was missing the 'Why'. When Ken revealed to me what lies beneath the human condition and what really makes us *tick*, it was like the floodgates had opened up. Those repressed memories and the exchanges I had with people leading up to my accident, came back to me in a wave. As we jotted them down and put the pieces together, we realised we were sitting on something enormous.

Consider a neurologist who contracts a brain disease. They'd be able to share first-hand knowledge of their condition. I too will share everything that happened to me leading up to, during and after my accident. What I felt, what I endured, the voices in my head, the bouts of depression, the low self-esteem, thoughts of suicide. Everything! It's an opportunity to know what it's like to have a near-death experience, without ever having one yourself. What you read in this book is exactly how it happened, captured with the precision of Ken's insights.

I think what I've learned the most throughout this whole process, is that if we continue to promote more of the same in our workplaces, how can we expect the results to be any different? Therefore, I want to leave you with one last thing before you commit to doing your work tasks. When you receive an instruction, check in with your 'higher' self to make sure it is something you agree with wholeheartedly. Does it feel right? If not, tweak it; modify it; talk about it; do whatever you need so that you follow through on that commitment. Simply go back and renegotiate the agreement until it feels 'good'. Whatever you do, be accountable to yourself for carrying out your promise as agreed. Please trust me with this. You'll be thankful that you did. If I had just followed my own advice here, I would not have had my accident. It's true, I promise. This book will show you "Why".

Theo Venter

 # Take care out there

"He who has a WHY for life can put with any HOW."
—Frederick Nietzsche

PREFACE

By Ken Roberts

We all make mistakes. It's what makes us human. But imagine you had to wake up every day living the same ill-fated mistake for the rest of your life. No one knows this feeling more than Theo Venter. We first met on a major mining operation in Western Australia. I was helping a contracting company meet their safety requirements when he presented the most remarkable story I had ever witnessed. A horrific workplace accident that should have taken his life. How he is still here, is a miracle. The only man to survive 22,000 volts of electricity through the heart, and live to tell the tale.

I can tell you it was a profound presentation. I was mesmerised and so deeply moved. We all were who saw him speak that day. Except, something strange happened to me while he was speaking. I had, like... an epiphany! I suddenly realised that all the accidents I had investigated throughout my career, had a common thread to Theo's. I was suddenly exposed to a deeper hidden secret that lies beneath all workplace accidents. Definitely a breakthrough that changed my view of safety forever. Still, what happened next was eerie. Our next assignments took us both to the same remote mining location, on the other side of the country—in the middle of nowhere. Out of the thousands of destinations, spread across three different airlines, and even an overnight stay in the middle, we would be face to face again within the week. How is that possible? I was desperate to share with Theo my experience of what happened during his presentation, and somehow the universe made it happen. Was this coincidence... or destiny!!?

We caught up at the local watering hole as soon as we arrived. We immediately shared ideas and stories of working around Australia and the world. It was inspiring as we talked for hours. Two kindred spirits. Theo shared more of his incredible journey to the brink of death and back. How he was supposed to die and how he is compelled to share his miracle with the world. He revealed that during the deepest darkest moments of his agonisingly long rehabilitation, he received flashbacks of the "red flags" he ignored which led to his accident. The outcome of which, has so drastically changed the course of his life. I shared with Theo what I discovered the day I saw him speak. An insight which explains vividly why he failed to recognise those warning signs. The mood suddenly shifted. "Wow," he exclaimed. "You nailed it, that's exactly what happened." I had captured the moment Theo's gloves were between his knees so vividly, that he was instantly transported back to the thoughts, feelings and more importantly, the motives for taking off his gloves. It became crystal clear what caused his accident. We sat in silence for a while staring at each other. It was a watershed moment. We both realised we had stumbled upon something remarkable. There and then we decided to let the world know of the "real" root cause of incidents and accidents. Together as a team. And here was Theo, actual living proof of our discovery. In the flesh thankfully and not a statistic.

We caution you however, as the title implies, Get Real

pulls no punches. We have an industry crisis on our hands and Get Real will challenge those cherished assumptions you hold so dearly. We offer an alternative to the academics and safety professionals on what motivates voluntary operational discipline, and a self-driven workforce. Having worked at the coalface our whole lives, we've combined both theory and experience. Both book-smarts and street-smarts. Because one is incomplete without the other.

Get Real is a hard-hitting look at Theo's accident, why it happened and how it relates to all accidents. It will challenge common workplace customs and practices and reveal parts of our humanness we rarely examine in the workplace. We offer refreshingly straight talk about what's wrong with the way we think and talk about safety. Firmly believing that we have the right to share Theo's story, warts and all. People need to hear the truth. Even if it flies in the face of our current model of understanding. We won't ask you to put your feet up and relax, but strap yourself in and hang on. Yes, you're in for quite a ride.

Although I say "I" as I write, just know that Theo sits on my shoulder. His presentation, *Just Another Day*, is why I'm able to put my concepts accumulated over forty years, into a book. We hope you get the same *Aha!* moments we received putting it together. We're convinced it's time to speak up and reveal those secret underlying reasons there are still incidents and accidents in your workplace. Very soon you'll discover why speaking up is so essential to our theme. But more importantly, you'll discover how to achieve "real" communication in your workplace for yourself. But you'll need to have an open mind.

Ken Roberts

"Do things worth writing or write things worth reading."
—*Thomas Fuller*

INTRODUCTION

If Theo and I were to justify philosophically all the reasons you should be safe, imploring you to start "thinking" about your personal wellbeing in terms of responsibility and integrity, it's the same tactics companies employ every day. With much the same result. People still take risks and they still get hurt. Why do we continue to 'think' our way through safety issues, when safety may not be a thinking process? What if personal wellbeing includes things like values, how we 'feel', how we respond? Persisting with thinking solutions, hype and rhetoric, expecting they'll create change, needs a re-think!

The "Real" Risk

The problem with our safety today is that no one truly believes in it wholeheartedly. There you go, we might as well just come straight out and say it now. At least not the industries Theo and I are involved with anyway. Beneath the games of charades played out across thousands of pre-shift meetings every day, in secret most workers (leaders too) think safe work practices actually hamper the progress of their activities. Of course, it's not something we shout from the rafters. Certainly not in the safety committees or management meetings we attend anyway. It remains hidden beneath the table. Swept under the carpet. Yet it's why Theo and I called this book "Get Real". We want to bring it out into the open and put it firmly back on the agenda. Not in a shaming way. But as a way of coming clean. So the truth can come out of the closet and we can talk about it openly. When I saw Theo speak for the first time, it hit me right between the eyes. Here I was, a safety practitioner, peddling a system that no one truly believed in. Not 100% anyway. Did I want to keep doing that? The answer is obvious. Who wants to be a salesman that doesn't trust their product? It's this notion, an overall lack of belief in our safety system, that motivates Theo and I to soldier on. Although we're a lone voice in the wilderness, we believe it needs to be addressed.

Living on the Edge

When Theo and I address the workforce and they open up, we hear things like, *"We are already safe,"* *'Workplace safety is too heavy-handed,"* or *"Safety treats us like children."* They don't imagine anything bad will happen as they begin their daily work tasks. Actually, we all do in a sense. It's how I operated when I was on the tools. It's why Theo calls his presentation *Just Another Day*. Workforces are saying they don't deliberately set out to hurt themselves. *"They're just accidents,"* they exclaim. This negation is relevant. It's basically how things get done. Otherwise, fear and hesitation would reign supreme (like it does sometimes). It seems that being "risky" empowers the human race. Or we wouldn't take the "necessary" risks to evolve. We wouldn't leave our homes to cross the street. Or mortgage our properties on a business idea. Risk and reward are the foundations of capitalism. Of all entrepreneurship and enterprise. Pluck and daring are traits we admire and praise. Even more than success. Chance and risk are pivotal to the growth and survival of the human race. Of any species. Yet this same entrepreneurial spirit is being crushed in our workplaces every day, in the name of safety. And it's making life a misery for both leaders and workers alike.

Daring and risk have become dirty words. The big question is, how do we embrace our inherent willingness to live on the edge, yet stay out of harm's way? Especially when it's in our DNA to engage risk. The problem arises when people take risks and emerge unscathed. This rewards risk-taking with a sense of pride. Though I sense it's more about the thrill than the reward. Unless of course you live in a developing country and taking risks is necessary for your very survival. In any case, a couple of key questions emerge. "What is driving people to take risks?" "Why do people sometimes place getting the job done before their own self-preservation and wellbeing? Well, you've come to the right place. You are about to find out.

No More Pleading

This book will challenge the idea that accidents can be avoided if we stop and *think* about them. That if people had carried out fully *reasoned* and *thought* out alternatives, there'd be no incidents. Truth is, you can't change ingrained workplace habits by "thinking" about them. Or by simply issuing instructions. It's impossible. Otherwise we would have solved all our problems by now. The terms "human error", "violations" and "unsafe acts" are outdated catchphrases from the 1940s that continue to dominate the discussion for no other reason than they are "logical, rational" explanations as to why people have accidents. Thankfully, safety research into human sciences and mental processes is at last challenging these beliefs. We are at last beginning to realise that safety is not a set of rules and procedures, but an innate sense of being, a way of life. A feeling.

Get Real is more than just a book. It's a manual that provides a core set of principles and proven strategies to get the best out of you and the people you work with. Do you ever ask yourself: Why do workforces sometimes do the opposite of what's expected of them? Dumbfounding you with their decision-making. Please make a mental note of your answer, or write it down. Because by the end of this book, you'll have a much deeper understanding of why people do anything at all.

We aim to show you practical and enjoyable ways to radically change the way you 'think' and 'feel' about the workplace. So that you can find more meaning and satisfaction in your work. We'll show you how to create firm 'boundaries' with colleagues and leaders, and how clear and concise 'agreements' define ways that work tasks can be carried out safely. Which won't feel like a chore. So leaders don't target an individual's behaviour. But can rely on autonomy and *voluntary operational discipline* instead. You will discover the secrets of accountability, based on establishing up front, the impact of not keeping agreements. Imagine, no more discipline or punitive measures. No more pleading with work crews to be safe. Instead, a sense of purpose and direction driving your safety. Which allows creativity and innovation to do the work for you. Do you even believe it's possible?

An Alarming Trend

If we take the emphasis off individual choice as the root cause of accidents, we start to see what is largely a systemic sociological problem. If not an increasingly disturbing trend. There appears to be a general lack of accountability emerging at the fabric of our society. Think Australian Cricket ball tampering, or Federal Parliament sex scandals. Even "Trumpism" is more predominant than it has ever been. These models are not serving us as examples we should be taking into the workplace. In fact, it teaches the next generation to pass the buck and turn their back on responsibility. The very thing that leads to accidents.

Theo and I believe it's time to shore up our current safety systems by challenging these misconceptions. By employing an accountability model that is refreshing and fun to employ. We'll also leave no stone unturned tackling what are largely taboo subjects. Shattering any myths along the way. Therefore, in the final preamble phase of this book, we feel it is our responsibility to issue you with our *authors' warning*.

> *"Feelings have not been given the credit they*
> *deserve as motivators of human culture."*
> —Antonio Damasio

AUTHORS' WARNING

If you manage or lead a workforce, run a company with staff or contractors, are the head of a business, or supervise people in any way, then this book is written especially for you. If you are a worker, labourer, technician, tradesman, contractor, consultant, or hired to carry out manual tasks or activities in any way, then you are going to get the wake-up call of your life, as you discover the real reasons there are still accidents and injuries in your workplace. Even if you follow procedures religiously, do you truly believe it's what keeps you safe?

Throughout this book we will offer you the viewpoint from either a worker or leader's perspective, and promise that you'll benefit from standing in each other's shoes. The problem is that in either case, work sites every day are being bombarded with myths about what creates an incident-free workplace. The mantra is that workers are safe as a result of immaculate housekeeping and everyone wearing their personal protective equipment (PPE). Or that written procedures and standards should be followed religiously. Or that safe work practices evolve when everyone proactively attends to machinery pre-start inspections and adheres to standard operating procedures (SOPs) without persuasion. Or that the workforce should report hazards enthusiastically, or aim for record low lost time injury frequency rates (LTIFR). Because as we all know, reporting everything as small as a paper cut will improve safety, right?

Well, if you've been in the workplace for a while, you'll agree that there's a kind of *safety weariness* that emerges when workforces continually pursue these nirvana, promised land, incident-free notions. Evergreen assumptions such as "All incidents and accidents are preventable" are starting to wear thin. The pressure on leaders to maintain "zero harm" is possibly contributing to an increase in the erosion of their integrity. In some cases, the pressure is aimed at minimising the impact of incidents on the "books". Lost time injuries are being disguised as medically treated injuries. Restricted work cases are being classified as first aid cases. That is if you can get the injured person to hang around the office while they convalesce. Should injured workers be assigned office duties under the guise of a return to work strategy? Some researchers believe it's time *"to rethink the way we attain progress in safety performance"*. [1] Using statistics to manage humans is probably having a negative impact which is not so easily identified... at first.

Much of the workforce seems divided on what creates a safe workplace. Craig Donaldson's article in the "OHS Professional" (March 2013), "Zero harm: Infallible or ineffectual", features prominent industry professionals from both sides of the fence. [2] Some say the absence of injuries or accidents in a workplace indicates a safe work culture has been established. Others disagree and say there's no connection between an absence of incidents and low incident targets. That their lack of injuries could simply be attributed to luck. Some declare that setting zero harm targets creates an unrealistic expectation, yet others believe it's immoral to do otherwise. Theo and I don't advocate you choose either side. Both views have merit and we'd prefer you to follow the science.

The fact is, no one wants to get hurt, and no one wants an incident or accident. No one! Workers don't deliberately set out to hurt themselves. In fact, they try to avoid discomfort at all costs. That much we can all agree. Yet a great deal of the workforce feel company safety programs are created by people who've never worked a day on the tools in their life. We know this isn't true. But that doesn't explain why workers aren't connecting with safety programs on a level that facilitates their trust and buy-in. The biggest casualty of course is that workers don't have faith in a philosophy that is designed specifically to keep them out of harm's way. The biggest industry concern appears to be the subject of control. "Behaviour" has become a major focus and a lot of resources have been allocated to "behavioural based safety" (BBS). Unfortunately, far less is allocated to uncovering "intrinsic safety values" which might inspire workforces to pursue safe work systems themselves. Rather than forms of manipulation or coercion. Professor Sidney Decker of the Safety Science Innovation Lab at Griffith University believes:

"We Should view people as a solution to harness rather than a problem to control" 3

Tactics to control the workforce creates an underlying tension that contributes in no small way to the rise in mental health issues and possibly the rise in workplace related suicides. OK, so attributing suicide to workplace stressors is quite brazen, but you can't escape the facts. A recent sample of remote mining and construction workers had higher rates of psychological distress than the general Australian community. [4] Therefore, Theo and I want to dispel the "Control" myth. Workplace safety targets, measured in the numbers of mistakes and negative events, must surely be amplifying our workers' personal sense of failure and disappointment. To the degree we seem obsessed with minimising "poor" behaviour instead of maximising "human" behaviour. For *psychic protection* in pre-shift meetings, workers are shutting down and switching off. That glazed look in their eye is not a deliberate lack of engagement, its disillusionment and weariness of the system.

Once beacons of hope, the slogans "safety first" and "zero harm" appear to be losing their shine. Perhaps we should spice them up a bit with an ingredient that's been missing all these years. An important step we've unwittingly omitted from our safety systems. Yet it's a key piece of protocol that would surely instil more trust and belief. Let's simply "Get Real". Surely a smidgeon of authenticity would not go astray. Or worker/leadership relationships based on trust. Perhaps the lost art of making and keeping agreements (accountability) needs to make a comeback. These attitudes seem like foreign concepts in today's workplaces. Yet such attitudes are imperative in terms of creating an atmosphere that promotes:

1) Constructive feedback,

2) Blameless accountability,

3) Ownership of our work tasks, and

4) Being *real* about the "disbelief" in the system"

Theo and I advocate that we should back things up a bit and integrate these "Psycho-technologies" before it's too late. That is, if we want to lift our spirits and ignite some passion back into the workplace. Workers are practical people. They've become sceptical when leaders campaign *safety is more important than production,* then stress the urgency of meeting a deadline. Just witness the last day of a shutdown to see what I mean. Feed-on deadlines can resemble peak-hour traffic. Inconsistent messaging has "hidden" repercussions that surface when you least expect them. Usually in the form of an incident.

This next point might sound alarmist, but behind management's back, workers are not buying into this kind of rhetoric or inconsistent messaging anymore. I know this one first-hand having eaten in lunch-rooms with the workforce for forty years. "Safety first" may be management's oratory on the surface, but it is cancelled out swiftly with dubiously optimistic production targets, or during the franticness of a shutdown. If leaders were to promote safety more genuinely, such as *'Safe Production'* or *'Take Risks Safely"*, they might come across as being more authentic. The point I'm trying to make is this: we either make it more "real" for workers with our messages, or continue to endure the lack of trust they have in our safety.

Lastly, we acknowledge that some workplaces are struggling to cope with a rapidly changing demographic, and face difficulties associated with an increasingly diverse workforce. Race, age, gender, sexual preference, ethnicity, and social background are marginalising workplaces and affecting morale. Traditional stopgap measures that treat the symptoms and not the cause, won't promote more acceptance. The best cure for intolerance is to look into a mirror. I've experienced workforces that simply reflect their own repressed anger. It's their cultural "shadow". But when I point my finger at someone, there are always three fingers pointing back at me. Usually highlighting my 1) blame, 2) excuses and 3) denial.

There's a need to openly promote further discussion in this space, or question whether our current safety model effectively handles gender and preference issues. There's been some discussion recently, and that's a good thing. However, there are many people who want to say more but are hesitant to speak out. It's unfortunate that our current safety paradigm doesn't eagerly foster healthy scepticism of our safety systems. In fact, there seems to be a sense of outrage when anybody challenges the status quo. *"Blasphemer"* they cry. Is it fear of change? We'll let you decide. But it isn't going to stop Theo and I from tackling these hard issues.

Therefore, our authors' warning is this... we are going to challenge existing beliefs and delve into the root cause of accidents using Theo's experience as proof. Besides, who would bemoan Theo his point of view? His accident should not fade away in vain. It's time we lift the lid on why people still get hurt in the face of current safety strategies. We need to "Get Real" about what's happening in our workplaces, beneath the rhetoric and the hype. It's the only way we'll ever touch the truth and get to the heart of the problem. If you are open to new ideas and alternative theories, we'll commit to showing you how we see it—bones and all. All we ask is that you drop your guard. We won't try to persuade or beguile you. But offer a profoundly different perspective. We've created a roadmap for "real" change. *If you always do what you've always done, you'll always get what you've always got.* We promise to reward you for thinking outside the box. So here goes...

It doesn't pay to ignore warnings.
Even when they don't make sense.
—*Debra Doyle*

SECTION I

WHAT

This first section is called 'What' because our aim is to explain things that might be happening currently in your workplace, from a deeper causation perspective. For instance, what really causes workplace accidents? What stresses are thinking solutions creating for your workforce, when it's really their feelings that affect day-to-day decision making? What motivates people to feel they need to get the job done above all else, in the 'heat of the moment'? What drives them to continue when something has gone wrong or conditions change. At what cost to their own health and safety do workers complete tasks in spite of existing rules and regulations.

However, be warned! Theo's accident is not for the faint-hearted. His story and pictures are quite graphic. We provide them here not to confront you, but to illustrate the depth of Theo's ordeal. And to communicate fully how incredible his journey has been.

So without further ado, let's kick things off with Theo's astonishing story.

THEO'S STORY

JUST ANOTHER DAY

It was *just another day*. February 13. Forty-fourth day in the year 2006. A new week begins. It's a Monday. Only three hundred and fifteen days until Christmas. That is, if you're counting of course. For Theo Venter, every day is Christmas. He's on top of the world. A healthy fit South African who landed a plum job as a "Liney" in Australia. Linesman are trades-people who construct and maintain high voltage electric power lines. Travelling to Australia alone at first, he fetched his wife and three kids from South Africa after five months of reconnaissance. They all settled into a lovely home in Perth, Western Australia. It's a beautiful part of the world. Life is good. In fact, it's great. But by the end of this particular day, Theo will be praying if he'll ever see his family again.

Like many Mondays, things kicked off clumsily. Theo's three-man crew are required urgently on a different job to the one they were originally assigned. A transmission pole has been struck by lightning overnight. Normally, a major outage of this kind would require the street's power to be isolated. But there's one stubborn customer who complains. No problem. Rather than create an inconvenience, Theo's team are instructed to fix the damage "live". It's normally a routine task. Of course there's always the risk of electrocution, but with all the safety precautions in place, it's a fairly standard procedure.

So the crew complete their safety risk assessment, like they have a thousand times before. Equipment in good working order, *Check.* Surroundings are safe, *Check.* Personal protective equipment, *Check.* The risk assessment done, it gets thrown through the window into the front seat of the truck. Theo and Nico, the most experienced lineys, are raised in the cherry picker. Leaving the third crew member on the ground as the safety observer. Things are going smoothly up in the basket and they are making good progress. That is until Nico comes across a tricky insulator. One fiddly twelve-millimetre nut is making things impossible. Not only is the sun heating up, but so are frustrations. How on earth do you reach into a tiny little hole, wearing thick heavily insulated protective gloves, to undo a nut the size of your thumb nail?

Nico gives up. He asks Theo to have a go. Whenever a job gets tough, you always give it to Theo. Mister Fix-it. The Go-to guy. Except this time Theo isn't able to do much better and struggles as well. But failing is not an option for Theo. It's not in his make-up to quit. Everyone relies on Theo to get the job done. Why should this time be any different?

A few Ideas enter his mind. He could lower the basket.

Call the boss. Go back to the yard and make a special tool. He could tell the customer they have no choice but to isolate the streets power, so he can remove his insulated gloves and remove the nut easily. *"How are other crews doing this?",* he puzzles. And then Theo recalls something that he's seen before. So while Nico is turned away observing the view, Theo clamps his gloves between his knees and withdraws his hands. Quietly, so Nico doesn't catch on, he reaches in and has free access to that stupid nut. It makes the job so much easier. The nut practically falls off. Theo feels a sense of relief, and a tinge of pride. He's beaten that impossible task. Then suddenly, without warning, the whole insulator begins to fall. Theo senses that his workmate below is about get clobbered. Unconsciously... instinctively... he lunges out to catch it!!?

⚡ S-M-A-C-K ⚡

Theo's left wrist makes contact with the power line. 22,000 volts rip through his body like a collision with a Mack truck, travelling at two hundred kilometres an hour. A bolt of lightning consumes his entire body. Raw electricity roaring through his veins. Every muscle distorts in a massive contorted spasm. *"I felt everything. I remember each and every second,"* Theo recalls. *"People say you block it out, but you don't."* The electrical force, looking for an exit point, rushes to Theo's right wrist which was resting against the metal cross arm. His left hand which contacted the power line is instantly disfigured for life. And then a miracle. At about two and half seconds, suddenly, somehow, Theo breaks contact with the beast. He falls back into the basket at Nico's feet. Nico thought Theo was dead, but kept his cool. All those years of training had primed him for this. He lowers the basket as fast as he can, with Theo's body smouldering and contorted on the floor. Unexpectedly, Theo regains consciousness half way down. His blood is literally boiling. Bones and flesh are smoking. Theo panics at the stark realisation that he is still alive. Then the screaming starts...

On the ground, cold water flushes and first-aid do nothing to ease the agony. Theo is literally cooking from the inside and he knows it. In a semi-unconscious state, he recalls all those training videos and a visit to his mate who died from an 11,000 volt hit. Theo visited him straight after his accident. But the next day—infection got him. No one survives a massive electric shock like that. No one. It will only be a matter of time and he will be dead too. In the ambulance journey to the hospital, Theo imagines what his wife will say. He promised he would always be careful. He swore he'd never end up getting zapped like his mate. But she is inconsolable when he arrives. Banging at his chest in anger she screams, "What have you done, what have you done?" They take her away, devastated.

Immediately doctors slice open Theo's arms to relieve the massive inflation. Then, antibiotics are pumped into him by the truckload. After a while, things calm down. There's a pause in the commotion. Theo wants to see his children. He pleads with the doctors. But they warn of the trauma they might experience seeing their father like this. It could have devastating long-term psychological effects. He's advised not to see them. For Theo, this is a fate worse than death. The one thing he can't survive. He wants to hug them and tell them he's sorry. More than living itself. He doesn't care about the smell, the disfigurement, the burning flesh. He doesn't care about the excruciating pain. He doesn't care if he loses his arms. But there's one thing he will never endure. If he somehow survives this disaster, can he ever be a good father again?

The thought of missing out on his children's love is more painful than his injuries. More depressing than his condition. Theo lies exhausted in a semi-comatose state. Drained equally from the mental anguish as much as his situation. The room is empty. There's only the sound of life support machines and the stench of charred flesh. Is this it? Is this how it ends? Theo lies in wait. But this is not how things were supposed to go. What on earth happened? *"What have I done to my family?"*, Theo gasps. This awful truth shocks him into considering his worst nightmare...

"Will I ever be able to take my kids to the park again. To sit on a bench on a bright sunny day. To watch my beautiful little princess dance around in her favourite dress, as she stops and smells the flowers. To watch my sons, play-fighting in the grass the way best friends and brothers do. What have I done?"

"It does not do to leave a live dragon out of your calculations, if you live near him."
—J.R.R. Tolkien

"Hello Australia." The last photo of Theo's arms intact. Immediately after his family's arrival in Australia. Theo left South Africa five months earlier. The longest length of time he'd not seen his children.

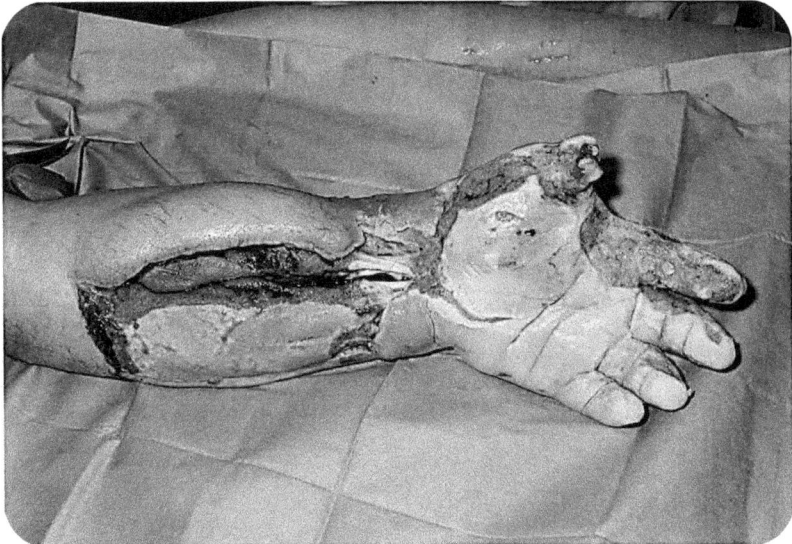

Theo's wrist was resting against the metal cross-arm when his other arm contacted the power line. A rush of electricity exploded from Theo's arm and hand as it searched for a way to earth/ground.

DEAFENING SILENCE

Theo had worked the lines for 17 years. Never even came close to getting "zapped". No incident, no injury, no close calls, zilch. In fact, you might say he had a rather unremarkable life. Yet his experience was vital for Theo's company, and they needed more good people like him. He was confident, knowledgeable and good with his team. It's why they made him a Leader. During Theo's presentations he is often asked, 'But Theo, why would you remove your insulated gloves?' His answer is astonishing and challenges what you'd expect to hear. Yet as his story unfolds, it is critical in understanding human nature (not behaviour), and why incidents occur, even when given the right circumstances—you truly believe they should NOT.

Skinny

When Theo speaks to audiences today, one of the most shocking revelations down to every last person in the room, is that not even a week before his accident he witnessed something he's never seen in all his years as a liney. The previous Wednesday, while keeping an eye on things from the ground, Theo looks up and notices Skinny, a big Maori guy, has taken off his insulated gloves. Skinny was having problems removing a nut from an insulator (ring any bells?). Theo freaks out, "What the hell Skinny, put your gloves back on—NOW!" To Theo this is incredible. Thousands of volts of electricity up there and Skinny takes off his insulated gloves. Sheesh!

Skinny yells something down to Theo which has reverberated in his mind a million times. "Sorry bro, but hey, let's just keep this between ourselves, OK?" It was in a tone Theo didn't particularly like. Kind of intimidating. Theo ponders, "Just what exactly did he mean? Is he asking me, or telling me?" Regardless, Skinny made it clear he wanted the matter to go no further. Skinny had only been in the game five months, arriving on a 457 visa like Theo. This visa allowed companies to sponsor workers from overseas. So it wasn't like either of their jobs were cast in stone. Theo must decide if he is prepared to rock that boat. It's a question he'll wrestle with for the rest of his life.

When Theo's audiences learn about Skinny removing his gloves, there is a sense of confusion in the room as they try to reconcile the illogical connection to Theo's accident. That Theo did the same thing, less than a week later, belies comprehension. There is a collective feeling of "What the...?" in the room. Yet the next piece of information floors audiences even more. Their astonishment is about to turn into a colossal "Oh no!"

The Meeting

It goes like this... just two days after the Skinny episode, a guy in a wheelchair arrives at Theo's workplace and presents one of the most heartfelt stories he's ever experienced. Everyone from work was there. Skinny, the crew, managers and supervisors. The whole workforce. Even the admin girls. They all witness an amazing story of survival. A tragic workplace accident that resulted in the guest speaker being condemned to a wheelchair for life. He appeals to his audience to never take risks and follow procedures, brandishing his disability as the tragic consequence of his actions. It's an inspiring talk. Theo immediately considers the burden this must be to his family. He silently makes a promise that he'll never end up like this guy. Theo went up and thanked him afterwards. Everyone did.

This is when Theo's presentation takes on a new twist. His audiences are perplexed. The irony melting their senses. You can carve the air it's that thick with confusion. People either frown at each other in pure disbelief, or gaze into space. "Geezuz Theo. Please don't tell us you witnessed a guy present a story of survival, a tragic workplace accident that resulted in permanent disabilities, then only three days later you have a tragic accident that leaves you with permanent disabilities too?" This is overload for some audience members as they struggle to come to terms with the paradox. The bewilderment and scepticism too much to comprehend. Then slowly comes "THE" realisation. Could an audience member witnessing Theo's talk possibly end up doing a similar thing? For most people what's difficult to fathom, is that the very conduct Theo scolded Skinny for, he actually perpetrated himself—and it came close to killing him.

The Manager

But just when you think you've heard it all, there's more. What you are about to learn is the single most important discovery of Theo's life. Why he believes he went through hell and back to share this lesson with the world.

So here it is…

After the wheelchair presenter finished speaking, Theo's manager stands up and thanks him for his courage. He turns to his staff, inspired by the presentation and delivers what he believes is the most important question he could ask. He may never get a chance like this again. "OK everyone. Let's consider if there are any activities we perform out in the field, that could potentially lead to a tragic life-threatening situation like our guest?" "Is there anything we need to improve and possibly prevent a tragic incident—or loss of life?"

There's a deafening silence! You can hear a pin drop in the room. Theo shifts uncomfortably in his seat. Skinny's transgression churning in his stomach. Pulse racing. He feels a burning sensation in his back. Skinny and the crew are seated right behind him, fretting on what Theo will do. The manager pleads again, "Come on team, there must be something you've seen that we can change and possibly avoid a major accident." "We owe it to our guest here." Again, there's an eerie silence! No one says a thing. Not Theo, not Skinny, not the guys, no one!

BANG!

Right there. That's when Theo's accident really happened. That's when Skinny, Theo and the work crew's underlying workplace culture, facilitated a tragedy. That's when Theo's family really had their hearts torn out. That's when the company shut down for weeks pending the investigation. That's when millions of dollars were spent trying to restore dignity and normality into Theo's workplace. That's when a man's life hung on the line. A fatality in waiting. It was only a matter of "when", right? Or was it?

Perhaps Theo's accident really happened a couple of

days earlier when he couldn't decide if he should do anything about Skinny's indiscretion. Removing your insulated gloves wasn't anything Theo had witnessed before. Yet in the heat of the moment, when Theo was up in a basket himself, it was his own alter-ego, *"Mr. Get The Job Done"*, who thought he'd give the "gloves thing" a try. I know it sounds illogical and irrational. And I can sense a hint of disbelief as you read this. I struggled to understand it too—at first! But I realised that this is exactly how humans work. They are illogical, irrational, contradictory! That's why logical, rational safety models aren't solving this problem. It really needs a paradigm shift to truly understand what's going on in these situations.

Gradual Cultural Creep

We like to imagine that we can pinpoint the root cause of any accident. Timelines and "5 Why" processes methodically investigate every step leading up to the point of impact. Yet it's more likely that the root cause of Theo's accident lies in years of cultural encroachments. [5] Perhaps people were removing their gloves way before Theo's company did. Just how did they remove that nut? Who knows? But one thing is certain, it's never what happens in the moment, or near it. There is always a series of values and beliefs that underpin any action or inaction in an accident.[6] Theo and Skinny's silence spoke volumes about their culture. Where suppression and non-disclosure, for whatever reason, ultimately won the day. Sadly, openness and disclosure was the loser.

And what about the Manager? For a leader to communicate real value and be authentic in the workplace, they must understand that their workforce is more than an organisational function. More than the study of human behaviour even. It's about understanding "human nature". Absent a trusting environment where people share their thoughts and feelings about the workplace, the manager is relying on a wheelchair-bound safety presenter for inspiration. Much like companies rely on Theo's *Just Another Day* presentation. Whereas, the workforce needs trust and a sense of empowerment before they'll communicate how they "really" feel. Even then, they struggle to put their emotions into language and words, preferring to bottle things up (like we all do sometimes). There's so much more to human communication than words. Subtle facial expressions and body language, or the simple discharge of energy, will signal something is awry. Without receptiveness of these cues, we barely touch the surface of what's really going on underneath. Especially if the highest workplace values are NOT trust, openness, inclusion and disclosure. If not having an accident is more important than a person's wellbeing, we turn to statistics and traditional safety gestures. Such as leading and lagging indicators. Unfortunately, we miss key "human" signals in the process... which this book will provide you the skills to do.

A Culture of Trust and Openness

Feeling the crew, means sensing the *frequency* of the room. Theo's manager might not have known the underlying cultural temperament of his staff. Nor Theo and Skinny's nervous energy as they sat there silently. But it must have been palpable. Theo likens his sitting there frozen and tense, wondering what to do, as one of the strongest body feelings he's ever experienced in his life. Perhaps there was something in the air and why Theo's manager posed his very important question. Whatever the reason, if the frequency in the room is not conducive to openness and disclosure, cultivated over years of practice and implementation, no amount of coercion will elicit the participation required to effect cultural change. The point I'm making is this. You cannot leave it to a wheelchair presenter, or even Theo's *Just Another Day* presentation, and expect work crews to divulge important life-saving information. No matter how powerful the performance. Culture is a character, a trait, an ethos, a philosophy. It requires intention and a commitment to openness that rivals any company mission. Yet I've never seen "Openness" or "Disclosure" listed in any company values. Never in forty years!

It took Theo a while to work this one out. For years he felt his presentation struggled to have the ever-lasting effect he craved. Then the penny dropped. His clients were relying too heavily on his message to create the culture they desired. He realised it was incumbent upon his clients to already have an established trusting relationship with their workforce before his presentation could elevate their culture to the next level. Companies tried to use Theo's presentation to bridge the gap. But then he wasn't just presenting his own story anymore. Somehow he'd become the poster child for a larger industrial crisis. What a burden. Should one man shoulder the responsibility for an entire industry's safety culture?

So what are the "spoken" or "unspoken" values your company embraces? If it is not openness, trust, inclusion or disclosure, how do you expect anyone to speak out about anything? We tell our workforce they have the right to stop a job or speak up every day. But they never do. In vain we might print little business cards that say, *"You have the right to stop the job"*, and expect this will somehow encourage people to speak up. A "logical" solution for an "emotional" problem. Except, never the twain shall meet.

Very shortly we'll reveal the solution to people not speaking up about safety. But before we do, we need to get to the heart of this issue and understand what makes people tick. In the next chapter we discuss why it's *human nature* to take risks.

"The most important thing in communication is hearing what isn't said."
—Peter Drucker

IT WON'T HAPPEN TO ME

Consider the wildebeest of the Serengeti. Dicing with death is a part of everyday life. Annually, they run the gauntlet across crocodile infested waters during the Great Migration. The herd know what besets them as they cautiously approach a torrential riverbank. Instinctively, they can sense the danger. Yet inexplicably, they thrust themselves into the rapids anyway. It seems to be a chance worth risking given the numbers. There are millions of them. Unfortunately, many unlucky creatures are snared in the jaws of hungry crocodiles. So what on earth are they thinking? Well, not much apparently.

Just Get the Job Done

Creatures like the wildebeest are driven by an ancient primal urge (emotionality) which overrides any common-sense thinking (rationality). It's nature at work. Even though many wildebeest become crocodile food as they cross dangerous rivers, it's nothing compared to the numbers that survive. The *odds-of-survival* gene is passed onto the next generation... and so on, and so on. It's a massive leap of faith as part of the cycle of life (habits). It appears that taking risks is a habit, as much as it is an instinct. Humans are no different in this respect.

People thrust themselves into work tasks, just to get the job done—every day. If nothing goes wrong, the *odds-of-survival* gene is reinforced and they are more likely to do it again. Out of practice/habit. But with less fear next time, as the risk becomes normalised.

So why do I compare humans to the wildebeest? Well, specifically, the same risk/reward function is hard-wired into both of our brains. Remarkably, we also share these features with sixty-nine thousand other vertebrates as well. [7] In an ancient neurobiological structure called the Brainstem. [8] The conviction that *"It won't happen to me"* resides deep within this very primal process. Which triggers our autonomic responses. [9] For instance, at opposite ends of the scale, this part of the brain will facilitate either fight/flight/freeze, or sleep/support/succumb. It's no wonder we are confused about what drives our everyday responses in the workplace. These seemingly opposite reactions are really two sides of the same coin. Coming from the same patch of grass: Our Brainstem, the "Habitual" brain.

Yet, we're far more evolved than the wildebeest, right? We are blessed with logic and reason. We are intelligent, yes? Well, maybe. Although self-preserve appears to be a logical explanation, it's not actually a *thinking* process. Risk and reward is not a rational concept or idea. Pleasure and pain is not a thoughtful experience. They are fundamentally hard-wired reactions, evolved over the history of biology, to protect organisms against perceived threat to their integrity or existence. These are feelings dictated to us by the brain's "pleasure centres". [10] Wildebeest and humans alike. Pleasure centres send a biochemical concoction throughout our bodies that signal to us if we are in danger—or not. These same impulses signal if we are on track with our purpose. Either a Wildebeest crossing the plains of the Sahara in search of greener pastures, or a homo sapiens trying to find a cure for cancer. Natural teleological drivers emerge from an ancient primordial sense of purpose that overrides the fear of risk. Without risk-taking, nervousness and fear would ultimately consume us. It is our inherent need to find durable fulfilment which gives us the drive to take risks to survive.

Stop and Think, or Follow Your Heart?

We are rarely in a state of poise. It's nigh on impossible to fight against feelings of fear or anxiety. Even though we wish we could. We simply can't shut down our impulses and feelings whenever we want to. Why? Because *feelings* are an independent fabrication of the brain. Feelings function as a result of a cooperative partnership between both body and brain, [11] whereas thinking is purely a mentation process. It's no wonder we default to thinking solutions in our workplace. They are so much easier to deal with. Consider this. There are three separate parts of our brain:

1) The *Rational* brain (Neocortex = logic, rationale).
2) The *Emotional* brain (Limbic system = feelings, emotions).
3) The *Habitual* brain (Brainstem = responses, instinct).

These three brain functions are tasked with specific duties: [1]Thinking, [2]Feeling, and [3]Habits. Feelings of pleasure or alternatively, states of frustration, are a combination of [2]*Emotional* brain and [3]*Habitual* brain functions. Not [1]*Rational* brain. Although rational thinking can sometimes trigger emotional responses. Confused? So was I at first. Until I discovered that feelings of either relaxation or frustration, are both the result of stored patterns of behaviour deeply rooted in a bionetwork of ingrained habits. They are steeped in risk and reward, pleasure and pain cycles. That's why habits feel compulsory to us when they happen. And why we don't engage in self-analysis when they take over our work routines. They simply operate automatically. The big question is; how can we change a habit—that ignores safety—when we don't even know we are doing it? Well, unless safe work practices are akin to a sense of pleasure, we'll continue to carry out our activities only ever trying to avoid pain (safe-work inconveniences). Short-cuts are really a normal response when there's no sense of purpose or pleasurable feeling enticing us to do otherwise. Something that inspires us to roll up our sleeves and carry out safe systems of work, because there's a sense of satisfaction in doing so. Otherwise, safety will "feel" like a chore. A right pain in the butt in most cases.

Convenience IS the Enemy

Are you starting to get the picture? Safety has to *feel* pleasurable, not irritable. Or our pleasure centres will simply resist safety efforts. Unconsciously or otherwise. The main issue is that we have to apply some elbow grease to be safe. Quite often, safety is just hard work. So the convenience (pleasure) our brain seeks, is countering the effort (pain) it takes to be safe. If safety is to win this battle, we must reward safe work practices in a way that celebrates the hard work it takes to be safe. It's that simple. Yet herein lies our dilemma. Workplace *safety* asks us to *"stop and think"*. Try and tell that to the wildebeest as they approach the riverbank. Not likely. The wildebeest are driven by a herding instinct that says "act now". A much deeper sense that if they risk their life, harm will probably not come to *them* given the odds. What is a worker thinking when they feel the urge to "act now". Use a chair or go back to the workshop and get a ladder. If a ladder was immediately accessible, it's a no-brainer (excuse the pun). But in the heat of the moment, "convenience" will always trump any other choice if it takes more effort to find a safer alternative. Unless some other motivation to go and get a ladder is more convenient than the possibility of injury, we are fighting an uphill battle. Because most workers believe like the wildebeest, harm will probably not come to *them* given the odds.

We believe somehow that *logic* controls our behaviour

in the heat of the moment. But unfortunately, thinking isn't what makes people act safe. Feelings do. We are trying to solve safety issues with the wrong brain. Safety is not the Rational brain's domain. Safety is rooted in the Emotional and Habitual brains. How do we know this? Because our unconscious is giving us a clue when we say, "I *feel* safe." No one ever says, "I *think* safe!!?" We tell our kids to use their heads (thinking), but really we want them to *follow their hearts* or *trust their gut* (feelings/habits). Therefore, we won't stop incidents and accidents solely through thinking solutions. Not without undergoing a completely different process, which you'll soon learn in this book.

At the risk of confusing you more, I'm not saying the answer lies in how we feel. In fact, it's our feelings that are causing the problem. I'm saying the solution is in providing our "Feeling" brains (Emotional and Habitual), with an entirely new focus, an entirely new mission... a *Safety Mission*. There needs to be a sense of reward for carrying out work practices that are aligned with the Emotional and Habitual brain's pleasure centres. To create a sense of pride and satisfaction. Managing risk should include safety goals that deliver a pleasurable sensation. By creating a sense of purpose around safety, it challenges the "Rational" brain's belief that safety is a hindrance. What? Safety a hindrance!!? Yep! That's right. We are in a constant battle with ourselves. A never-ending struggle between Rational brain and Emotional brain objectives.

The War of the Brains

The Rational brain and the Emotional brain both believe they are running the show. But the Emotional brain has a trump card. It has "total control of your body". So the best way to create safety is to appeal to our pleasure centre in a language it understands. And that language is *Purpose, Mission, Values* and job *Satisfaction*. The term *"Use your head"* is associated with behaviour (thinking and logic), but *"Follow your heart"* is associated with passion and purpose (values and emotion). Which one inspires workers more? That's a loaded question of course. But crucial to understand.

This interpretation is critical to bridging the gap between safe work practices and a workforce who's not buying into your safety philosophies. You do have a safety philosophy don't you? If not, your workforce will be making up their own. And it won't be pretty. Until now, companies have struggled to communicate to the workforce in a way that their Emotional brain understands and buys into. This book's entire premise is built around setting targets and goals in a language the Emotional brain understands. Avoiding numerical and quantitative targets and goals (zero harm or injury statistics). If safety is a *feeling* problem, then quantitative numerical targets is like hammering a square peg into a round hole. When you're holding a hammer, everything looks like a nail.

Driving Force

I know it's ironic, but we need to forget about safety for a while. Our sense of self-preserve and the conservation of our wellbeing is directly proportionate to the levels of personal satisfaction we have in our workplace. Not safety. Our work tasks must necessarily adopt a higher ideal than our own self-preserve. That is if we are to achieve a higher degree of safety. A sense of teamwork can create a feeling that we are part of a greater cause. A sense of pride can create engagement and enthusiasm. That's why Mission and Purpose are the single biggest motivators to humankind. These principles reside deep within our being, evolving through thousands of years of survival in clans. It's the Emotional brain's influence again. Throughout the ages our feelings of self-worth necessarily revolved around pitching in and assisting the tribe. If you didn't pull your weight, you were shunned from the community and your chances of survival were greatly diminished. Let alone your yearning to belong.

We've been working together as a species to achieve great things, since the dawn of humankind. Throughout the Bronze Age, the Agrarian Age, the Industrial Revolution, Space Exploration, the Tech Age, etc. The construction of the Great Pyramids, the Great Wall of China or Angkor Wat for example. Incredible human feats are endless. The sense of pride that is cultivated in coming together for these achievements cannot be underestimated. Pride is a powerful motivator. Unfortunately, so is shame. Except, more like a DE-motivator. Both states of being have completely opposite outcomes in our workplaces. Which one is driving your safety? Shame or pride?

Theo and I believe there's a need to reconsider our safety systems from this perspective. That we can't solve our problems through purely 'rational' concepts. Emotional intelligence has to be in there somewhere. Especially because it's emotions that affect our safe work decision-making. Not rationality. Truth is, the workplace is full of irrational, emotionally unstable human beings. We don't act rational at all in stressful situations. None of us do. We are ALL irrational, ALL emotional. I suspect this news will hit safety policymakers the hardest. They may have to acknowledge that the mountains of procedures generated over the years, has been aimed at the wrong part of the brain. Having written countless procedures myself, the emphasis was always on rationality: regulatory compliance, conventions, rules, processes etc. Not exactly concepts that get the blood pumping. But when I introduced *humanness* into my technical writing, people started to absorb them more sincerely.

I 'Feel', Therefore I Am

Antonio Damasio, the famous neurobiologist, discovered that emotions play a critical role in high-level cognition. [12] It's an idea counter to the 20th-century view on emotion, reason and the human brain. René Descartes, the French philosopher who coined, *"I think therefore I am,"* may have sent us down the wrong path for over four hundred years. We are only just now starting to realise that, *"I FEEL therefore I am"* is actually a more apt description of what's really going on. Damasio made a ground-breaking discovery while studying people who have damage to the part of the brain where emotions are generated. He found they all have something very peculiar in common. They can't make decisions. They can describe what they "should" do in logical terms, but they found it impossible to make even the simplest choices. In other words, we may use logic (Rational brain) to reason ourselves toward a decision, but the actual "Decision-Making" is governed by feelings (Emotional brain). Our workplaces are missing this vital ingredient... an "emotional connection" to safety. That is, the incentive to undertake work activities safely, based on the expected satisfaction it provides. Otherwise known as, "Intrinsic Motivation". 13 This is the real issue. Lack of buy-in. If we matched our efforts to control risk, with the same focus on a sense of personal fulfilment in doing things safely, would we not have safer workplaces?

In the next chapter we are going to discuss the science of safety further. How we think, act and communicate. And what works and doesn't work when we design our safety programs.

"Everything happens for a reason, the hard part
is finding out what that reason is."
—The Alchemist by Paulo Coelho

INSIDE-OUT SAFETY

Nico turns away, so Theo slides his hands out of his insulated gloves and clamps them between his knees. Immediately, voices enter Theo's head. "Don't do it Theo, your training says NO." Then instantly another voice arrives, "No problem, I know what I'm doing." Suddenly, a menacing growl barks, "Hey it's hot up here, get on with it will you." With all these thoughts, Theo must make up his mind. Because he's going to get that nut off right or wrong. What is driving him at this point? This is the moment of truth for a million incidents. Why does anyone do what they do—in the 'heat of the moment'? Answer this question and you've cracked one of the greatest workplace riddles known to man.

The Billion Dollar Question

How come *getting the job done* causes so many accidents? Surely, knowing the answer to this one question would go a long way towards fixing workplace accidents. In fact, in one of my roles, I interview work crews immediately after an incident. Once I've created their trust, we talk about what was on their mind just prior to the point of impact. The same story emerges time after time. In the *heat of the moment* there is an overbearing voice which says, "Come on, let's just get this job done." It trumps any safety oratory or safe work procedure. Split-second decisions default to the most convenient option or short-cut. Whether it's right or wrong doesn't seem to matter. There are no thoughts of impact, of long-term consequences or potential injury. As Theo slipped his hands out of his gloves, there is no flashback to the wheelchair guy or the manager's plea. It's a phenomenon really, and confounds safety professionals no end. The awareness that things might not turn out so well is overridden by an incredible impulse to finish the task. I can put up my hand and admit that I am susceptible too. We all are. What? You've never exceeded a speed limit or made a U-turn at an intersection? You've never negotiated a pedestrian cross-walk while the animated man was still flashing red? Of course you have. There seems to be a fundamental principal at play here. An impulse to get the job done that overrides procedures and downgrades risk. Why don't people simply follow procedures? Answer: They aren't motivated by procedures. Nor by the threat of punishment for not following them. So what are they motivated by?

The IOS Model

In his book "Start With Why", Simon Sinek explains that depending on how we translate information, defines the way we *think*, *act* and *communicate*. He draws three circles inside each other, calling it the Golden Circle. Then he labels each circle starting from the inside-out with *Why*, *How* and *What*. Sinek explains that our effectiveness is greatly enhanced when we operate from the inside-out, starting with 'Why', not from the outside-in starting with "What". [14] The amazing thing about this model is that it's not just conjecture. It's real. It's not human behaviour, but human biology. The *Why, How* and *What* model corresponds exactly with the three major brain functions I introduced in the previous chapter: *Rational, Emotional* and *Habitual.* A cross section of the human brain looking down from the top reveals that the *neocortex, limbic system* and *brain-stem* line up exactly with the Golden Circle.

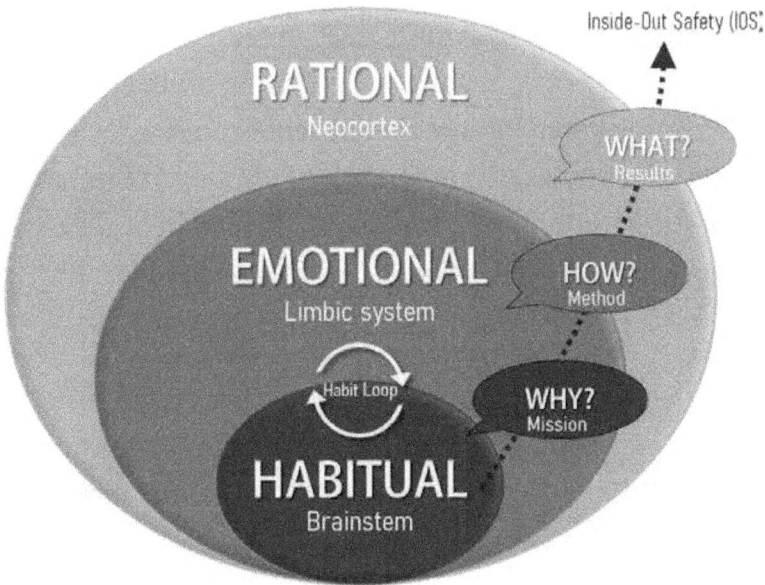

Diagram 1— Inside Out Safety (IOS)

It's an extraordinary breakthrough and encompasses a wide variety of applications. When you apply the Golden Circle in a safety context, following an instinctual biological pathway, you discover why some organisations generate safe workplaces and others don't. It explains why safety will emerge when our motivation starts with 'Why', a sense of purpose. I've called this version of the Golden Circle the IOS Model, like the Apple iPhone operating system. To suggest that "Inside-Out Safety" (IOS) is a *mind operating system.* Each region of the IOS Model corresponds with the three functions and characteristics of the human brain. These functions each have their own purpose, agenda and even a personality. Just like people do, for obvious reasons. Diagram 1 on page 26 illustrates the relationship between the three functions. Unfortunately, if we only focus on "What" we do (the results), more than "Why" we do it (our mission), the "How" (process) is misled and *getting the job done* overrides doing things safely. This is outside-in and represents how most workplaces operate today. Because it takes a lot more effort to start with "Why" and operate inside-out. Operating from either outside-in or inside-out greatly influences how you think, act and communicate in the workplace. Regrettably, starting with "What" can be disastrous. Because we can't control *results*. Here's an example why.

Safety Should Not Be the *Last Line* of Defence

Following is a brief explanation why we are prone to operate from the outside-in. Put simply, it's more **convenient** to focus on results ('What') than to create a 'Why'. Can you discover the same patterns of behaviour in your own workplace?

- ✗ We all know 'WHAT' we do. That's easy. We build things, make stuff, deliveries, repair or maintain equipment, pack products, provide a service or advise people in some capacity. It's crystal clear. It's 'What' we do to exist. It's the *results* we achieve. Anyone can see what we do.

- ✗ Then some workplaces have developed a further understanding of 'HOW' they get things done. Whether it's skill, experience, supply and demand or plain simple luck. 'How's' define our level of competence and proficiency. 'How' is stuck between following the 'What' or the 'Why's' orders. Whichever one is the most influential, gets more focus.

- ✗ Very few workplaces know 'WHY' they do what they do. A 'Why' means what's your cause, what's your *mission*? What's your "intrinsic motivation" or sense of purpose. What is it that underpins all decision-making? In most cases, this is not so clear. Or no one is buying into it.

You've probably experienced an *outside-in* workplace, where the Rational brain wrongly assumes that 'What' we do is our purpose. Except 'What' is *results* oriented. So getting the job done becomes a greater focus than *ways* (How/method) of going about things safely. It is likely that rules, regulations or threats of dismissal misguide your workplace. Workers might consciously or unconsciously place a higher value on getting the job done (What/results), rather than good communication and team-work (How/method). Leaders might place following procedures (What/results) above openness and disclosure (How/method). Habitual safe work practices come from gut instincts (Why/mission) and should not be relegated as a "Last" line of defence. Safety habits must come "First". Conscious or unconscious Habitual safe work practices must lead the way. When they do, the Rational brain's logical processes such as procedural compliances, rules and regulations, numerical goals and quantitative targets tag along accordingly, as a secondary line of defence. Get it? Good safety habits first, then mainstays of the Rational brain last. There can be no other way.

How 'What'-based Safety Evolved (Maslow's Hierarchy)

If we take a trip back to the '1970s, a global push for safety revolutionised our workplaces, it was a watershed moment. 'What'-based procedural compliance and regulatory authority intervention was actually a godsend. It cleaned up a massive problem. Why it worked is because it was a solution created at a higher level than the problem which existed at the time. As mentioned earlier, we inherited terrible safety standards as a hangover from the industrial revolution. Although harsh penalties and sweeping changes to workplace legislation was an outside-in 'What'-based solution, it was higher than our existing position on Maslow's Hierarchy of Needs. We were on the bottom rung of the ladder then: "Physio-logical needs". People were desperate for jobs, and proprietors were embracing capitalism in a huge way. Children in the workforce was not uncommon and fatalities were an accepted by-product of progress. It took another level of cognition to solve this problem. Possibly, if there was a 'Why' attached to the introduced legislation at the time, it was that the numbers of fatalities and injuries were more than society could tolerate. The pendulum had swung too far in favour of the company. These 'What'-based solutions were effective under the circumstances and the number of fatalities and injuries plummeted. Then we elevated ourselves to the next rung on Maslow's Hierarchy: "Safety Needs" (how appropriate).

That is, until we hit a glass ceiling, or was that a glass floor? Although fatalities and injuries declined steadily for many years, about twenty years ago those numbers started to level off. There is evidence coming out of the US and the UK that injuries and fatalities are steadily increasing again. Therefore, the pendulum needs a reset. It appears we need another big shift. Punitive measures enforceable by law and threats of dismissal are worn out doctrines for our current sociological model. They worked a treat for their time, but we are definitely now onto the next rung in Maslow's Hierarchy of Needs. We have risen to the next level: "Social needs". How apt considering the explosion in social media.

But wait, my sense is we are about to leap yet, onto another rung. Up into the realm of "Esteem needs". If it isn't required already, a new level of solution will be needed in line with this higher level of cognition in our workplaces. A shift from the 'What' to the 'Why'. If not all parts of the IOS Model working in harmony. If implemented, when would we know this new science is working? The answer is when trust and disclosure come out of the closet. It will require leaders and workers being real with each other about their (dis)belief in their safety system. It just can't be done any other way. Very soon as a leader, you won't be able to issue instructions that you don't truly believe in. That is, if you want to achieve the levels of safety you desire.

Charting a Course for Change

It is reasonable to understand why workplaces succumb to Rational brain tactics when there's no 'Why' (purpose) charting their course. It's obvious really. They operate from the outside-in when there's no higher cause motivating their decisions. The Rational brain takes over and safety becomes logical and rational. There's no *Emotional* connection to safe work practices. Outside-in workplaces produce more incidents and accidents without this connection.

Workplaces gravitate towards Rational brain, 'What'-based solutions (statistical and quantitative targets/goals) because they are much easier to define. It takes a little more effort and skill to go through the process of defining a 'Why' and operating inside-out. Maybe even requiring more training to understand how the IOS Model works. 'Why's' are developed through the Emotional brain and the Habitual brain working together. Without their common cause or sense of purpose driving safety, the Rational brain expects that those brains will simply buy-in to its rules and regulations, and that they'll treat those as their purpose. But as we know, rules and procedures are largely uninspiring to the Emotional brain. Buy-in of our safety systems is an emotive experience. It is feelings that make Safe work practices Habitual. Although it's harder to define the

Emotional drivers (values) to support safe work habits, it's absolutely essential if you want to combat outside-in practices.

In later chapters we'll provide you with a step-by-step method to create your workplace "Why". I call it a *Safety Mission*. But it can be called your Game Plan, Purpose, Work Crew Charter... anything you like. Just as long as it aligns with the workforce's values. I'll definitely be explaining more later.

Safety is the 'What', not the 'Why'

I get that this is a heavy chapter to digest. But the underlying point I'm trying to get across is this: **Safety is NOT your goal**. It's a result! When a work crew is alone and there are no leaders around, and no one else is looking—what will motivate them to do the right thing? Which habits will emerge? When we understand that safety is the "What" not the "Why', we begin to realise that focusing on results is ultimately out of our control. It's OK to *monitor* results for *comparisons*. Results are how you gauge *progress*. But you can't create your 'Why' from a result.

With repeated reinforcement of a "Why", created through the emotional connection to a vision of the ideal workplace, workers build a sense of pride in "How" they want to achieve it. It creates a sort of collective *'conscience'*. A moral compass. I know of no other model that will have the same impact as Inside-out Safety (IOS). It's what all workplaces crave. That is, accountability, autonomy and the emergence of voluntary operational discipline. Not because workers have to, but because they want to. Mostly because it's fun and empowering. When these two motives are combined, there's increased learning, attention and buy-in. Next, we learn why!

> *Your beliefs become your thoughts. Your thoughts become your words. Your words become your actions. Your actions become your habits. Your habits become your values. Your values become your destiny."*
> *—Mahatma Gandhi*

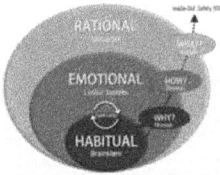

Safety is Not Your Goal—It's a Result

Outside-in-thinking is logic driven, not emotion driven. Instead of being guided by a sense of purpose, workplaces have the potential to put "dare in front of care". If you can't access that 12-millimetre nut, will you remove your insulated gloves because it makes sense (logic), or will you "choose" to look for a safer alternative because removing your gloves 'feels' wrong (emotion)? Logic will override choices if there is not a strong "emotional connection" to safer ideals. Such as trust, openness, camaraderie, teamwork, clear communication, authenticity, or disclosure, as examples.

If your workplace operates from the outside-in, people will always take the most convenient choice. Because it's the easiest solution. It's a rational, logical 'What' oriented thing to do. Unfortunately, logic and rational thinking can't sense (feel) risk in the heat of the moment. Those split-second decisions are not theirs to make. Gut instincts are the Habitual brain's role with input from the Emotional brain. Workplaces without a concise 'Why' guiding their decisions, will allow 'What' to influence the 'How' to seek convenience and short cuts. The Rational brain's forte.

Most workplaces don't have a 'Why' because it's harder to define. Identifying a 'What' is much more convenient, so they settle. In most cases, workplaces don't even know they do that. Defining a 'Why' and planning for a safer 'How' requires higher focus and commitment. It may even require further training and resources. However, intrinsic safety motivation cultivated from a clear 'Why', means a workforce will ultimately roll up their sleeves and carry out what's required to be safe. If you are a leader in a 'What' driven workplace it's more likely that you're constantly pleading with the workforce to be safe, rather than relying on them to take responsibility for their own safety. Pleading is *outside-in*. Leaders who create a 'Why' and drive safety with a sense of purpose are *inside-out*. Creating an emotional connection to safe work practices will ultimately guide people's decisions away from convenient choices. Creating a "Why" is a small price to pay if you want to slash your incident and accident rates.

(White paper excerpt)

CONVENIENCE KILLS

Theo makes a conscious decision to remove his hands from his insulated gloves, perceiving it more convenient than the personal cost of conceding failure. What of the other possible alternatives then? He could have isolated the power, consulted the engineers or possibly a dozen other solutions? Except it would inconvenience the crew, the customer, or possibly dent Theo's ego. Besides, the insulated matting was in place, everything was covered, and Theo knew what he was doing. He had always found the easiest way around things before. And this time he had a model... Skinny. Although he'd never seen anyone remove their gloves before, why would Theo even consider it after scolding Skinny? What could possibly tempt him?

What is Actually Real?

In an experiment where participants watched a screen with a cloud of dots moving either to the right or to the left, they were instructed to move a handle in the direction of the dots.[15] They were good at that. But when researchers added a directional load to the handle, making it slightly harder to move it the way the dots were moving, the participants unconsciously avoided the effort and moved the handle in the opposite direction of the dots. Stubbornly, the participants swore the dots were moving in the same direction of least resistance. But they weren't. The effort of least resistance changed their perception of reality. It was difficult for them to admit, but their brains had tricked them.

When convenient choices work out we say, "Great." But if they don't, our Rational brain vindicates there was no better option. "Oh well, better luck next time." Convenient decisions make us proud when they work, and bring shame when they don't. It's our Emotional response to Rational decisions. Our Rational brain is tasked with getting the job done with the least amount of effort. So it creates logical justifications why convenient choices are required. This creates an inner conflict with the Emotional brain whose moral conscience is safety. But if the Rational brain is convincing enough, and the Emotional brain doesn't have a compelling 'Why', then carrying out convenient options is a done deal. Once the Emotional brain is on board—it's over. Whether it's right or wrong. I'm sure you've met people who are so attached to their opinion that they will fight to the death to defend it, even if they are dead wrong. [16] In a battle for the soul of a person whose Emotional brain is swayed, it's pointless.[17] We must give the Emotional brain something safe to fight for... or we're dead, literally.

Overcoming the "convenience trap" means planning work tasks using the IOS model, starting with 'Why' and being aware of the mental forces trying to persuade us to be convenient (like the dots experiment). Finding this wisdom out in the field—in the *heat of the moment*—won't happen. Having conducted incident investigations over many years, I started to see a common thread. Many people said they experienced a brief, almost lightning fast internal conversation, debating whether they should take the actual short-cut that ultimately resulted in the incident. They chose the most convenient choice because they missed the most important step. They didn't challenge if the choice really is the most convenient option over the long term. A quick exercise to measure the potential short-term gain against the potential long-term costs may have alerted them towards making a 'better' choice. But this wisdom rarely occurs in the field. We try to make this happen with "Take Five" risk assessments. But ask the wrong questions. We aren't looking for hazards in these moments, we are looking for motivation to take the less convenient choice. What if we asked in the Take 5 checklists, *"Are you tempted to take the most convenient option?"* Would this create a different outcome?

Another problem is that humans have a propensity to extrapolate the present and project it into the future. In other words, we tell ourselves that nothing can go wrong based on current conditions if they stay the same. This creates pride (Emotional brain), which reinforces the Rational brain's conviction that nothing will go wrong. The more inventive the rationalisations, the more confident we are in our conviction.[18] However, rarely in industry do conditions stay the same. It's kind of "irrational" when you think about it. But then, that's the Emotional brain's influence. Rationality is reserved for the logical 'What'-based Rational brain, always looking for ways to make things simple and "get the job done".

Humans are creatures of habit. Left to our own devices, the Rational brain will try to make almost anything into a routine—a habit. Because habits allow our minds, thus our bodies, to ramp down more often and conserve energy.[19] Except that habits are relegated as a function of the Habitual brain's subconsciousness, waiting for a trigger to wake it up. Once the Habitual brain has anything to do with it, the thinking process is replaced with automatic responses. This is our brain operating at our most basic human level, without much thought at all. It's natural that our instincts seek convenience.

We are also very good at following other people's choices remarkably well, especially if we believe they have discovered an easier way of doing something. The herding instinct and mimicking propensities in humans are natural preservative behaviour. [20] Powerful because they are impelled, regardless of reasoning, by a primitive system of mentation that is trying to save our life. The irony of course is that in the modern world and the advent of heavy machinery, herding doesn't consider potential short-term gains against potential long-term costs. Those same impulses trying to save you—will get you killed.

The Law of Efficiency

Nature is most efficient. It always chooses the pathway of least resistance. Fatefully, when Theo touched the live cable, he became the electricity's pathway of least resistance too. Our 'What' based Rational brain is programmed the same way. To use the easiest means, to do whatever is required with the least amount of effort, to conserve as much energy as possible. This includes social concepts. Like seeking approval rather than talking to our peers about questionable conduct. Or keeping quiet in the pre-shift meeting to avoid discomfort. Remember Theo when his manager asked if anyone knew of questionable work practices? Maybe it needs to be more convenient to say something before people will. But actually, it is! Understand-ing the true nature of convenience is the first step to realising that seeking convenient options is a trap. The pathway of least resistance is Physics, whereas seeking convenience is Biology. Unfortunately, human nature and human behaviour do not operate on the same level. One is naturally occurring while the other assumes an incorrect human assumption. Let me explain.

Efficiency, or making the most possible use of the resources at hand, is the single biggest concept on how we run the world. It's what incited the wheel. Things like the dishwasher, the refrigerator, computers or even the venerable potato peeler were all invented to make our lives easier. But there's a problem if you think making things easier comes without a catch. The First Law of Thermodynamics tells us that energy is always conserved.[21] So the ratio of energy you save is equal to the energy spent somewhere else. It is always in unity, a 1:1 ratio. There is always a corresponding consequence to making a convenient choice. You think you are reducing effort, but you introduce a new inconvenience somewhere else. This is the first step to viewing the workplace from a completely new perspective. I hope it changes the way you view safety forever.

This aspect of our lives is not very well-known or discussed much. But scientists have always known it, physicists swear by it and all breakthrough philosophies are built upon the idea that nothing is ever created or destroyed, just transformed. Did you know that every atom and molecule in the universe was already made available to us in the Big Bang? This is it. It's all here. There is no atom-making machine producing more things in the universe. Every element we are ever going to have is already at our disposal, constantly being transformed from one thing to another. Energy is transformed into matter, matter into light and light back into energy ($E=MC^2$). Around and around it goes.

Why aren't our safety systems acknowledging this fact? Why do we persist with the fallacy that we make anything safer by relying on external barriers? It creates a false sense of security. Implementing 'What'-based risk controls are Thinking brain stopgaps. If we consider 'What'-based risk controls in the context of the IOS model, you realise it is an incomplete assessment. Risk controls are great if they have been coupled with a 'Why'. 'Why's create the personal responsibility to carry out the 'How's safely. 'Why's ensure risk controls get used.

Risk controls should be written in context. Such as, "This Danger Tape is in place to remind workers it is their personal responsibility to be aware of Mobile Equipment". Unfortunately, it seems more "convenient" to use danger tape as the physical barrier itself. Our confidence in flimsy red plastic tape, somehow supposed to protect a pedestrian from 5 tonnes of moving metal, is grossly misplaced. Instead we should be making a concerted effort to create a 'Why' which enhances personal responsibility. A 'Why' that places pedestrian safety where it should be, squarely in the hands of the pedestrian. Too often we rely on barriers to keep workers safe. Like insulated gloves when working on 22,000-volt power lines. This creates complacency. It is an illusion. It is up to workers to keep themselves safe at all times. Barriers are simply a reminder, a Rational brain solution to an Emotional brain problem. Barriers shouldn't be a control. If workplaces had a 'Why' around workers taking 100% responsibility as a pedestrian—we wouldn't need barriers or flimsy danger tape.

Convenience vs. the Conservation Law
You'd be amazed at what it takes to make solar panels. The massive consumption of energy and resources might make you

reconsider if solar panels are good for the environment. Quarries produce Quartzite and are trucked to Smelter in semi-trailers. Trucks and machinery consume fossil fuel around the clock. Thousands of Hectares of forests are burnt in massive kilns to create charcoal for the carbon billowing tons of black smoke into the air each year. Pine Trees are ground down into woodchips and added to the ingredients to fuel the chemical reaction in a furnace. 132,000 volts fuel the submerged-arc silicone furnaces 24 hours a day. The electrodes are 500mm in diameter and 3 metres long. They are so massive the electricity buzzing through them makes a frightening sound. All of these "resources" and huge amounts of "energy" burn away furiously around the clock, day after day, year after year to meet the demand for silicone solar panels. Good marketing lull people into believing solar electricity is "free" and "convenient". It's a false sense of security if anything else.

No one talks about these kinds of offsets. They are rarely taken into consideration when we speak in terms of convenience versus conservation. There are other setbacks in our eternal quest for life's luxuries. Plastic bags, fossil fuel products, fertilisers, chemicals. Not to mention the human costs such as the loss of life at Chernobyl, Bhopal, Deepwater Horizon or the Piper Alpha disaster. There's the impact on the environment, the forests, the sea, the atmosphere and the list goes on and on. We all pay a price in our quest for convenience. Convenience does not come without a cost. We always pay a price. ALWAYS!

Short Term Gains Against Long Term Costs

Convenient options appear attractive in the *heat of the moment*. But they often expose us to peril when those options have not been weighed against a more accurate time frame. In other words, when you slow things down, what is the potential short-term gain versus the potential long-term cost of this option? For Theo up there in the work basket, the voices in his head are getting moodier. Mr. 'What' has a problem and is hell-bent on removing this stubborn 12mm nut. Mr. 'What' is backing Theo to solve this tricky situation by shoring up his fighting spirit. Even though it's not lost on Theo, that only last Wednesday he was yelling at Skinny for taking his insulated gloves off. Now he suddenly finds himself compelled to take his own gloves off. What the hell? This is going to take some skilful justification from the Rational brain, Mr. 'What's' specialty. Eventually, the Emotional brain is persuaded and applies feelings of frustration to support getting the job done. The IOS process is nowhere to be found. Convenience beckons and catastrophe looms.

"I wonder," says Mr. 'What'. "Perhaps Skinny is onto something." "Maybe gloves-off is the only way of getting at this thing." To cement the deal, the Emotional brain amps' things up a notch, being convinced Mr. 'What' is right. "Damn Skinny, who does he think he is?" Theo considers his training, his experience, what's right and wrong, his pride, his ego, the past, the present and the future—all in a nanosecond. Most importantly though, he isn't weighing up any short-term gain against the potential long-term costs. Of course, short-term gain is an attractive proposition from Theo's perspective, way up there in the basket. By getting his fingers into that tiny space, there's the convenience of not having to come up with another plan, convenience for the crew, convenience for the customer and for the company. Convenience to Theo's ego versus a bruised one if he fails. Convenience overrides company values (or at least the expressed ones) and even Theo's own values of personal wellbeing. Convenience overrides everything.

Complacency vs. Convenience

Much has been said of the word "complacency" in our industry. I would say however, that nothing gets said of "convenience". Yet in every incident investigation I ever conducted, and there have been countless, I would attribute all of them to people choosing the most convenient option. If they are complacent at all, it's about accepting convenience so easily. Only after the incident do we discover that the so-called convenient option was actually the most inconvenient after all. Incident, injury, hospital, investigations, they are all more inconvenient in the end. But these are the obvious impacts. What about the subtle ones? Let's say a work crew needs to carry out work-at-heights. Instead of fetching the appropriate fall arrest equipment, they decide to quickly climb onto a structure and perform their task before anyone notices. They finish their task ahead of schedule. It's not uncommon for a supervisor, unprepared for the crew's early completion, to allocate a quick but unpopular task to tide them over until the next job is available. Damn it! The law of equivalence wins again.

"For every action, there is an equal and opposite reaction." Sir Isaac Newton probably wasn't thinking of the workplace when he discovered his third law of motion. However, convenience has both a positive and negative effect simultaneously. We humans are simply not open or aware enough to see it. Making the extra effort that safer choices require, will reap the corresponding quantum physical benefits. This is the key to job satisfaction, doing what it takes to get what you want. In Theo's case, he would give anything for the chance to reconsider his options again. But alas, as always, we usually only consider the consequences after it is too late.

Our best decisions occur when we accept natural law in the moment. The greater the effort, the greater the benefit. Balanced decisions are a finely tuned blend of 'Why, 'How' and 'What'. The precise mix depends on each situation, but it must flow IOS (inside out) to be safe. If students were warned in the dots experiment that a directional load would be applied to the handle, they'd be more aware. Their response would have considered the "reality". That's why I warn work crews about how "Convenience Kills" before they go out in the field. When they are aware of this fundamental principle, that convenience is out to get them, it's amazing how it pulls them up before taking a short-cut. You should warn your crews too, and watch their reaction when they get it. I love the AHA! moments when people realise this principle is real. As work crews become more aware of how much convenience is always trying to trap them. They will report back to you their successes if you remind them before they head out for the day, "Hey team, remember that CONVENIENCE KILLS!" It has a remarkable effect on morale. I'm often told how this one message has saved them from heartache time and time again. How "Convenience Kills" popped into their head before they took a shortcut. Imagine how many incidents have been avoided. Imagine how many injuries have been prevented. Just imagine what's really going on underneath what you think is real!

> *"Everything that depends on the action of nature*
> *is by nature as good as it can be."*
> —*Aristotle*

THE SAFETY BRAIN

Most people felt Theo should have followed the company's mantra: "Safety Before Production". Except, Theo's Emotional brain smelled a rat. Was repairing a power line "live" for one customer, downgrading "safety first" as simply rhetoric? Without an emotional connection to a 'Why', the Rational brain waits on the sidelines to implement its own plan and creates a storyline to shore up Theo's self-identity as the Go-to Man ("You can do this Mr. Fix-it"). Problem is, it's a 'Get the job done' identity. Without a 'Why' to steer Theo's ego, he relies on Mr. Fix-it for a solution. Unfortunately, an alter-ego is not a reliable first (or last) line of defence. Safe work habits are.

The Habit of Safety

Safety Habits are formed through a symbiotic relationship between the Emotional and Habitual brains. As indicated by the *Habit Loop* (circular arrows) in *Diagram 1— Inside Out Safety (IOS)* on page 26. If workers connect safe work practices with a pleasurable experience (feeling), they become good habit loops to be repeated as much as possible. An example is rewarding openness and disclosure, or celebrating incidents as lessons learned. However, if a workforce experiences safety as being unpleasant, such as disciplinary measures for procedure breaches, it will create a "resistance loop" (bad habit). You may experience this as low morale. Unfortunately, revealing minor infractions or potential incidents and hazards will be stifled, for fear of further reprisal. You never want resistance to become a habit. But it does so easily. That's why shaming people after an incident can manifest into low morale rapidly. Most people develop some form of shame early in their lives. It doesn't take much to trigger those habits again as adults.

Just to rub more salt into the wound, the "Golden Rule of Habit Change" as espoused by Charles Duhigg in his book the Power of Habits, states you can never extinguish a bad habit. Only change it. That's why some incidents die hard. Have you ever been dumbfounded after a "lessons learned" session that the same incident happened again? Hello habit loop. It's imperative that you adopt a purpose driven workplace that routinely indoctrinates a 'Why' into the Habitual brain. You'll be able to modify those persistently bad habits into good ones.

Habits and routines form 90% of our workplace culture. Louis Gerstner, former CEO of IBM said, "Culture isn't just one aspect of the game, it is the game." Therefore, if culture "is" the game, how do we go about winning it and building a safe workplace? The answer is you have to embed safe systems of work into the Habitual brain, by attaching them to pleasurable experiences utilising the Emotional brain. Rationally crafted safety slogans or zero accident targets are not effective. Because workforces rarely create an emotional connection to them. Logical messages are a 'What'-based endeavour. Any message worth its salt, has to be "felt" by the pleasure centres of the Habitual and Emotional brains—to have lasting impact. The Habitual brain is also responsible for self-preservation, defence mechanisms and personal wellbeing. [22] If good safety habits are cultivated by a 'Why' before being passed onto Mr. 'How' and Mr. 'What' for implementation, leaders wouldn't need to hang signs with safety slogans or curb worker behaviour. Behavioural Based Safety (BBS) is a brand of Psychology better left alone. I'll explain why later. Needless to say, focusing on behaviour is dangerous enough in itself, as it always leads to blame. We should focus instead on human *nature*. If we follow the IOS Model and cultivate a safety mission aligned with the entire workforce's values, we can trust that behaviour will take care of itself. By understanding the relationship between the different functions of the brain in the IOS Model, you'll appreciate how Theo had his accident, all accidents actually. I'll be referring back to the IOS model regularly throughout the book to explain why we carry out our work tasks the way we do. So let's take a look at each IOS brain function to understand their impact on the workplace and how work activities might operate more safely if we adopt the IOS technique.

Rational brain—The *What?*

Our Neocortex, or Rational brain, drives the 'What'. It is responsible for the Cognitive Revolution in Homo-Sapiens. [23] Setting humans apart from the animal kingdom. The Rational brain sits outside of the emotions, acting as our seat of reason. It is responsible for our logical 'What'-based responses to incidents, and doesn't understand the irrational behaviour that creates them. It's into blame. That's why you'll hear, "Why did you do it?" It seeks to box humans into a logical concept (which is nigh-on impossible). The Rational brain carries out higher level processing such as logic, reasoning, creative thinking, language and the integration of information. It focuses on the things we do and getting results. Not on who we are and how we are feeling. It has no attachment to safety or survival at all. The Rational brain isn't even concerned or aware of physical risks. It can't sense danger. Rather it is driven only by data, reasoning, facts and figures. Not physical stimulus or body feelings. The Rational brain will say, "No to drugs". While the Emotional and Habitual brains say, "Yes please." That you're reading this book means the Rational brain is working just fine. Without it, you would be nothing more than a vegetable. A vegetable with feelings none the less. The Rational brain doesn't connect with the "feeling" of being safe. Only the "concept" of safety from a logical viewpoint. So it doesn't make decisions with your wellbeing in mind. It's the Rational brain that says you'll be fine, when you really should see a doctor. It thinks it has all the answers from a logical standpoint.

The Rational brain cannot comprehend emotions. Only an approximation using words and logic to express feelings. Desire, fulfilment and compassion are all foreign concepts and it has no interest in pursuing these silly notions. Let alone trying to understand them. If you are an artist, the Rational brain is more concerned about the brush strokes and palette colours or texture than it is in creating a mood. Moods are the Emotional brain's job.

Emotional brain—The *How?*

By far, the star of the show is our Emotional brain. The Limbic System. It drives your 'How' and cooperates with the 'Why' and the 'What' when looking for direction. The Emotional brain is used primarily for learning, creating beliefs and building trust. Feelings play a vital role in learning. That's why you feel the way you do given certain situations. To make an event more memorable. Feelings help you learn to avoid something painful or seek something pleasurable. Feelings determine what the

Rational brain needs to justify and rationalise for decision-making. Decisions are a product of pleasure and pain seeking, the Emotional brain's most basic function. [24] Most people tend to make decisions based on how they feel, not what they think. This is an extremely important part of your life and controls more of your behaviour than you realise.

The Emotional brain only understands images and experiences and cannot decipher language. Trying to tell the Emotional brain to act safe using signs, posters or procedures, and other rational thought processes, is like speaking a totally different language. You'll need hand gestures, body language, sound and physical stimulus to communicate fully with the Emotional brain. The Emotional brain only communicates in terms of ease or unease, purpose, pleasure or frustration. Without the Emotional brain's buy-in, you have no loyalty, allegiance or alliance. Nicknamed our "trust centre", the Emotional brain draws upon internal and external experiences to decide what to believe in, and defines our sense of values. It must buy-in to whatever is being presented before it is persuaded to change. Even if change is for our own good. Otherwise, the Emotional brain sends a message to your "gut" that it doesn't trust what's going on. That doesn't mean it's true. It just means your sense of values are being challenged. Find that confusing? There's more.

The Emotional brain is duty-bound and passionate about WHY things get done. Not WHAT gets done. Goals not results. Unless of course, there's no 'Why'. Located between the 'Why' and the 'What' (refer to the diagram on page 26), it will collaborate with whoever has the most conviction. The Emotional brain places more emphasis on safety when it attaches a strong sense of *belief* to work tasks. It's more than just turning up each day to earn a living. It wants to believe in a cause, a 'Why'. The Emotional brain loves statements and creeds about who you are. Such as, "We are product innovators" or, "We are industry leaders". "We do it right the first time," or a million other 'Why' inspired causes. The Emotional brain will persuade your 'What' to pursue goals and targets with the 'Why' in mind. It's always the Emotional brain with a sense of purpose that will inspire safety. Without the Emotional brain's buy-in, watch out! You'll likely get a backlash worth remembering. Such is the Emotional brain's temperament sometimes. Having clarity of purpose and a clear and concise 'Why' allows the Emotional brain to press upon the Rational brain to find ways of achieving it. Even more so, it helps create good IOS habits within the Habitual brain. Creating a foundation of habits worth referring to when challenges arise.

Habitual brain—The *Why*

We refer to the Brainstem as the Habitual brain because it operates subconsciously. Controlling autonomic functions such as heartbeat, blinking and breathing. The Habitual brain only communicates in terms of trigger and response. Like "fight or flight". When the Habitual brain senses fear it releases a chemical cocktail throughout your body that changes your state instantly. It's immediate. For instance, you suddenly see a snake (trigger), which causes you to flinch (response). It works in tandem with the Emotional brain to create habits and routines that lessen our load. Imagine if our brains had to figure out every piece of information as if it were new for the first time. We would be constantly in a state of overload. Memory and habits are critical to our survival. Memories and habits form and operate unconsciously after the Emotional brain has filtered those experiences through cycles of pleasure and pain.

The purpose of a 'Why" is to pump some juice into your

work day. If workers are focused and equipped with a sense of direction, they are more likely to be proud of their workplace and act more safely. Ill-defined 'Whys' lead to ill-defined outcomes. Well-defined 'Whys' sidestep the Rational brain from running the show. The Rational brain doesn't believe in anything other than getting the job done. So you really have no alternative than to enlist the Habitual brain and start with 'Why'. It's unfortunate when we don't, as Theo discovered.

The Safety Brain in Action

Let's explore the personalities of each brain function and their characteristics in the workplace. Starting with Mr. 'What'.

MR. WHAT: Avoiding frustration and effort is hard wired into 'What's' psyche. Always seeking convenient choices. If there's no sense of purpose (a 'Why'), then Mr. 'What' is in control. And this will affect day-to-day activities in terms of safety. In this context, safety is considered an inconvenience. He will employ Mr. "How" (Emotional brain) to vent frustration and impatience, and to hurry things along if he doesn't get his way. Mr. 'How' has no choice but to do whatever Mr. 'What' asks. Because the job has become the 'Why', instead of an attitude or value. It's a typical outside-in situation when we start with 'What'.

MR. HOW: Without attitudes and values as its moral compass (accountability, camaraderie, good communication etc.), Mr. 'How' gets confused and thinks the job is his purpose. But really, its task should not be production oriented. Production goals are for the Rational brain to focus on. It's about the journey for Mr. 'How' and the "way" we should go about things. If there's a clearly defined 'Why', then Mr. 'How' is in good shape. He would much prefer to follow a purpose-driven cause. If Theo's 'How' had been functioning with a sense of purpose, he would have been more focused on carrying things out in line with the mission. Instead, Theo's 'How' (feelings) was immersed in helping Mr. 'What' get that "stupid" nut off. Those feelings should have been immersed in a 'Why'. When getting the job done becomes a higher value than the 'Why', accidents happen. It's only natural.

MR. WHY: Under this scenario, Mr. 'Why's' safety habits have been left as the last line of defence, because things are outside-in (refer to the IOS Model diagram on page 26). Out of the three brain functions, the Habitual brain (Mr. 'Why') is mostly concerned with your self-preservation (fight or flight). It operates subconsciously. Either triggering a response from its instinctual programming, or running habit loops from the lessons you've learned. [25] But lessons learned are too late in this instance. The Habitual brain can only transfer the lessons from a painful experience back into a safe habit loop (a 'Why'), after the incident has occurred. This is a "lagging" process. An example is that after his accident, Theo would never take off his insulated gloves again. But it's a tad late unfortunately. We need a "leading" process, the 'Why', to be up front. That's why we must start with 'Why'.

Summary

Relying on 'Mr 'What', the Rational brain, to connect with safety on a deep personal level is illogical and will create more confusion. It's not in the Rational brain's wiring to "connect" with anything. It's a tool for rationalisation only. When there's an incident, your Rational brain gets confused and relegates whatever it deems irrational—as a failure. It will look to blame incompetence or carelessness. Scratching our heads and jumping to conclusions we say, "Someone has acted unsafely." We rarely consider that a deep-rooted cultural or organisational shortcoming exists. "It doesn't make sense," we lament.

When there IS a 'Why', it is a hallmark of the Rational brain to maintain accountability, rationalising why we must follow 'Why's' purpose. This is a great Rational brain quality.

When the Emotional brain is focused on results (the job), instead of it's purpose, it will try to put into words it's disappointment or anger that another incident has occurred. But the Emotional brain is unable to "do" language. To communicate, the Emotional brain creates an uneasy physical reaction throughout your body instead. The Rational brain interprets this physical negativity as a sign that something needs fixing fast, and tries to approximate the uncomfortable nature of the feeling with correspondingly harsh corrective safety measures. But of course, this is just a logical reaction to an otherwise personally affective issue. Any emotional connection to a 'Why' has been lost in the mayhem, and the think/solve/implement cycle will start all over again.

Believing that people will be inspired by the Rational brain's procedures and regulations without a 'Why' often leads to disappointment and frustration for leaders. Yet it is largely how we respond to incidents, creating more paperwork and rules, and somehow expecting things to be different next time. The idea that "every" incident requires a mandatory set of corrective actions, is creating more heartache for workplaces than anyone is prepared to discuss. This is a great example of a 'What'-driven workplace using 'What'-based solutions.

Conclusion

Repetitive tasks are constantly being relegated to the Habitual brain, to make the brain's life easier. The problem is that our brain can't tell the difference between good and bad habits, and they get activated or "mis-activated" unconsciously. [26] If you have a bad habit stored away, like reaching into a moving part to free up a troublesome process, it will always be lurking in the shadows, waiting for the right cue to rear its ugly head—when you least expect it. [27] Unfortunately, these types of incidents (repetitive) were far too prevalent in the past. Our acceptance of injuries as part of the furniture was a huge problem. In as much as habitual unsafe work practices were claiming victims far too often. Fatalities and injuries were destroying the fabric of our society. Therefore, logic-based safety programs, punishment and reward, legislation, regulations and penalties became the order of the day. They became the new habit. Statistics showed that incidents and accidents steadily declined for many years. However, more recently they have tended to flat line. [28,] [29] In some countries, fatalities and injuries are on the rise again. So we need a new approach, new habits.

Another problem of course is that the rate of work related stress, anxiety and depression is on the rise too. Workers compensation in the form of "psychological injury" may soon surpass traditional injury claims. [30] We'll have to watch and see where this one takes us. Though I fear we are witnessing the birth of a new epidemic, much like traditional injuries boomed in the '40s and '50s. I'm certain 'What'-based solutions will have no effect on mental health and wellbeing issues. It's imperative we discover more 'Why'-based answers.

If we want safe work systems to prevail, we must have a 'Why'. Relying on Mr. 'What' to come up with a safety mission will disappoint, and may even end in disaster. 'What' and 'How' are foot soldiers, awaiting orders from the Commander-in-Chief... Mr. 'Why'. Without 'Why's' leadership and guidance, sound judgment and decision-making will go AWOL. Safety is not your goal. How you *think, act* and *communicate* is.

*"A few times in my life I've had moments of clarity
where the silence drowns out the noise and I can
feel rather than think."*
—Tom Ford

HEAT OF THE MOMENT

In the absence of a coherent "Why", and faced with this tricky nut situation, Theo's 'What' has taken over. But it's outside-in thinking. It's back-to-front and logic driven—not safety driven. When Mr. "What" is running the show, he instructs the Emotional brain to inject a sense of impatience and irritation. Making the situation more problematic. He enlists the Habitual brain to dig up a bunch of old memories from childhood, forged in the crucible of punishment and praise. Mr. 'How' starts barking orders. "C'mon Theo, let's get going will you?" Echoing some distant parental command. Theo imagines the work crew's reaction if he can't remove this stupid nut. He somehow believes they'll be disappointed in him. He's the "Go-to guy", Mr. Fix-it. But without a "moral compass" (a 'Why'), Theo is in real trouble as the 'heat of the moment' takes over.

What If...?

February 13, 2006 could have ended up vastly different for Theo. But it didn't. Something happened that day we can never change or comprehend. We've reconstructed every nanosecond leading up to his accident. We call it *"heat of the moment"*. It means the internal conversations, temptations and motives behind any rash decisions people make when things change. Or when all of a sudden, workers are faced with a flurry of choices. In this chapter we'll describe how Theo was operating from the outside-in. He developed a back-to-front mindset because there was no 'Why' to convince him otherwise. His decisions bypassed the 'Why's' protective devices and penchant for self-preservation. The result was devastating. Let's analyse Theo's accident step-by-step, overlaying the IOS model... in the *heat of the moment*.

Your 'Why' is the Risk Assessment

Up there in the basket, the problem for Theo right now is that the original mission, "repair the power pole safely" isn't resonating through the fog of frustration. Besides, it's a result disguised as a goal anyway. The safety controls for each job step, written in the risk assessment, is now sitting in the front seat of the truck. Not obviously coming to mind. A full understanding of the purpose of the risk assessment was not fully translated into a 'Why' anyway. When there is no 'Why' driving the risk assessment, risk controls become lip service. Instead of sound safety habits, they are pretenders. *Slips, trips and falls, housekeeping, dropped objects.* Every day, these fraudsters end up on a risk assessment. Stopgap measures filling in spaces on an otherwise worthless bit of paper. Without any real underlying sense of purpose, we echo the "Do it safely" mantra. Good safety marketing, but that's about all. Hardly practical advice. It's like saying, "Stay out of trouble" to your kids, or "Be good" as they rush out the door. In one ear and out the other. What exactly does "Be safe" mean to a work crew in the *heat of the moment*? Habitual safety is triggered automatically from a sense of commitment to a cause. It doesn't require reference to any risk assessment. Your 'Why' is the risk assessment... written in blood!

Decision Time

There's a certain electricity in the air when liney's work "live" (pardon the pun). And right now, Mr. 'How' will accept any instruction. Whether it's from the Rational brain or the Habitual brain. It's whoever has the clearest purpose. So, if Theo's 'Why' is crystal clear, the 'How' will bring that vision into fruition. But if the 'Why' is not concise, then Mr. 'How' will look to the Rational brain for direction. More than a willing cohort in these situations. The problem is, the Rational brain seeks convenience and short-cuts, and just wants to get the job done. The 'What' brain's logical choice is to make things go easier. Whereas the 'Why' is prepared to roll up its sleeves and do whatever it takes to create safety. These are two vastly conflicting motives being passed on to Mr. 'How' for implementation. And will have vastly different outcomes. In light of the absence of a coherent 'Why', you can always count on Mr. 'How' to get things done anyway. It's what 'How' does best, get it done no matter what. Although Mr. 'How' is revved up and ready to go, his instructions are about to come from the wrong direction. Outside-in. A tragedy is about to unfold.

Seal the Deal

It's time to get creative and the 'What" (Rational brain) has been given the reigns. It will tell Mr. 'Why' to sit back and relax. The Rational brain's approach is getting the job done and to seek approval from the crew. Without the 'Why' espousing a cause that encompasses safe work systems, or motivating the drive and effort required to be safe, Theo simply follows the growing voice in the back of his mind, which seems to have all the answers. "OK Theo. You've seen how it's done. Remove your gloves and you'll have easy access to that difficult nut." This logic provides the perfect ammunition to support Mr. 'What's' penchant for short-cuts, and it starts to rationalise why this scenario is best, comparing Theo's experience to Skinny's. "Domkop five-minute liney. I've been doing this stuff for seventeen years and forgotten more than Skinny knows. Who does he think he is anyway?" All that needs to happen now, is for the Emotional brain to inject a few *warm fuzzies* into the equation that entices Theo to stay on this chosen path, and voila! The deal is sealed. The next thing you know... Theo's gloves are between his knees. Unfortunately, he is so far off-track from the original mission (repair the pole safely) that the train has completely derailed. You know the rest.

The Right Message

What if Theo's 'Why' was more encompassing than get the job done? What if it included a sense of purpose around innovation, or the idea that a companywide solution to this nut problem would benefit the whole industry? What if Theo's Rational brain took a back seat and allowed the correct IOS pathway to unfold. Instead of 'get the job done' it could have been, 'let's slow things down and consider things step-by-step'. How might

Theo's life be vastly different today? When we are 'Why' inspired, the Rational brain becomes an ally and rallies behind the worthwhile cause. Be it a company value that everyone has bought into, or a personal value that places safety before pride.

Doing things safely is not a 'Why', it is an action, a 'How'. You can't adopt "do it safely" as a slogan for your cause. But you can use "Do it right every time" or "Communicate with your team". These are values that could have had vastly different results for Theo. Values that could have been turned into good habits. Because they are specific, they are a 'Why'. "Safety first" is vague, so the Emotional brain ignores it. Safety slogans are both geographically and archetypically foreign to the Emotional brain, so it simply cancels out the word "safety" as rhetoric. Plus, the Rational brain doesn't understand what "safety" means in terms of danger. It's just a word. *Don't get hurt* is just a concept. When the Rational brain is unsure, it seeks convenience. When the Emotional brain is unsure but guided by a 'Why', it will pause and send an uneasy feeling to your gut, to remind you to check in with the mission. It's not a voice in your head. Your gut instinct is a total body experience.

If Theo or anyone has been getting away with risky business, where there has been no 'Why' to warn otherwise, your pleasure centres generate an agreeable feeling with the gut, and signals that it's OK to do it again. This is a disaster in waiting and why the Emotional brain can be your knight in shining armour, or your worst nightmare. It just depends on who is feeding it. From the inside-out, or the outside-in. Safe work habits are simply implants/memories stored in the Habitual brain. It will attach a nice sensation in support of an action, or an unpleasant sensation to resist one.

Perhaps if there was a well-defined 'Why' up there in the basket that day, Mr. 'How' the action man, may have been more emotionally connected to Theo's wellbeing, instead of injecting impatience to push things along. If 'How' had collaborated with the 'Why' to complete the task more in line with a quality or safety value, or any other empowering intent, the 12-millimetre nut problem may in fact have been inspiration for an innovative new approach. Perhaps an industrywide solution.

This "nut" problem needed solving at a higher level than it was created. Higher on Maslow's Hierarchy of Needs. For your interest, a new innovation has recently come onto the market for lineys. An insulated tool that removes that 12mm nut. Fifteen years later and a tool arrives? That's safety for you. And there's no guarantee that this new product will get used. That's stubborn habits for you.

Safety is not your goal, it's a result. It's not even tools or PPE (How/method). It's finding meaning and purpose in 'Why' you carry out tasks. Without input from a 'Why's' good habits, your 'How' will keep reaching for bad habits, over and again. Not learning from mistakes. Without a daily process of tracking and correction (accountability), your 'How' doesn't know any better. Soon you'll discover how easy it is to introduce this type of daily reckoning, an accountability model, that workers love.

"Safety is discovering a WHY in WHAT you do."
—*Theo Venter*

WALK THE TALK

After his accident, Theo was troubled that the incident investigation might not include a deeper metaphysical evaluation of the bizarre circumstances leading up to his accident. I.e. Skinny's gloves, the wheelchair guy's presentation, the manager's unheeded safety plea. Surely they all played a role. Except, these were never explored. Theo was too embarrassed to raise them. The report concluded with what all incident reports arrive at: "Procedural Violation". Yet, it's too easy to pass things off as an indiscretion. It only scratches the surface, a cop-out. What lies beneath the transgression? Theo didn't shirk his responsibilities or avoid ownership of his poor judgment. Quite the opposite. But he has gone through too much pain and agony to hang things on low-hanging-fruit conclusions. His accident should not have occurred in vain. It's time to reveal all, walk the talk... own everything!

Aligned with Reality

The problem with today's safety paradigm is people often confuse how the world is, with how they feel it ought to be. There's a huge difference between "what is" (fact) and "what should" be (values), otherwise called the "fact/value distinct-ion". It's that thin line between what is truth and what we think is the right thing to do. It's a source of conflict between science, and indeed a source of conflict at the core of our workplace. People will say, "Why did Theo take off his gloves when he knew it was wrong?" They'll advocate, "he should have", "he ought to", "was supposed to". These are phrases to describe "judgements". While injuries are a "fact". The problem is, that these values statements target an individual's character. It's an assumption that their actions were unconscionable or immoral. Whereas, to uncover the facts, we must target reality. Only then can we do something about it.

We could throw around things like integrity, accounta-bility and ownership and belt people around the ears with them. Saying you should have done this, and you ought to have done that. But how does that serve anything after the fact? Except to target people's behaviour. That would shut the door on discovering other causes that may have had considerable influence. What if there's more to it than people's behaviour? We'll miss the real root cause. Targeting people's behaviour, comparing them against our values (judgement), is self-defeating and only creates more disconnection and resistance to change.

Whereas values will have more meaning when they are something to aspire to, coupled with a few other important ideals such as support, openness and trust. Throw in the acceptance of human fallibility and then we can be more congruent with the "true" intention of a safety system... to protect us from ourselves. After all, safety means the wellbeing of people. This includes emotional and psychological safety too.

I don't think workplaces fully understand the effects that shame has on a workplace's psyche. I'll go further and say, targeting behaviour has an adverse effect on safety overall. I mean it.

Walking the Talk, Painlessly

Quite often we only look to improve things when something goes wrong. Yet how has it been safe for years and now only after an incident we deem it unsafe? How can we blame a person's behaviour when we only give lip service to safety, "real" safety? If Skinny, Nico and Theo couldn't get their insulated gloves into that tiny space, how was it done before? Who knew about it? How far up the chain did it go? Congruence means a company's words, thoughts and actions are aligned. Both internally and externally. The company safety oratory matched with a strong belief in the system. A workplace with a high value on congruence... walking the talk.

But congruence for the real world. We can't be all "Captain America" about it. More like "Deadpool", warts and all. Meaning that integrity, accountability, ownership and personal responsibility will emerge in a natural visceral way. So it's believable and dare I say it, fun. If a workplace's integrity accepts the limitations of being human, it will also accept human physio and psycho fallibility as a matter of course. It's more important that trust emerges before leaders adopt a moralistic high ground. A "zero target vision" doesn't allow for this kind of acceptance. Yet the workplace is a team effort. Everyone is part of both winning and losing. Everyone. It's integrity because it's fun, not right. It's accountability without judgement. Incidents valued for their learnings, not resisted because of their failings. To develop an air of ownership and personal responsibility, openness and disclosure must be valued higher than collecting evidence and witness statements after an incident. It's the opposite of culpability and blame, thus shame. Shame is so prevalent in our industry. We should be promoting, that if shit happens someone will "own" it because they will be honoured, not hanged. Congruence is cultivated, not enforced. It's an ethos and philosophy that leaders and workers believe in because it's in their DNA, not a slogan on a poster in the lunchroom.

At the Heart of the Problem

The Oxford dictionary says "congruence" means "agreement or harmony". This is a great analogy. If there is no harmony or agreement with the stated company values, workers will not feel a sense of devotion to honour them. Telling workers, they are bound by company standards when they sign their letter of employment, doesn't inspire loyalty. Nor will threats of disciplinary action if they don't abide by the rules.

It is all well and good to say that workers are being paid, so they should comply. But if their heart isn't in it, they simply won't buy in to the company ethos or speak out about safety when it matters. Consider Theo. They had his mind, but not his heart. Workers need to feel it in their "bones" before they trust and believe in a program or system. If workers get a sniff of incongruity between what leaders declare—and how they act, you'll lose them.

This is so important. No amount of manipulation, coercion or force will establish voluntary operational discipline. If the workforce and leaders are not congruent with stated company values (or otherwise), loyalty evaporates. More than likely there will be a hidden secret unspoken value that neither the workforce or company leaders acknowledge or even (want to) realise. Because it might destabilise the externally communicated "Safety first" reputation. And that would be akin to blasphemy under our current paradigm.

To enable open and inclusive safety discussions, the work environment must consist of trusting relationships between leaders and workers, built on a congruent foundation. It's not always pretty, but trust can be brought to life if we are dinkum with each other about our levels of belief in the system. This may mean raising your hand at the pre-shift briefing and saying, "You know what? I think these Take-5 safety observation checklists have become a tick and flick exercise". In a trusting environment these comments would not be struck down by leaders. Quite the opposite, leaders would encourage further discussion around creating alternative programs or repairing the one they have. Solutions created around a 'Why'. Possibly influencing the entire industry with their innovations.

The BS Detector

BS stands for "Brain Stem" right? I'm joking. But it's no coincidence that when we detect BS, our 'Why' is responsible. The 'Why' works closely with the Brain stem as part of the Habitual brain function to create trust. If a company is (perceived to be) carrying out activities below the standards they espouse, workers will never buy in to upholding them. Whether leaders realise it or not, work crews instinctively sense when things are not authentic, real or genuine. Workers develop a kind of sensitivity for directives that contradict stated company values. Our "trust centre", the 'Why' (Habitual brain), sends sensory messages to the Emotional brain to be watchful, that we may be in danger. It's the IOS model in action. Our defence mechanism sensing things are askew.

If the safety oratory doesn't match what really occurs on site, the Emotional brain will interpret that "something's not right", and this inner conflict will have a subtle but distinctly noticeable effect on worker morale. Never spoken to out loud, only alluded to under their breath in lunchrooms and corridors. The real places where safety cultures are cultivated. When leaders direct more haul trucks into an already congested area, or classify a potentially serious incident as a "near miss" to avoid the paperwork, workers begin to feel that these vague interpretations of the standards are a green light to do the same. Ultimately it creates disbelief in safety systems generally.

The Psychology of Congruence

In psychology, when we feel congruent. Our internal beliefs agree with our external experience. [31] We walk the talk, negotiate with confidence, seek things that match our viewpoints, create plans for the future and are self-motivated and inspired to carry them out. We accept personal responsibility, take ownership of our workplace and are willing to be held accountable for our commitments and agreements. When standards are consistently achieved, intrinsic motivation and a general belief in the system will emerge.

Quite the opposite however is when we feel things are incongruent. It manifests as a conflict between internal beliefs and external behaviour. Expressed usually as negative emotions.[32] Such as anger (you disappoint me), depression (I disappoint you), and anxiety (fear of disappointment). These are all manifestations of incongruent feelings. Feeling this inner-conflict leaves us uninspired and powerless to speak out or change things. When a workplace is not congruent, then persuasion, coercion and manipulation is required to convince a workforce to be safe. How many workplaces are pleading with their workforce to be safe today? Is that congruent with our safety values?

Model Leadership

Although it is not common, a company who places a real value on the integrity of their relationship with the workforce, greatly influences the safety culture. By "real value" I mean the unfathomed commitment to the satisfaction of the workforce. More than loyalty to the customer, more than caring about the shareholder, more than pandering to management. Not just lip service, but unparalleled compassion and a true understanding of the power of relationships. It's when a leader's performance and delivery of their instructions are measured in how well they relate and support the workforce. This models a true commitment to the workforce, and workers will reflect it back to the company in spades. It also communicates to the world how a company wants to be perceived. In this case, totally committed to its people first, above any other value.

Unfortunately, or fortunately, depends on how you look at it, a leader's conduct and integrity is always under the microscope. When the leadership team and work crew are in accord, the journey towards continuous improvement seems inevitable. But any seeming contradictions in a company or leader's conduct, is permission for workers to surreptitiously do the same. You'll find workers will not buy in to stated rules and procedures as a result. They may not bother to wear seatbelts, will talk on the phone while they drive, or not adhere to speed limits. These may not necessarily lead to incidents, but it's a sign that double-standards exist and much worse, no trust. In this environment workers decide to do as they please. Especially when leaders aren't around to enforce operational discipline. On the other hand, if leaders are congruent and walking the talk, most workplace activities will be carried out as agreed, if not enthusiastically. When leaders practice what they preach you'll find workers are willingly on-board with the agreed purpose and direction of the company.

In his Just Another Day presentation, Theo mentions how his Safety Manager and the Workplace Health Inspector entered his hospital ward as part of their investigation. "Stop it right there", Theo demands. "Let's cut the crap. I took off my gloves. I don't know why, other than to finish the job. There's no other excuse, it was me." The inquisitors looked at each other, close their notes and thank Theo for his honesty. It was an easy conclusion for them. *"Procedural breach"*. Maybe they could have conducted a "5 Whys", but it would have led to the same question every time. "Why did you do it". Perhaps not then, but they could have delved deeper. What was Theo's mood? What was his relationship with his boss, the crew, his wife? These answers may have changed the course of history. May have uncovered a deeper hidden cause. Like this book will.

"Trust is the congruence between what
you say and what you do."
—Peter Drucker

SECRET VALUES

During Theo's agonising rehabilitation, he has more time on his hands than he cares to remember. He repeatedly asks himself why he let so many people down. After the millionth time it sends him into a deep, deep depression. At that level, when all dignity and ego has vanished, he confronts his own soul and drifts into deep philosophical contemplation, delving beneath the 'real' root cause of his accident. A man with all that experience doesn't just throw his life away. What really happened means reaching down to some bedrock of truth. The foundations upon which the workplace culture truly operated. Then it occurs to him. There was something! A deeply hidden code that no one talked about. "You didn't speak about it, but you knew it was there," he recalls.

What's Really Going On?

Theo reflects on the culture, its customs and beliefs. What was really lying beneath the safety oratory and the rhetoric? Was there something going on that no one was talking about? There was no outwardly blatant disregard for safety or work procedures, or the suppression of known discrepancies. But clearly, that is what was happening. Theo discovers in hindsight that his workplace was actually governed by a host of secret and unspoken values. If Skinny couldn't get his gloves into that tiny space, and Theo couldn't either, then how on earth did all the other lineys get that 12-millimetre nut off? This wasn't only a company problem, but the industry as a whole might have been accepting this practice.

It's what lies beneath the company's stated values, the secret values, that's really motivating a workforce's cultural leanings. These can have either a positive or a negative effect. More often or not they are negative. Even well-meaning values, if they are not driven by a 'Why', will invite the opportunity for workforces to deviate unwittingly from their original intention. Consider that Theo wanted to remove the 12-millimetre nut so as not to inconvenience the crew or the customer. It was well-meaning enough, and unspoken. But not congruent.

Getting It Done

Do things really get done "by the book" with all the obstacles and constraints that occur daily in an ongoing operation? When the pressure is on and things have to get handled, get made, delivered, dug up, erected, maintained or carried out as quickly as possible, what becomes accepted practice? What is the real company value, the real bottom line, when things get expensive, hectic, pressured or stuck? When stuff has to be expedited to meet a deadline or meet production targets, what is the "elephant in the room"? What are the secret values, those motives that contradict company expressed values, which conflict the company's public message and reputation? Which are condoned arbitrarily to get things done. These are the real underlying causes of accidents. In their research paper, "Earnings Expectations and Employee Safety", Caskeya, Bugra and Ozelb state that:

"Higher injury/illness rates are associated with both incr-eases in employee workloads and in abnormal reductions of discretionary expenses". [33]

Unfortunately, there's resistance to uncovering secret values because it may suit both leaders and workers alike to have them maintained. It might mean they can relax the rules a little. It usually takes an upheaval to break the status quo and clean these incongruences up. Yet congruence is the only path to job satisfaction. No one ever truly finds empowerment trying to cheat the system. Not over the long term anyway. Secret values are those references that workers absorb consciously and unconsciously but never communicate openly. Such as "you can't beat us", "we get it done", "we are the quickest, strongest, fittest, the best", we make it happen".

On the face of it, these seem harmless enough. If not great attributes. But if they are not connected to a 'Why', the 'How' will have a field day. This is when we carry out tasks trying to seek approval or succumb to the ideals of punishment and reward. Even machoism or bravado creep in, or peer pressure. In any case, much of this conduct certainly isn't congruent with the expressed company values. So what is going on here?

IOS Culture

An IOS culture aims to reveal the secret values that exist and openly discuss their impact. Their revelation encourages the emergence of trust, creating further openness and disclosure. When a workplace is operating back-to-front instead of IOS, secret values are tolerated because they support 'getting the job done'. The clandestine nature of secret values means that on the surface, the use of hollow safety language and shallow communication deceives leaders into thinking they are getting the message through. Theo's manager would argue that his culture was strictly "safety first". That personally, he would never tolerate anything less. And to be honest, a man in his position is obliged to say this. However, the events occurring within his company tell another story. Critical PPE was deemed arbitrary.

To learn anything from Theo's tragedy, perhaps we should go deeper and be completely honest with ourselves. In other words, let's *get real*. Can every person in an organisation put their hand on their heart and say categorically, "I believe our company operates with the utmost integrity, congruence and accountability". If so there are probably no secret or unspoken values operating in your workplace—and there will be the emergence of trust and voluntary operational discipline. Is this true for you? If so, you are to be commended.

Planting New Seeds

It's only conjecture, and perhaps we'll never know, but did Theo feel a sense of inner conflict for not acting upon Skinny's transgression? Could taking his own gloves off be the Rational brain reconciling the 'Emotional brain's guilt? It's drawing a long bow for some people. However, this type of deeper psychological contemplation is the brave new world of safety science. Dare I say it; our humanness is being considered. I envisage in the future these types of hypotheses will be the starting point. As soon as we recognise secret values as a cultural realism. If you think about it, unspoken and secret values may influence workplace culture more than you realise. If conduct is NOT being driven by regulatory compliance or corporate governance, then it must be some sort of values, secret or otherwise, driving worker conduct. If congruent workplaces create trust, and trust creates safety within a spirit of continuous improvement, where should we start? The answer is practicing "extreme ownership" and walking the talk. It's about creating clear and concise agreements and a system that upholds them. It's unearthing and cleaning up any vague interpretations of the rules or acceptance of procedural deviations. By implementing an operating model that integrates accountability and ownership as a "true" value. Where safety is no longer lip service, but a cultural truism.

Easier said than done right? Not really. I've been running an accountability and agreements model in the workplace for years. It is amazing how eager workers want to "clean things up", let alone the positive impact accountability principles have on their personal lives. Soon I'll be sharing with you these techniques that you can start applying yourself. Leaders who embed accountability into their leadership model use their own conduct as an example. This encourages workers to respond by taking personal responsibility for their activities and ownership of their conduct too. They both walk the talk.

> "I am master of my spoken words and slave to
> those which remain unspoken."
> —Ankita Singhal

DECISIONS, DECISIONS

Theo's decision to remove his hands from his insulated gloves was made after weighing up all of the possible scenarios in a heartbeat, in a nanosecond. Any number of choices could have transpired, but they didn't. He recalls the instance he saw his hands revealed as he slid them from his gloves. He freezes that moment in his mind. The last time he saw them intact. Those appendages that served him so well. He visualises the tone of his skin, the hairs bristling in the sun. Delving deeper into those thoughts, his feelings, the environment, sounds and smells—he suddenly recalls something. A self-concept. He remembers how invincible he felt. Untouchable, bullet-proof. The Habitual brain's caution and self-preserve were nowhere. Only self aggrandisation and invincibility. What causes this?

"Rabbit" Proofing the "Fence"

Before you make a decision, your Emotional brain rages all over the place. Then, when you've made the decision your Rational brain sets about rationalising it. Watch people carefully and you'll see the flip flop between the emotional state and the rational state. "I want a new car" (feeling). "But I can't afford it" (rationalising). "But I want it" (feeling). "You don't need it" (rationalising). Let me explain how this roller coaster works.

To decide means to kill off choices. 34 The Latin *de-* means 'down from' and *-cide* means the 'act of killing'. Think of suicide, insecticide, infanticide or homicide. Words that end in "cide" refer to the extermination of something. *De-cide*-ing is the art of choosing which choice will die. In just about every case, the inconvenient choice will get the bullet. If you've got lots of cash, your ego is inconvenienced by driving around in a crappy car. If you're broke, your finances are inconvenienced if you buy a new car. That's why capitalism and credit boomed simultaneously during the industrial revolution. They both create more convenience. Until you have to pay back the debt of course. And this is my point. Why does short-term gain trump the potential long-term cost so much? Well, everyone values a person who can make decisions, right? These people often become leaders. We frown on those who can't make the tough decisions when it counts. When we are faced with narrowing down multiple choices, we naturally kill off the "inconvenient" ones. Removing selections that require greater effort, personal cost or are a threat to our ego. This is instinctive. It's hard wired. How can we re-wire ourselves to select the tougher, safer choices in the *heat of the moment*? Well, you have to understand your motives.

A "rabbit in the headlight" describes a situation when none of the choices available are convenient. There's a fear of having to choose because any choice appears to have a negative outcome. Whereas "Sitting on the fence" implies the opposite. That all of the choices are convenient and we suffer a sort of *fear of missing out* if we let one go. We have developed these expressions to be derogatory towards people who can't make decisions. It's part of our culture to honour those who are decisive. Decision-making therefore is rewarded more than wavering in our society. People fear that a *rabbit in the headlight* or *fence sitting* sees them as being weak. Faced with a tough situation, we are geared unconsciously to jump at any opportunity to make life easier. It's nature's way, to take a short-cut in the *heat of the moment*. But the consequences are often the opposite of what we expect. Here's why.

Nature's Way

The levels of trust between workers and leaders play a significant role in decision making. If trust is low, management's instructions and safety communication have far less significance. 35 If there is no connection to a common vision or cause, the workforce is more inclined to make decisions based on convenience—than follow instructions or procedures. Buy-in of company standards decrease considerably when there is no link to a 'Why'.

Expecting workers to be loyal to company regulations and standards when Rational brain concepts create them, without evidence of a 'Why', will feel like manipulation and not achieve the required buy-in. The workplace will not *feel real* for workers and a sense of going through the motions will emerge. On the face of it, being efficient and choosing the most convenient option seems to be in tune with nature. The problem is nature can be devastatingly efficient. Earthquakes and violent storms for example can level the playing field instantly. Even so, in that devastation is the seed of change and renewal so vital for the ongoing survival of the planet. There's that conservation law again.

The problem for us however, is we don't have the resilience to outlast Mother nature's procreative qualities. Therefore, we can't cave into our convenience instincts and expect to survive. Taking short-cuts over the immediate term exposes our fragility. If we compare our workplace decisions against convenient versus inconvenient choices, we have a tool that will greatly enhance our survival. But how can we be aware of such wisdom in the *heat of the moment*, bringing the unconscious back into consciousness? We can't. But we can plant unconscious habits that do it for us.

Follow Your Nose

After repeated exposure to the same risks, we become desensitised to those potentially fatal consequences. This is also human nature and a huge problem for us. To see what I mean, let's try something. If you focus now, you can see the end of your nose. It's there, take a look. It's always in your view. But our minds have become so efficient at blocking it out we never notice it. When you decide to pay attention to your nose, your perception changes and you experience another point of view that is closer to reality. This is what is meant by Get Real. The idea that things are happening right under our noses but which we ignore or overlook. We naturally avoid looking at our nose like we naturally avoid things that inconvenience Mr. 'What's' determination. The 'What' relegates nose awareness as nonsense and places it in the unconscious. Making it the Habitual brain's responsibility. Ridding itself of the toil and energy it takes to process this information.

These parts of our brain have made up our minds for us. I bet that if you tried, you couldn't focus on your nose for more than a minute while you read this book. Such is the power of habit. We only become alert to the Habitual brain's fight or flight responses when they are triggered. We don't have a conscious choice in any of its decisions. Therefore, we must combat habit patterns relegated to the unconscious mind with different trigger and responses. That's why missions are so valuable. They change existing habit loops, bringing about awareness to what's important when triggered. Are you still focusing on your nose or have you forgotten it already? Get it?

Trained for Danger

Ironically, we are also trained to block out the fear of dangerous work activities otherwise we wouldn't have the confidence to perform our tasks. Think of skydiving, military exercises, aircraft test pilots, bomb squads, underground miners or even lineys. For instance, Theo's training involved a unique experience. Raised in an elevated work platform next to a live transmission line, Theo must reach out and touch the live electrical cable with a metal shifting spanner, wearing his insulated gloves. He can hear the tremendous power buzzing through the wire. Every part of his being screams not to do it. But this is an important part of a liney's education. If a liney doesn't have the confidence to trust their specialised PPE, they aren't equipped to make calculated decisions as part of their high-risk work activities. Did desensitising Theo to the risks of high voltage transmission lines contribute to his accident? Or was it simply part of his training and the absence of a well-defined 'Why' that is to blame? Perhaps we'll never know, so we shouldn't take a chance. All high-risk work activities need 'Whys' too.

I once led the investigation of a serious incident in an open-pit mining operation in Laos, South East Asia. Nineteen Lao nationals in two personnel buses were picking up the remaining drill crew at the end of the shift. Parked just twenty metres from a fully charged drill-hole pattern, suddenly it went BOOM! The drill and blast supervisor, safely in the firing shed, initiated detonation. Luckily everyone on the pad was on the protected side of the blast, and the percussion blew away from them in the other direction. Everyone survived, but they were badly shaken. The root cause of the accident turned out to be *"desensitisation of the safety check sequence"*. Over time, incremental shifts in shot-firing habits had crept in, to save time. What's interesting is that the local national workforce was new to mining. It was the first western-styled mining operation in Laos. They started from scratch. No pre-existing shot-firing sequence prevailed. No existing bad habits. In fact, the locals had a deep respect for explosives. Un-exploded ordinance (UXO) was a massive problem after they were bombed relentlessly during the Vietnam War. Every member of the drill and blast crew could relate a horror story where a family member was maimed by UXO that littered their villages after the war. Therefore, the drill and blast crew were trained to a very high standard with a heightened sense of awareness to the dangers of open-pit blasting. Those responsible for the incident could not blame a pre-existing company culture. It was simply the safety checks slowly eroding over time to make their job more convenient. Human habits in action, right before my eyes. I recommended in my report several changes to the drill and blast operation. One of them was to rename pit locations after villages and the drill pad areas after streets. "Rue Sam, Huay Xai" meant Bench 3 in the South Pit, for instance. No one had thought to link safety checks to local Laos values. Where real life UXO problems existed. By creating a "Why" linked to village life, the safety check sequence would have much more significance. The firing sequence would (necessarily) become the hallmark of the highest safety standards for the entire operation. The Laotian's loved the idea but the westerners baulked. A little too "out there" for the traditionalists. Pity.

Instinctively, our brains automatically seek shortcutting the blast sequence or taking off our gloves to access a tricky nut. The extra effort it takes for a safe alternative is countered by the Rational brain logically reducing the workload. The Rational brain constantly relegates repetitive tasks to the Habitual brain to conserve energy. Except the Habitual brain works unconsciously. Therefore, if we relegate a bit of risky business into the Habitual brain it will be triggered again unconsciously. Scary to think that our inbuilt brain efficiency can pose such a grave danger.

Who or What Is Really Guiding Us?

Liney's will tell you that after a while, working around 22,000 volts soon becomes second nature. An underground miner will tell you working around explosives becomes matter-of-course. If our safety compass loses its bearings, it's because the Rational brain has done such a good job. But good for who or "What"? Researchers from the "dots experiment" in the previous chapter wrote that when we try to decide which apple to pick from a tree, the brain avoids visual stimulus about colour, size and shape, which is the real information required to choose wisely, and instead we focus on the effort required to obtain the apple. [36] We perceive apples at the top of the tree to look less tempting than the lower ones:

> *"Our brain tricks us into believing the low-hanging-fruit really is the ripest," says Dr. Nobuhiro Hagura.*

In the workplace our decisions constantly seek low-hanging-fruit solutions. Our perceptions being misled. In fact, it does not make any sense to pick low hanging fruit at all. Typically, if you carry a bag and pick the low hanging fruit first, you would have to work your way up the ladder with an increasingly heavy load. Therefore, we must brace ourselves in the face of our natural human propensity to avoid "reality" and bring the end of our nose back into focus. (Got you again!)

Given all of the information, how can we possibly know our choices are guiding us in the right direction? How can we stop our emotions, our pride, even our dignity from leading us astray? How do we discern the Habitual brain's seemingly harmless decisions that will ultimately save us or kill us? What will steer us in the right direction when it's needed most? Because in the *heat of the moment* everything feels 'real'. Somehow, we need a process that guides us to make default IOS decisions that are reliable, safe and productive. Like a 'Why'.

Keep Ego Out of It

In the harsh realities of the Savannah, a Lioness may adjust her litter size to suit her ability to raise her offspring. She's not attached to the decision whether to kill off her cubs or not. She doesn't have a 'How' sense of remorse. Scientists have detected some stress levels in her decision but believe it's a sense of vulnerability from her situation. [37] She makes her choices based purely on survival, comparing any short-term gains (keeping the cubs) against long-term costs (her own life).

The point I'm making is that in the workplace, we are left to our own devices all the time, making decisions based on our own personal ego preferences and values. If our values are steeped in 'team' performance, then asking for help is convenient. If our value system prides itself on 'individual' performance, then NOT asking for help is convenient. Two value systems, both with convenient options. But two completely opposite outcomes. When we introduce ego or side with our self-identity, our decisions are greatly affected and varied. Nico admits he cannot get the nut off and asks Theo to have a go. Theo couldn't get it off either but refuses to admit defeat. What makes Theo fear the possible discomfort to his ego that he would take a risk, before thinking of his own wellbeing? Before Nico's, the company, his family? Was it purely convenience?

The truth is we'll never really know, so why leave it to convenient choices in the first place? We should never be making decisions in the workplace that relate back to our ego and subsequent emotions. But since it's the only possible way we can, the best defence against convenient choices is to attach pleasurable outcomes as motivation to carry out the additional effort required to be safe. Creating a sense of purpose that is aligned with the workforce's values if powerful motivation for this. Intrinsic Motivation can be achieved when the workplace has a value in line with their own personal beliefs. If we don't discover what those beliefs are and put them to work, we relegate safety habits as a last line of defence. Too late she cried!

"When your values are clear to you, making
decisions becomes easier."
—Roy E. Disney

CULTURE SHOCK

Theo loved what he did and was attracted to the "thrill" of live-line work. He was good and knew it. Everyone trusted him and his judgement. They respected his experience. However, it was different working in Australia than his homeland South Africa. People were different. He had to adjust to his new environment and do what he could to fit in. He wanted to do well, and was not going to rock the boat if he thought things were unsafe. His job meant everything to him and his family. It was a case of adjusting to the new environment at all costs. Both culturally and work-wise. It's a tough gig trying to fit in. But when everything you have is riding on it, you just do it.

What Does "Good Safety" Look Like?

In his ground-breaking book "Sapiens", Yuval Noah Harari explains how humans evolved to become the most dominant species on earth because of our ability to imagine myths and stories. Imagination enabled us to communicate with each other on a mass level. Hence societies were born and the emergence of values and cultures. Ideally, safety values would create safe-work cultures. Except when we say "safety", no one can *imagine* what it really means? Instead, we'll talk about what it's NOT. For instance, we'll often say safety is having *no* incidents, *no* accidents, *no* hazardous conditions or *no* injuries. For sure there's "good" housekeeping or wearing the "right" PPE. But what does that really mean? Is it a safety value, quality value or an instruction? Or all of the above! If being safe is "not" having an incident or accident, well that's a pretty broad characterisation. Yet, even the Cambridge dictionary describes it that way: "Safety is not being in danger or put at risk". So how do we articulate what "good" looks like when we unwittingly communicate safety in terms of what we "don't" want? The answer is to focus on mindset and attitude, and not focus on things over which we have no control.

Harari shows us many examples of how imagination, myths and stories create culture. Some are good, others not so much. Think dictatorships or racism. Even workplaces are prone to dogma. We can create good safety by not painting vivid pictures of what's bad and what to avoid. We can inspire staff and contractors to create a *vision* of what good looks like. Something they can see in their mind's eye, that gets their juices flowing. Perhaps it's why workforces don't fully buy into our safety systems. They struggle to SEE it. Instead they perceive safety as hampering the progress of their activities.

That's where a "Safety Mission" comes in. By facilitating workers to create their own version of "good", they communicate safety in terms of what they imagine it looks like. On their terms, not ours. Something they'll believe in and trust because THEY own it. I've facilitated hundreds of Safety Mission processes where even the roughest toughest work crews will protect and embody their declaration because it was drawn from deep within their own value systems. Then we reinforce their vision daily in the pre-shift meeting. By encouraging their imagination, we allow them to create the dream of what a great place to work at, would look and feel like.

A definition of what good safety looks like—according to them.

If You Feel Safe, You'll Act Safe

Like most businesses, you've probably tried to develop your safety culture through an intricate web of "information". Such as inductions, emergency response provisions and safe operating procedures that point you in the right direction. All the things that make up the various do's and don'ts we tell people they must follow to be safe. Problem is, it only works on the surface. People still take risks and they still have accidents. Why do they do that? Because you can't create an impeccable safe work culture through information packs and training. Cultures are cultivated from the impressions people form about whether they trust your operating model—or not. It's either loyalty or dissent filtering through the social networks that exist in your organisation. You hope it's loyalty from a safety perspective. Because when people "feel" safe, they will "act" safe. Dissenters will see safety as an inconvenience.

Newcomers experience a company's culture in lunch rooms and work fronts. By chatting with people over coffee or a couple of drinks after work. They learn about the bureaucracy, who to avoid and who gets things done, when to speak up or when to be quiet, through daily social interactions. This "true" demonstration of your existing culture is captured through the informal power structures, relationships, alliances and even conflicts—that make up your workforce's daily work habits. If teamwork emerges through a sense of trust, then a positive safety culture will evolve. If there is friction, stress and a punitive atmosphere, a negative safety culture will evolve. But worse, belief in your safety system will erode.

Inductions, procedures, the safety manual or handbook can only convey information, never culture. Cultivation of the desired culture is far less about information, promotional material, catchphrases, procedures and systems (although very important)—and much more about people's "feelings" and their value systems. I.e. What's in it for them. It always has been. Yet we rarely take a snapshot of our existing culture in terms of the workforce's "emotional connection" to safety, or relationships with the leadership team. We seem to rely on facts and figures and whether we've met our numerical targets or not. Lost time injury frequency rates (LITFR) and zero harm comes to mind.

Going Through the (e)Motions

An instruction to double the amount of Take 5s or field interactions in response to an incident won't improve safety. Instead it lowers the crew's morale. Trying to solve 'Why' problems with a 'What' solution is counterproductive. Chevron oil and gas in Western Australia realised this problem, so they removed Take 5s and trained their personnel in a self-governing risk analysis program. No more tick and flick, just a 'Why'-based solution that creates ownership instead.

Einstein said, "You can't solve a problem at the same level it was created". Yet there are crazy programs out there where workers write pretend letters to their family, promising to be safe. Or they place the names of their children on their PPE. Gory posters of injuries are placed in the lunch room or on safety notice boards. These might feature the Rational brain's creativity, or the 'What's' clever use of manipulation, but it has no impact on the real issue. That is, a lack of intrinsic motivation to be safe. Workers don't buy-in to WHAT they need, they buy into WHY they need it. Plotting your work crew's attitude against the IOS model is far more effective. It will highlight the current status of your safety culture more accurately than relying on statistics and graphs. Next time, try assessing your workplace through the IOS model and match your current situation against it. For example:

- Any time the workplace is going through the motions, following systems they don't truly believe in, they operate at the level of the 'What'.
- If workers are stressed or pressured to complete tasks, the workplace is operating from the level of the 'How'.
- When workers are internally motivated to carry out safe work systems with the intention of satisfying a higher ideal, the workplace is operating on the level of the 'Why'.

Key Performance Attitudes (KPA)

Rational ('What') based solutions want to solve the human "issue" through the use of control. The problem is while the 'What' is running the show, the 'How' will always be tagging along, following along aimlessly, creating impatience and a dynamic that forces you to "get it done". If it could, the 'What' would eliminate humans from the equation altogether. But until we've all been replaced with robots, the 'What's ambition won't go very far. You'll never get rid of humans. Who will run robot programming and maintenance? So, we either solve this dilemma, start looking for 'Why'-based solutions or continue to experience accidents. Unfortunately, with all our efforts to track workplace performance, we still haven't discovered a device that gauges authenticity or belief in the system. Or perhaps we'd be able to pinpoint much of our difficulties.

Another area we should be monitoring is a performance category nearly impossible to measure. Trust! If we could, we'd have at our disposal a Key Performance Attitude (KPA) that could tell us if workers are buying into a company's safety culture or not. I call these types of indicators KPA's because I believe they are more important than KPI's (key performance indicators). But how do you gauge authenticity? How do you plot "attitude"? Well, that's easy. How have we always measured our friends' and colleagues' mindset? We check in with them to see how they are "feeling". Except somehow authenticity has lost its way in this regard. Somewhere along the line, "How are you" started getting responses of the obligatory, "Good."

Getting Real

Maybe as a species we've never been good at connecting with others on this level. But whether our mindset is positive or not, has a massive impact on our commitment to safe work practices. And this deserves our attention. Sometimes we feel like crap. We have bills, the cat died, Johnny is sick etc. Yet we always reply "How are you" with, "Good." Your body language never lies however, and your colleagues can usually smell a rat. It's just they don't have the tools to deal with a situation that isn't "Good". Have you sat in a pre-shift meeting and the mood is decisively down? Particularly after an incident. Everyone wants to get to work and avoid the discomfort. There's no cure for this. No magic wand. We need to be clear about our commitment to workplace agreements in these situations. "Are we 100% clear on the agreement to wear our PPE today?" "Check." "Are we 100% clear on our agreement to follow the Working at Heights Procedure?" "Check." "Joan, you've got the bins, right?" Check! "Jim, you'll refill the parts shelves, yes?" Check!

Simply acknowledging the down mood and offering support is all any of us can do. If all our agreements are clear, concise and committed to 100%, we can still go to work. But let's be human about it. We can be authentic. Sweeping bad feelings under the carpet is when the problems start. Communicating in terms of being real is probably the last thing we ever consider in our workplaces. In my programs I introduce the idea of relating how we feel in terms of "mad, glad, sad or bad". I avoid "good". Actually I forbid it. Sure, someone might say "glad" when they're not. But the exercise simply highlights when we are not being authentic. Workplaces that don't operate authentically may even create an environment prone to accidents. What most people don't understand is that authenticity in the workplace must be of higher value than shareholder or customer experience, or it's like learning to run before you can walk. An authentic workplace must emerge even before productivity, to be truly effective. Otherwise performance targets will feel like a hollow victory.

So here's the deal. If we seek durable fulfilment at home, we are usually authentic with our spouse or friends, right? If work is an extension of our lives, then finding personal satisfaction in the workplace hinges on the same principle. Being real is not easy sometimes, but creating safety depends on it. Our attitude doesn't always have to be "up", just real. Are you beginning to see why we called this book Get Real?

Developing Trust

A company does not own its culture; it is only a facilitator. Workers own it. The best thing a company can do is promote a cultural brand that ignites trust and allows a workforce to embrace it and pass it on to the next generation. Placing shareholder or customer value before your workforce, violates that trust. Trust does not emerge simply because a supervisor makes the rational case for safety, or because a manager promises that trusting each other will create teamwork. Trust is not a tick in a box. Trust is a feeling, not a rational experience. It's Emotional brain—not Rational brain. It's 'Why'—not 'What'. When leaders implement a commitment to their workforce above all else, a natural empirical order is realised. They believe a satisfied and inspired work crew will create a safe workplace; a safe workplace ensures quality and productivity; quality and productivity enhances shareholder value and customer experience. In this order a natural hierarchy exists. A balance and evolution that corresponds with the natural sequential progression of all three parts of the IOS Brain:

1. Define your *Cause* first ('Why')
2. Then the *Planning* ('How')
3. Safe *Productivity* follows ('What')

Trusting relationships are not something that can be produced on command. Trust will emerge when there's a sense the organisation is driven by things other than self-gain, when authenticity and honesty is a higher value amongst leaders. Workers will believe in the system even when things go wrong. That's when a leader's authenticity can emerge, in the face of adversity. That's when workers can see their relationship is worth much more to the leaders than blaming them after an incident. In the same way, workers might lose trust in their leaders when everything goes as planned, if there's an air of pretentiousness or a sense they are going through the motions to meet regulatory requirements. Workers won't put their heart into it. No heart means no 'Why'. Without 'Why' involvement our safety programs can only ever arrive at the level of the 'What'. It's an incomplete model.

With trust comes a sense of value—real value, not just value equated with money. Value by any definition is the transference of trust. Leaders can't convince workers that safety has value, just as you can't convince people to trust you. Leaders have to earn that trust by communicating and demonstrating that they share the same values and beliefs as the workers. They have to talk about safety as their highest value by demonstrating their dedication to workers wellbeing. No secret or unspoken values. Just real ones.

Charades

One of the biggest game of charades in any workplace is the use of safety systems or programs that neither workers nor leaders believe in. But I see it all the time. Are you surprised when I tell you most people cannot see the value of completing Take-5 pre-task hazard assessments? Or they are sceptical of Job Hazard Analysis (JHA) worksheets when they have to sign them? Particularly if they are pre-filled on a computer and printed off, or even hand written off-site, not even completed at the work front. Even after they sign the document, most workers never refer back to them anyway. It's assumed they will, but they don't. Most workers aren't referring to owner equipment manuals (OEM) or procedures either. Having spent many hours translating safety procedures into layman's terms, I soon discovered it wasn't that workers couldn't understand them. It's that they are not inspired enough to read them. Procedures are a product of the Rational brain and have more appeal when they are written from within the spirit of a 'Why'.

Being Part of a Tribe

As I've mentioned, we are very good at following other people's habits because of mankind's herding instincts and mimicking propensities. This is natural in all humans as preservative behaviour. [38] Cultural herding developed through a primitive system of mentation that is trying to save our lives. Sticking together we survive. Assimilate with the tribe and we get to hang around. Don't assimilate and we get shunned from the tribe, facing life's dangers alone. It can be either a blessing or a curse to act like everyone else. If you are part of a work group that has a 'Why' with embedded safe work systems, it is a blessing. If the work group operates without a 'Why' it will cultivate a "get the job done" culture, a curse. Although we don't realise it when we are being like everyone else, these cultures may adopt questionable tactics to get the job done and accidents may become more prevalent. Leaders sometimes scratch their heads and wonder how things could have turned out like this. But it's because there is no 'Why' driving the culture.

When no 'Why' exists that values safe work systems as a higher value than getting the job done, workers take all of the data available at the pre-shift meeting, all of their instructions from the supervisor, gather all of their experience and simply work according to their own instincts anyway. They trust their gut. Except it's not their gut making the decisions. Gut decisions are driven by the Emotional brain. 39 What we think are gut decisions are actually self-identity patterns being supported or challenged by our conditioning. For instance, if I have a schedule to keep, I'll be punctual because "I'm the type of person you can count on". When I meet someone, I'll be pleasa-nt because "I'm easy to get along with". When I write a report, I'll be thorough because "I'm detailed in my analysis". These are concepts developed around self-identity. How we see ourselves. If we are dictated to by these identities, they will dominate our decisions. The Go-to man or Mr. Fix-it might be great attributes if they have a corresponding safe work mindset. Otherwise, with no sense of purpose, our decisions are influenced by punishment and reward, our self-concepts acting out stored patterns of behaviour according to pleasure seeking and pain avoidance. Or trying to impress the tribe. The problem is when these patterns are (mis)activated at inappropriate moments, it can take the focus off the mission at hand. Do the job safely will sometimes morph into 'get the job done now'. Just ask Theo. No one knows more than he, the power our self-identities have over our decisions.

"Never apologise for what you feel.
It's like saying sorry for being real."
—Lil Wayne.

ZERO CONTROL

Theo was a great golfer. After healing, he needed to know if he would ever play again. However, the first time he picked up a club he discovered it was never going to be the same. His disfigured left hand hampered his swing. He'd have to re-learn to play with only his right arm, practicing over and over again. When he eventually played his first game, he out-drove his friends. By focusing on the things he COULD control, he remains very competitive. It's now about technique and timing. Not his score or handicap. He only concentrates on the mechanics of each swing. He doesn't have the power he once had, but he regained something more important... his dignity.

Stop Focusing on Results

What I am about to say might shock you. So here goes... It's a big mistake to set quantitative targets, or aim for numerical goals. I'm more shocked that our safety industry hasn't worked this out yet. We have absolutely no control over these types of performance targets. None! And we are kidding ourselves if we think we do. Because these are not goals at all. They are RESULTS, disguised as goals. Successful golfers don't focus on results: breaking par. Baseball batters don't focus on results: hitting home runs. Sprinters don't focus on results: breaking records. Why? Because they know they have absolutely no control over results. There are so many variables. Stiff competition, wind, temperature, landscape, chance etc. Often it's a game of inches.

Successful athletes focus on what they CAN control. Fitness, preparation, condition of their equipment, refraining from playing outside of their competence (i.e. shots they don't practice). They focus on mindset, their mechanics, on making a pure swing. If they get those things right and they've stuck to their game plan, the *results* will take care of themselves. It's a flawed assumption that numerical quantitative targets ever work in the workplace. We simply set ourselves up for failure. If you want a safe workplace, you must not set quantitative targets, quotas or percentages. No such performance goals whatsoever. None of that, never! Those are things over which you have no final control. You can only control your own actions and attitude. What you say; how you say it; your use of time; planning; your mission and purpose. These are goals that improve your actions and behaviours. They are the only valid goals, because they are the only ones you can CONTROL.

What does Zero Mean Anyway?

Is saying "Don't get hurt," then tracking incidents and accidents a paradox? Would tracking attitude, planning methods or mindset be a more effective metric? Would alternative methods of goal setting empower the workforce and create the buy-in our safety philosophies need? Over the last few decades, industry has overwhelmingly embraced the concept of *zero harm* as an overarching workplace strategy. However, lately it tends to polarise leader/worker relationships more than bind them. There is a lot of research currently investigating zero accident policy effectiveness, both in theory and in practice. The results are not good. Firstly, the term is confusing because not all injuries are applied. It seems minor injuries like paper cuts and bruises are acceptable. Whenever the Habitual brain experiences this kind of conflict, it will cancel the concept out. Also, in the spirit of continuous improvement, we shouldn't ignore the evidence that zero target policies are facilitating the concealment of reporting, and encouraging the non-disclosure of incidents and injuries.

An Infinite Vision

Finding common ground between statistical targets and "soft" metrics, is no easy task. Though it might make things easier for work teams if their targets feel a little more fulfilling, more visceral and organic. I have immense respect for our current safety programs. However, workers don't seem to be inspired by lost time injury frequency rates, because they rarely achieve them. It's like a coach who sets world records as a goal. Average athletes have no chance, so they give up hope. Sound like any workplace you know? I will admit that as a statement of one's commitment to safety, zero harm is quite aspirational. It's downfall however, is that it's not real. Imagine a world without harm. Yeah sure, right? Herein lies another problem. Trying to imagine a world where no one is harmed, is quite hard for people. It's like trying to imagine global financial equality, freedom from hunger, or a world without religious conflicts. Although they are highly desirable, they're hard to visualise. Lin Yutang, the famous Chinese philosopher, wisely wrote: "A tendency to fly too straight at a goal, instead of circling around it, often carries one too far."

Let's invite our workforces to speak their truth and say how they really feel about the pressure of maintaining zero harm. We might just find some bedrock of truth we can build the foundations of our safety systems on. Workers crave any opportunity to be real. We just need to create the space where they can be. I don't advocate throwing the baby out with the bath water, but I think instead of creating an environment where injuries are not acceptable, what if we promoted more life affirming targets. The energy it takes to invent ways of keeping statistics at zero might be better off spent discovering *infinite* ways of finding durable fulfilment, or achieving the desired levels of personal satisfaction. Instead of stifling our endeavours by limiting things to zero, should we embrace more unrestricting targets? What about happiness or camaraderie?

Believability

Craig Donaldson's article in the "OHS Professional", "Zero harm: Infallible or Ineffectual", explores the evidence for and against zero harm as a philosophy and if it influences workplace behaviour positively—or not. [40] It raises the issue of what zero harm really means for professionals in our industry.

Does it mean "no harm to anyone, anytime while at work?" Or is it, "no incidents yesterday, therefore we achieved zero harm?" When I ask people to explain what "it" means for them, I get many different answers, mostly disbelief. The problem is, if the workforce doesn't truly believe in its safety goals, we may have built our safety systems on a house of cards. What might have been meant as a universal vision, may actually turn out to be something people can't visualise. This is a problem for mission and vision goal setting objectives. The ability to "see" the vision creates the momentum to achieve it.

Here's the thing. Whether it's zero harm or any other philosophy, an organisation that is secretly (or openly) going through the motions with its safety program will struggle to be believed. We all know what happens when a salesman doesn't believe in the product they are trying sell. People see right through them, right? Therefore, workers see when an organisation washes over existing programs and call it zero harm. They just don't buy it. Of course, zero target programs have created many improvements over the years too. Yet programs must be continuously built upon to keep up with the times.

I commiserate with management who are tasked with meeting zero targets set by the board. Unfortunately, the result has been the implementation of a carrot and stick mentality. Punishment and reward, lagging indicators pretending to be leading indicators, gifts and incentives as enticements and many other manipulations. The problem is that in chasing *zero* we stifle openness and disclosure. Which is essential if you want your workforces to champion safety. There's no doubt that striving for zero facilitates the under-reporting of incidents and injuries. It's a fact. And the workforce resists engagement too. The suppression of *free speech* in our pre-shift meetings around this subject is so palpable; it's amazing to think we don't address it more often. If we eradicated the idea of incidents as a negative; stopped trying to force statistics to be zero; if we removed the frustrations this creates between management and the workforce—how might that change the whole paradigm around what "zero" means? Let's give zero a facelift.

Giving Zero a Facelift

What if there was a positive vibe around incident investigations? What if we rewarded reporting of incidents with a name that celebrated the spirit of continuous improvement? Would we even call it zero? Perhaps "unlimited", "infinite", "boundless", "tremendous" or "colossal" are more inspiring terms. What if we encouraged imperfection? For instance, is it better to force your children to be perfect, or entice their growth in the spirit of creativity and learning from mistakes? What is going to get the best results, expression or extraction?

The vector that zero programs have, is the opposite to growth and expansion. It's constrictive and creates a deflating mindset. Just sit in a pre-shift meeting after an incident to see what I mean. So depressing. Safety innovation doesn't thrive in this type of atmosphere. Innovation needs freedom of expression and infinite creativity to succeed. When we record our mistakes and errors as statistical data, trying to steer them towards zero, we are driving our workforces downward and inwards. Putting a cap on their spirit and enthusiasm.

A Problem to Control or Resource to Harness

Workers are not inspired by messages that say, "Don't get hurt". They never have. Never will. Yet we say it all the time. They need less patronising instructions if you want them to be honest about their workplace. Furthermore, the struggle between zero and disclosure is not really the battle here. If you want a war, it should be against insincerity, duplicity or the status quo. Besides, zero is so finite as a target, there's nowhere else to go except "1". And in this context, "1" incident is a fail. Therefore, workers are hesitant to speak out or share near-miss learnings under this environment, for fear of failure. We won't ever truly learn the real root causes of our incidents until we stop feeling punished for having them.

The truth is, we have no control over incidents. Because we have no control over human beings. As counterintuitive as it sounds, more acceptance of incidents would reduce them. Implementing numerical and quantitative targets are pointless. Yet, how can a workplace be courageous enough to say, "We accept that you may have accidents?" We can't. But what if we drop numerical safety targets and try better communication? The quality of the discussion after an accident is more important than not meeting some target. Even if a worker was careless and disregarded a safety barrier, how we conduct ourselves as leaders will have more influence over the crew than a meltdown. Self-control and the capacity to rise above the situation is more important than a tarnished statistic.

In his article, "Employees: A Problem to Control or Resource to Harness", Professor Sidney Dekker points out that there is no evidence a zero vision is having a positive impact on safety. [41] Therefore, the jury may still be out as to whether the drive for zero is the right approach. Unfortunately, we still see promotional material with the following theme: "If safety goals are not set at zero, an employer sends a message to employees that incidents are acceptable." But how is that true? It's such a strong statement. There's no room for an employer to move. It means they are evil if they don't support zero. As free-thinking individuals I'd like to think there's room for any challenges to the status quo. It's what makes for a progressive society.

Professor Dekker believes Behaviour Based Safety (BBS) programs try to influence human behaviour so that it will fit our workplace, when perhaps it should be the other way around. Maybe we should be shaping our workplaces to fit human behaviour. We seem insistent on squeezing people into a fixed system rather than engineering a system to fit people. Dekker mentions that BBS does not really ask why we do what we do or explain a model of the mind. Rather, BBS actively resists such introspection. BBS intervention assumes that with the right incentives and sanctions, people will naturally engage in safety. However, I'm not seeing this. So let's flip BBS on its head. Instead of discussing activities in terms of behaviour, unleash our 'Why'. It really wants to find a purpose and goal to pursue. Given the right 'Why', perhaps behaviour doesn't need controlling at all, but is enticed and inspired.

The word behaviour is Old English from the compound "behabban" which means "to contain". Whereas the Latin word "inspiren" was used in the sense of "influence or animate with an idea or purpose". Therefore, inspiration is the "spirit" from "with in". Whereas, behaviour is always spoken in terms of restraint. Unfortunately, autonomy and voluntary operational discipline cannot emerge from an atmosphere of suppression. A self-driven workforce is inspired from within. Is placing a poster in the lunchroom saying "Zero Injuries Is Our Goal", telling workers to be safe or to be perfect? Is that even possible? By focusing on injuries, we kind of rehearse them enough times in our minds until we get them right.

In my experience there are often many signs to warn us that an incident is looming, but our receptiveness to them is stifled by zero target demands. Rather than sharing safety challenges in the pre-shift meeting, we are predisposed to hide them to maintain zero. The only people that speak up in a pre-shift meeting seem to be those who want to move things along, so they can *get to bloody work*.

"Anything that puts downward pressure on honesty,
disclosure, openness, and learning is bad for business."
—Sidney Dekker

SPEAK YOUR MIND

Theo's crew are asked by the manager if there is anything they can contribute that would improve safety. A simple request, yet it goes unheeded. Everyone would have benefitted from a discussion of the 12-millimetre nut problem, most of all Theo. But it was never spoken of again. Not even in private. Without sharing openly, we miss out on our biggest asset—the hindsight and wisdom of collective experience. Continuous improvement and learning from our mistakes hinges on our capacity to speak up confidently on any issue. Problem is, when we give workers the opportunity, for many reasons they rarely speak their mind.

Apprehension

What an organisation says and the message it sends are sometimes two different things. Underneath the leadership's plea for workers to speak up is often a countering force quietly opposing it. If there is a flow on effect from the continual drive to discourage incidents, it's an underlying tension that discourages openness and disclosure. An organisation's communication may convey a resistance to bad news.

Generating a level of apprehension amongst workers which discourages them from being outspoken. For the most part, it occurs on a subconscious level. Yet the apprehension to speak up in meetings is tangible, it's like pulling teeth. Industry is aware of the benefits a healthy discussion creates and has introduced peer-to-peer programs to tackle this kind of thing. Field interaction programs are designed to enhance more participation. Except nowadays field interactions have been turned into a KPI. Transitioning from an engagement tool into a numbers game. Such as weekly/monthly targets for the number of hazards observed or take time talks achieved. Pity.

Why are workers weary of speaking out? Is it a fear of looking silly—or stage fright? Probably both. Is there another reason? For instance, has there been negative responses to people speaking their truth? Or to raising a "sticky" issue? I venture to say it is outside of most company comfort zones for work crews to be too vocal. Conformance is king in today's workplaces and speaking out about existing safety programs is akin to blasphemy, judging by people's reactions. Just step onto a traditional mine site and say you don't believe in the JSA process (risk assessment form) to see what I mean.

Maybe it's fear of the annual performance review, which can be a particularly vengeful tool if workers are found to be too much trouble for a leader. Speaking out may be interpreted as criticism and leaders bite back. Would anyone logically speak up if there is stigma attached? Would anyone report unsafe behaviour if they thought it would incriminate a friend or colleague? Would anyone report an injury or incident if it attracts a negative response? Do you fear reprimand or even mistreatment if you step out of line? If most people feel Take-5 hazard assessment checklists are a tick and flick exercise, why don't they just come out and say it? For fear of the backlash of course.

Downward Pressure

Theo's friend Cindy worked on a remote mine site for two years servicing accommodation rooms. It was a brutal schedule. Forty rooms a day. She decided to fill out her Take 5 safety checklist in her room the night before to meet the demand. One day she received a written warning and underwent counselling. But it wasn't for prefilling the Take 5s. It was because she'd failed to meet her quota. Not enough take-5's. Go figure. Companies say speaking up is paramount. Yet if workers are dissuaded to, they'll just circumvent the process and not feel enthused or encouraged to participate.

My wife landed a job at a mine site I'd been assigned to recently. She is a hairdresser but worked as a cleaner because it paid well. The physical work was much more than she was used to, and she often came home with a few aches and pains. After a while the aches and pains developed into tennis elbow. She was hesitant to report it because the contracting company's culture was "anti-injuries". In fact, there were rumours that if people had time off to heal an injury they were dismissed once it healed. Contracting to a major mining operation creates this environment. There is immense pressure on all contractors to avoid injuries because it affects the whole site's lost time injury frequency rate. I told my wife to report her elbow immediately.

As expected, her manager reacted and demanded to know why she didn't come forward sooner. My wife's worst fears were realised, and she was embarrassed. She wanted to do the right thing. However, the message at the daily pre-shift briefing was that injuries were to be avoided at all costs. The gossip in the lunchroom led her to believe that a few aches and pains should never be mentioned, or else everyone suffers recrimination. The pressure applied from the mining company, pushed down through the subcontractor, onto the work crew, was translated by staff to suppress the reporting of injuries. The repetitive nature of the injury could have been avoided if she had mentioned it earlier. She was put onto light duties. If she had done so earlier the injury would not have developed.

The Regulator's Impact

I don't blame my wife's manager, her company or the mine. Regulatory authority intervention is creating a pressure cooker atmosphere and a heightened sense of threat to industry survival. Amidst an increasing duty of care and corporate liability, companies are losing sight of the real reason for their safety strategies, fearing regulatory reprisal and litigation instead. It was interesting to watch the fallout of the Queensland Dreamworld fatalities in 2016 when a pleasure ride malfunctioned. The Queensland Premier stood before a packed news conference prior to the investigation, before the inquest, even before the funerals. She came out swinging:

"We all know how important workplace safety is and how important it is to have strong deterrents. That's why Queensland has the best record in Australia at prosecuting employers for negligence—and we are now examining current regulations to see if there are any further measures we can take to discourage unsafe practices". [42]

My heart sank. What a lost opportunity. Instead of

backing industry and offering full support, the Premier hung them out to dry. The window of opportunity to provide an environment of openness and disclosure quickly evaporated. The investigation had no chance of uncovering the real root causes of the accident. The Premier had blown any chance of key players speaking candidly, because of fear of litigation and culpability. She sealed the deal with:

> *"An audit will consider whether existing penalties are sufficient to act as deterrents, and whether these should be strengthened to contain provisions relating to gross negligence causing death".*

It saddened me, the whole tragic circumstances of the accident and the dreadful fatalities. I just wished that years of workplace reform hadn't perished with them. What did we learn I wonder? Did this create an environment conducive to transparent open workplaces? Did a bond of trust and cooperation emerge between the regulator and industry so that the real reasons the accident occurred were revealed for the betterment of everyone concerned? True to form during the inquest, everyone fled for the exits. Denial, excuses, avoidance of ownership and blame, became the order of the day. Of course it did. The Premier basically threatened witnesses with life imprisonment if they owned-up. It was a travesty.

Suspicious Minds

Why do companies make workers sign Job Hazard Analysis (JHA) worksheets today? They never used to. I assumed it was to reinforce personal responsibility. Until workers were being told in their inductions that a JHA is now a legal document. The biggest victim was trust. Workers become sceptical of safety programs developed out of the fear of regulatory reprisal. It suggests worker safety is not the real reason they are being implemented. They sense something's not quite right. So they play along but not buying-in 100%. They need the job and do what they have to. Perhaps you leaders might admit that you play this game too. Are you using the threat of legal prosecution to keep your workforce in line? Stop doing that. It doesn't work.

When secret or unspoken values (unconsciously) conflict with company expressed or stated values, it becomes a case of safety charades. How many workplaces say things like "we put safety first" then implement production targets that seem at odds with their assertion? How can we even say "safety first" if we do not plan for safety first, if we do not spend the time to ensure people understand the why/how/what and operate within this understanding? If we do not spend the effort to systematically ensure and provide safe systems of work.

What about the expression bandied around freely on work sites these days, "Look after your mates"? Theo looked after Skinny, didn't he? By not exposing him. If you look at things from another perspective, would letting Skinny off the hook appear to be looking after your mate? It was certainly well regarded by Skinny and the crew at the time. My point is that safety rhetoric is confusing at worst, misleading at best. Emotional responses and knee-jerk reactions to incidents are steering workplaces via the rear-view mirror. Low-hanging-fruit safety has become the order of the day. Are mandatory lids on our coffee cups, hard hats for open field workers and benign signage at pedestrian walkways, motivating workers to develop a safe work culture? We mistakenly believe low rates of incidents in these areas are a green light that the programs work. Realistically, they were already low incident areas.

Autonomy

We place a lot of emphasis on our workers having the right to stop work if it's unsafe. However, the courage to speak out—no—the sense of duty to speak out can only be achieved if leaders promote ownership, openness and trust as the highest value. Regardless of what the company's stated values are. Workers need to feel a bond of trust with their leaders before they are going to disclose information willingly and enhance safety.

Voluntary operational discipline will emerge if the workforce sense they have nominal control over the decisions in their workplace. The problem is when leaders don't trust workers to make the right decisions and blame them for incidents. It takes courage for leaders to accept ownership for their part in any incident. It takes courage to release the shackles and encourage workforce autonomy. Especially when the pathway of least resistance is geared towards workers harming themselves. However, the last thing a company needs is a workforce going through the motions, blindly following safety goals without buying into the program. Whether we like it or not however, this is what seems to be happening. Remember, safety is not your goal anyway. It's a result.

"Speak when you are angry and you'll make the best speech you'll ever regret."
—Laurence J. Peter

SECTION II

HOW

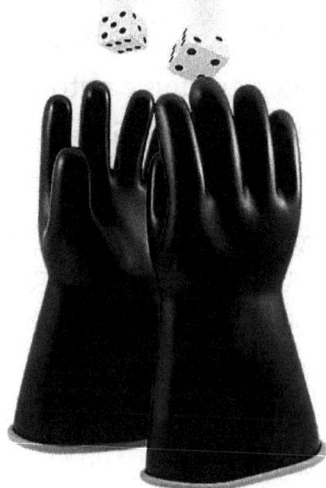

Section II, the 'How', is about principles rarely spoken of in the workplace. But which influence how we perform our day-to-day activities greatly. It's what drives how we go about getting things done. Underneath the actual activities we perform. How can we tell if things like incongruence, inconvenience or secret values explained earlier, are covertly having an impact on accidents and injuries? What are the signs to look for and how do we fix them?

Section II explains human performance in terms of our natural instincts and tendencies, avoiding the "behaviour" trap. It might give you another perspective that doesn't focus on conduct or conformance. But more importantly we focus on natural human disposition and tendencies.

THEO'S STORY

PRIDE AND PAIN

Theo's wife returns to his bedside and is shocked at the smell of burnt flesh. She is only allowed five minutes to relive fourteen years of marriage. To say all that needs to be said before she's hauled away. Perhaps for the very last time. Strangely quiet, the commotion seems to have quietened down now. It's just Theo, the smells and sounds and his own thoughts. It's quite calm. No one is preparing him for emergency surgery. No one is running around or preparing him for anything! Helpless, arms raised and wrapped in a kilometre of bandage, death lays silently in wait. Luckily, Theo finds himself a patient at the renowned Royal Perth Hospital. It's the finest burns unit in the southern hemisphere. But medical staff are not doing much "burns unit stuff" beyond relieving his pain. Theo believes they are resigned to him dying, he's just not going to survive. Frustrated by this he refuses to sleep, determined to meet his fate head on. It has been a long, long day. It feels like it's been an eternity.

On day two, there's no sign things have changed. The lack of medical attention heightens Theo's concern. For sure, the medication takes care of the pain, but nothing subdues his ghostly unease. He concludes the medical team are simply waiting for him to die so they can reallocate his bed.

On day three there's a knock on the door. Who on earth knocks on the door in a hospital? Suddenly, a familiar face emerges. It's his Dad. Theo breaks down. How could he let his mentor see him like this? Theo's father flew immediately on a panic-stricken flight from South Africa. Theo imagines the anguish he must be putting his father through. It is more than the concern he has for his own injuries. It's a sight his father never imagined he'd see. No father does. And an electric shock of all things. As an old Liney himself, Theo's father always pushed it out of his mind. It's not something a father wants to consider.

On day four, Theo finally succumbs to drifting in and out of sleep, in and out of consciousness. Yet the medical team are perplexed. They don't understand why Theo isn't dead yet. Mystified, they send him over to radiology to check out his vital organs, an ultrasound should confirm their worst fears. After a long probe around, Theo asks the Sonographer, "Am I OK?" The Sonographer doesn't reply and simply retrieves another machine. "What is it?" Theo asks again. Without a word the Sonographer scratches his head. He tells a technician to go and get one of those new ultrasound machines that arrived last week. These two machines are faulty. "What's going on," Theo pleads? The Sonographer checks one more time and stares at Theo blankly, "It's a miracle," he says. "Your heart is strong, your kidneys seem fine, and your lungs are unscathed. Somehow your organs have escaped any damage."

Only now do the medical team swing into action. There's

a flurry of activity for the first time in days. The famed Dr Fiona Woods tells Theo they'll operate around the clock. Cycles of surgery with one day to operate and a day to recover. Relentlessly removing damaged flesh and tissue from Theo's arms. His left arm doesn't have much chance, and the exit wound in his right wrist doesn't look good either. They take muscle from his back and harvest skin from his legs and graft it to his arms.

It took seventeen surgeries in twice as many days. But thankfully, somehow, they save both of Theo's arms. Although there will be permanent disability to his extremities. After three months the medical team have done all they can do—physically. However, Theo needs to go home. He's far from healed, but his soul needs healing now. There is a marked reduction in Theo's spirit. Once a proud man, he always looked after his wife and kids. Now he relies on them personally, physically, hygienically... for everything.

His arms are useless, and it is all too much for him to endure. He shuts down the blinds. He shuts down his feelings. And he shuts down on his wife and kids. The guilt and shame is all too consuming. He spirals into an abyss. The black dog bites him hard. 'It's just not worth it, IM NOT WORTH IT.' Ending his life seems like the only answer. *"After you think about suicide more than a thousand times, it becomes perfectly logical,"* Theo recalls. Before he makes this ultimate decision, he will try and do one last normal act.

Emerging from the darkness of his cave, Theo plans to drive to the shops and buy a packet of cigarettes. A perfectly normal thing to do. Except with two incapacitated limbs and a heavy dose of painkillers, he fumbles for hours trying to get the keys into the car's ignition. Then something happens, he does what he has always found it difficult to do. He asks a passer-by for help. Rather shocked, they start the car. He basically drives with his elbows, somehow making it into an empty parking space.

He will need money. As he walks up to an ATM, he wonders how he will get his wallet from his pocket and the card from its sleeve and into the ATM. How will he key his PIN, or even retrieve the money? Humiliated, again he asks for help. Again, people are willing. This is a new experience, asking for help. Even newer is accepting it. The money is ejected but he can't grab it. Eventually he has to get on his knees and remove it with his teeth. He hasn't thought this through... thankfully. Or he might never have had the breakthrough he experiences driving home.

The humiliation turns from anger to resolve. A realisation that if he is to survive the thoughts of suicide, he is going to have to reach out for even more help. It wasn't so bad at the shopping centre. If he can ask someone to take a wallet from his pants pocket, he can surely sign up for physiotherapy. A phone call and it's done. He attends two years of treatment. It's an agonisingly slow journey. After many, many months he can just wriggle the index finger on his right hand. His change of heart to accept help, finally starting to pay off. After what seems like an eternity. Yet, if being able to ask for help was an adjustment of his pride, it did not stop the further spiral down. Massive bills, the alarming toll on each family member.

Eventually the Venter's were poor. More emotionally than financially. His wife and the mother of his three children could take it no more. The toll on her spirit, seeing her husband the shell of the man he once was, too much to bear. She had done all she could. Her dreams of the perfect family were shattered. It was over. She leaves.

Theo is left to suffer another long-term consequence of his choices. Certainly, nothing will ever be the same again. With the hellhounds snapping at his heals, Theo must decide if he will start making the new agreements required to kick-start his life. What will it be? Survival or to start living. It is time to believe that things can eventually be normal again. His life is now in what's left of his hands. What decisions will he make? What actions, attitudes and commitments will be required? What should he believe?

"Unravelling external selves and coming home to our real identity is the true meaning of soul work."
—Sue Monk Kidd

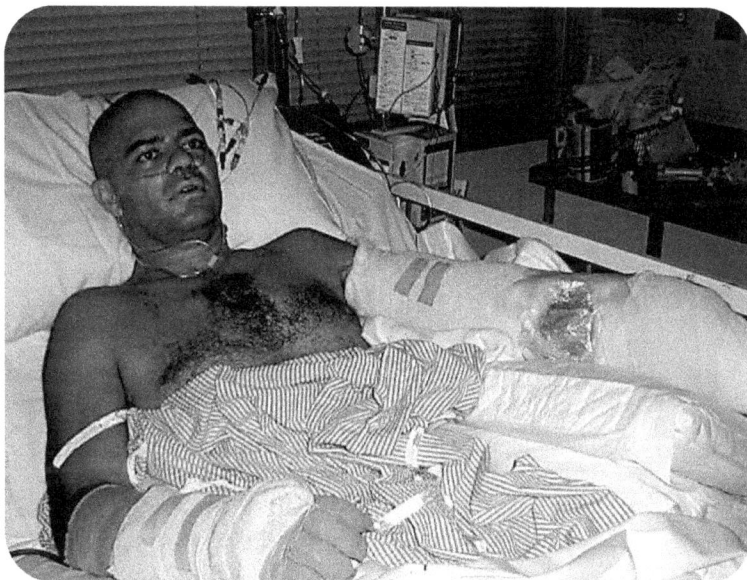

"If I'm not going to die, then kill me!" Theo is frustrated that no one is rushing around to save his life. The Doctors believe that no one survives 22,000 volts. Hospital beds were in short supply Theo recalls.

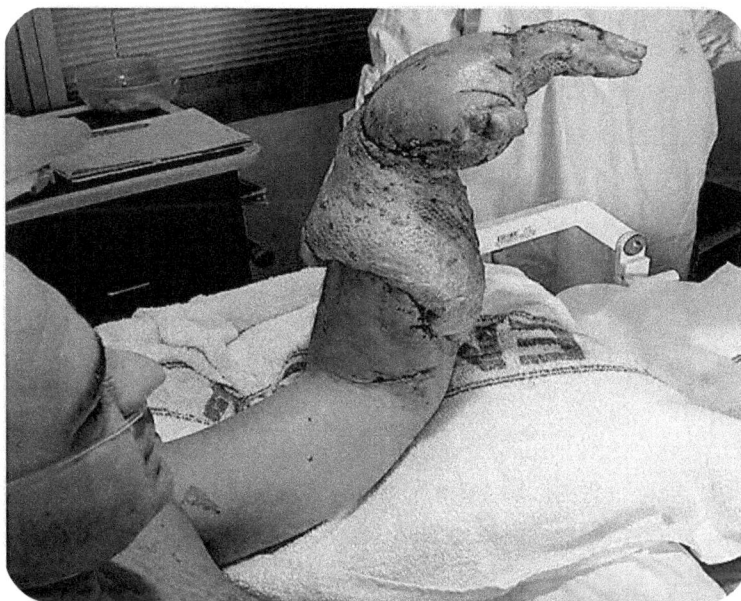

"Let's shake on it". After 3 months it doesn't look pretty, but it's actually a work of art. Surgeons thought they would have to amputate initially.

BELIEF

Theo's manager prided himself on communication. However, after the special safety meeting when no one spoke up, he feels the crew aren't fully engaged. When he learns of Theo's incident he is dejected and blames himself. It doesn't add up. He questions the employee surveys, the daily safety reinforcements. He wonders what went wrong. When he visits Theo in hospital, he tries to reach into Theo's soul and download the reason he took off his gloves. To unravel the mystery. He is very thankful that Theo is still alive and promises to himself that he'll never allow something like this to happen under his watch again. Problem is, he thought he was doing everything he could. What now?

What Do You Believe?

As a Manager, would you be alarmed if you discovered your workforce isn't truly invested in your safety system? Team Leaders know what I mean, and I can see you workers nodding in agreement. I say this because in forty years of industry, I have never met anyone who can put their hand on their heart and honestly say they believe wholeheartedly 100% in their safety program. No one. Theo and I find this staggering. It's one reason we called this book "Get Real". Whenever we run a workshop, we gauge the true levels of belief workers have in their safety systems. But starting the conversation is like pulling teeth. Because people are afraid of reprisal if leaders are present. So we start with the leaders:

"Are there any leaders who can put their hand on their heart with 100% conviction and confidently say their workforce believes and trusts in your safety system, to the degree they would not take off their insulated gloves, like Theo?"

Remarkably, not one leader has put up their hand yet. Belief in our safety systems, or the lack thereof, is probably one of the biggest problems facing companies today. Too easily, leaders promote 'safety before production' and believe it's true (it's not); They believe 'Take 5' hazard checklists are being completed sincerely (they're not); they are ignorant to un-spoken and secret values because vocalising them would upset the apple cart, and the dogma *'all accidents are preventable'* is simply low-hanging-fruit jargon. Are we not sweeping things under the carpet when we don't acknowledge the truth? Like a dark family secret. Unfortunately, all family secrets come back to haunt us eventually. And in the workplace, shady pasts usually appear in the form of an accident. Shouldn't challenges to our current safety beliefs be as legitimate as creating new ones? Sadly, there is a genuine fear of reprisal if workers speak out. Challenging long held beliefs doesn't 'feel safe'.

So let's consider when Theo really had his accident. Was it when he touched the electricity? Or was it the moment he put his hands between his knees and withdrew them from his gloves? Was it the moment he saw a colleague remove his insulated gloves a few days earlier, when Theo decided not to take it further? Or was it years of cultural impingements that gradually overlapped each other until they became normally accepted practices? What do you believe? Well firstly, to answer these questions we need to understand what a belief is. For instance, is *reality* what you see? Or simply photoreceptors reflecting light in your eyes. Is *reality* what you hear, or your ears encoding sine wave vibrations? Do things only become real when our brain attaches meaning to these sensory perceptions? I'm leading you on, of course it does. Ultimately, it's our interpretations that create beliefs. Otherwise 'experience' is just our senses sending information to the brain, without judgement or opinion. Usually, human beliefs become real when everyone else believes in them too. Only until then, it is quite possible, that nothing is real. Therefore, we should be able to effectively create our own beliefs, right? Then we wouldn't have to follow the herd. We could instil our own safety values in the face of our current beliefs. However, the problem is that beliefs are not formulated in the Rational brain. So this kind of logic doesn't make sense. It's our Emotional brain that attaches meaning to our perceptions and stores them in the Habitual brain for a rainy day. Beliefs are in fact—a habit. Always there lurking, waiting for the right cues and responses to emerge when you least expect them. How can we create the kind of beliefs we need to act safely?

Here's an Idea

Imagine a completely different belief system took over our workplaces. One where near-misses and minor accidents were totally acceptable, because of the retrospective analysis and consequent improvements we'd glean. What if, counterintuitively, these incidents were regarded as a "proactive" learning experience? What if near-misses and minor accidents were treated as inevitable products important for the success of a continuously improving workplace? Imagine a world where leaders did not react to incidents with frustration, but were calm and supportive. Imagine there was another purpose for incidents altogether. Instead of chalking them down as a negative, creating resistance and fear—we valued them for the important lessons they provide. Would we elicit positive emotions in the workplace by linking incidents to learnings, compassion and understanding? Bear with me here. I'm not trying to be facetious. By avoiding frustration and fear, we would see a rise in worker responsiveness and changes in their willingness to open up and divulge near misses at our pre-shift briefings. Imagine this type of environment—voluntary disclosure—influencing our incident investigations. Where we might uncover deeper meaning than those same old evergreen conclusions: "Insufficient information in the JHA, or "Didn't follow procedures", "Didn't identify hazards" and etc. Instead we came up with: "Worker having problems at home", "Didn't believe in the system", "Insufficient clarity around the 'Why'." Imagine there were no low-hanging-fruit conclusions. Bliss!

If we were open to exploring a deeper mental and metaphysical understanding of what causes accidents, we may see the benefits they could provide and possible decreases in injuries in the future. Can you picture yourself seeing things from this perspective? OK, so it's not that easy from our current conditioning. But if it reduced injuries and fatalities, how willing is industry to give it a go? Is it too far a stretch? Well, probably in today's climate. Beliefs are changed gradually or it rocks the boat too much. I've tried... believe me.

Controlling Beliefs

Industry would do well to abandon controlling tactics and adopt a "coaching model". A coaching model that creates accountability and self-belief. If people are the heartbeat of our industry, then a strong pulse obviously is a satisfied, ambitious and trusting workforce. A drive for this type of culture is the hallmark of a self-sustaining and continuously improving workplace. Where everyone on all levels, not just managers and leaders, have the opportunity to grow their skills, enhance their value and achieve personal and professional goals. Coaching— *real* coaching—creates a meaningful focus that lifts spirits and creates trust. A trust that ultimately fosters belief in the system.

The fundamental principle which underpins coaching and the Get Real philosophy, is that to achieve engagement and responsiveness, it is the result of believing in the workforce. Believing they are creative, resourceful and holders of the keys to their own success. If a work team needs direction to complete a complex task, or colleagues need to resolve a problem or meet personal challenges, coaching can facilitate that process. It builds self-belief in people so they can overcome their own challenges. By allowing them to discover, to clarify and align with the problems they want to resolve. They will self-generate solutions and strategies, and seek support to achieve desired goals. Self-belief is one of the main endorsements for a company adopting this kind of engagement and a primary driver for voluntary operational discipline and a continuous improvement environment.

Let me ask you again, as a manager or leader, can you put your hand on your heart and say with 100% conviction that you have full faith and belief in the safety system you want your workforce to believe and buy in to? This means you believe that Take 5 pre-task observation checklists are effective and all staff should enthusiastically engage in them willingly, to improve safety at every opportunity. If so, I applaud you because your workplace must be remarkable in terms of performance and worker satisfaction. If not, I also applaud you. Self-evaluation is critical in taking the first major step to change. However, unless you are prepared to do what it takes to find your 'Why', cleaning up incongruences in your workplace will be impossible. Even if you find just one 'Why' worth pursuing.

Good Habits Die Hard

In October 1987, Paul O'Neill gave his first speech as CEO of the aluminium manufacturing giant, Alcoa. "I intend to make Alcoa the safest company in America," he said. [43] In '87 Alcoa was a basket case financially, and no one talked about safety. Investors thought a lunatic had taken the helm. All anyone was thinking about in '87 was profits. Yet when O'Neill retired thirteen years later, Alcoa's annual net profit was five times higher than when he started. Alcoa had become the richest company on earth—and the SAFEST!

I don't mention this analogy because it is about safety. The moral of this story is how finding a program that aligns everyone's vision and direction allows a workforce to believe and buy in to one common goal. So what was the secret? In a word, "Disruption" O'Neill said. "I knew I had to transform Alcoa but you can't order people to change. So I decided I was going to start focusing on one thing that would spread throughout the entire company. By changing one keystone habit." Except, the problem for us in today's workplaces is that everyone focuses on safety now, and it's become overbearing. Necessary of course. But hammered to death. Just ask any worker. It's far from new or inspiring like it was in '87. You can't flog a dead horse. In '87, thousands of CEO's jumped onto O'Neill's safety bandwagon. So much so that we still have the remnants throughout our industry today. Zero harm being one of them. Get Real advocates you search for a new idea. But still ground-breaking like O'Neill. An idea that focuses on changing one keystone habit across your workplace.

Operation "Respect"

If you transform one routine so that it spreads throughout your entire company, or even an entire industry, it becomes life-affirming and uplifting. Such as a habit that promotes openness and disclosure, or trust and ownership, personal responsibility, voluntary operational discipline or dare I say it... *respect*. I recently implemented a program to the "Modifications and Projects" department on a major mining operation. We called it *Operation Respect*. This site was notorious for disrespectful behaviour and social issues. It was resulting in their online complaints service being log jammed. So with very little effort, *Mods & Ops* (MOPs) took the lead and announced they were implementing a program called *Operation Respect*. We created a mission and were very clear about its highest value: Respect. Everything we instructed or communicated was channelled through the impact respecting everything had. Amazing, right? Big tough miners adopting a respect-yourself and others attitude. The upshot was that Respect actually transformed everyone's attitude towards each other and the job. The result was swift and desirable. In fact, it was easy to channel everything we did through the prism of Respect. It flowed into safety, production, budget, schedule... everything.

I guarantee if you try O'Neill's little gem and implement one keystone habit, just one keystone value, it will create such enormous gains that you'll wonder why you never thought of it before. The place where I believe it was most effective for MOPS was at the daily pre-shift briefings. Instead of the Supervisor kicking things off with, "OK, who has a safety share?", they announced *"OK everyone, are we clear on our Respect goals? What about our agreements, all good? And who needs support with their accountabilities, anyone?"*

Why don't you try it and see? Define your biggest issue, create a one-word mission to fix it, and channel everything you do through it. You'll be amazed at the results.

"Once you break a habit into its components, you can fiddle with the gears."
—Charles Duhigg

TRUST

Theo had always prided himself on his communication. When he was young, his mother encouraged him to recite poetry and express himself creatively. He won the annual recital competition seven years in a row. Speaking openly in front of people was not normally a problem. It did not make sense that he would say nothing at the meeting when his manager asked if there were safety issues they could learn from. Certainly, he could have mentioned the insulated gloves without implicating Skinny. If he can recite poetry in front of a hundred people, why was it so difficult to speak up at the meeting? He'd do anything to have that moment back again.

What Do Workers Trust?

People not only go to work to earn a living but also to derive a sense of self-worth from their achievements. Call it pride or job satisfaction, feelings of being valued for our contribution is a key motivator in the workplace. That is of course if we are operating higher than the survival rung on Maslow's hierarchy of needs. 44 According to the UK Department of Health, the workplace is one of the main environments that affects mental health and wellbeing. [45] They are not the only country who is saying this. Yet, the relentless pursuit for perfection in the form of a zero accident vision may be catching up with us (much like a zero Coronavirus vision). There's a trend globally where dissatisfaction and low-fulfilment is affecting workplace morale. And mental health issues appear to be on the rise. Tom Harkin, a youth worker that appeared on the ABC TV series "Man Up" sums it up wisely: "Humans have emotions and if you put a bottle on it, it's going to explode." [46] The National Alliance for the Mentally Ill states:

"Work is at the very core of contemporary life for most people, providing financial security, personal identity, and an opportunity to make a meaningful contribution to community life". [47]

Facebook and the advent of social media is revealing that workers want to make an impact. Oddly, our organisations are saying the same thing too. They want to hear workers speak up more. So it's a little confusing to say the least. Somehow, contrary to what we experience outside the workplace, there's some underlying reason workers aren't communicating on the level they and their organisations desire. Perhaps there is a lack of trust that's creating this apprehension to speak openly.

On the surface, all workplaces are encouraged to communicate freely on safety issues. And they do to some extent. Especially at committee meetings and pre-shift briefings for example. But it's like pulling teeth sometimes. When 'control' is a higher value than 'openness', our systems of operation will resist people speaking their truth. Especially if it challenges the status quo. It's interesting that self-driven workforces who naturally experience continuous improvement, are motivated by the same desires as those workforces with no empowerment or sense of autonomy. They both desire personal satisfaction and to have a voice in regard to their workplace. The difference is the confidence to do so. Creating an open environment where a worker's beliefs and feelings are as important as the company's bottom line, is often countered with a perception that it's wrong to criticise an organisation's processes.

Credible Communication

Perhaps implementing safety programs which involve the workforce's values and beliefs would generate more buy-in and trust that is essential for workplace success. Dr. Gretchen Mosher is an assistant professor at Iowa State University and published an article called "Trust, Safety, and Employee Decision Making". Mosher wrote that "trust" enables the communication and openness required for timely sharing of accurate and relevant information, and that transparent decision making and sincere delivery of knowledge in turn creates trust:

> *"Openness plays an especially key role in (building) trust between managers and subordinates".* [48]

Focusing on mistakes (incident rates) and counting them, trying to steer them towards zero, may create an underlying mistrust that cultivates concealment or the suppression of incident reporting. If the workplace had a high value on openness it would pave the way for workers to divulge things they might not normally reveal, but which is imperative to creating a desirable safety climate. Typically, what we experience after an incident is workers going into their shell to avoid condemnation, instead of being open to the learnings and opportunities for improvement. **In reality, this is the most important time for a workplace to pull together, take extreme ownership, support each other and arrive at a mutually beneficial solution for them and future workforces.** Often it's left to the supervisor or safety representatives to come up with corrective actions that often treat the symptoms but not the cause. If the cause is seen as behaviour, no one is equipped to explore further what it is about the behaviour that should be addressed. We are not psychologists after all. We simply come to work to earn a living, right? Well maybe. Perhaps we come to work to thrive and to be all of who we are as an extension of our lives and lifestyle. We don't need psychology, just our humanity.

Our workplaces are normally equipped with the best tools available to handle these situations. Tools that work fine if we give them a go. Dr Mosher notes:

"Consistent and credible communication plays an essential role in workplace safety programs, letting employees know what the expectations are in terms of safety behaviour."

Depends on what "credible" communication means I guess. Is it leaders cultivating a strong relationship with their work crews? Is it leaders who create meaningful dialogue and who encourage inclusion and disclosure? Would allowing workers to voice their disbelief in the system provide the consistency and credibility that Mosher refers to? Or is that just something too scary to consider? Especially in light of our current paradigm. Unfortunately, openness is shut down more than encouraged. Especially if it criticises the system.

Work/Lifestyle Conundrum

Recent campaigns asking workers not to use their "common sense", though well intentioned, may have unwittingly disconnected them from a sense of ownership and personal responsibility. Workplace inductions were suggesting that workers should not apply their own sensibilities to their work tasks. They offered that strict adherence to the procedures was the only contribution a worker needed to provide. I watched this create a kind of introspection over the years. The enemy of self-discovery. Hampering the outspokenness of safety issues and the opposite of continuous improvement.

A leader who indulges the work crew's enthusiasm and leaves out the safety jargon, avoids the risk of desensitising important safety messages. A sticker on the mirror above the wash basin saying, 'You're looking at the person responsible for safety', will never achieve the buy-in that the significance of taking personal responsibility needs to convey. This is another example of a Rational brain ('What') solution.

It goes without saying, no one person is responsible for the success of a workplace. It's a team effort. An interwoven chain of cooperation needs to happen in any workplace to achieve results. People rely on each other. That reliance can't exist without trust. People will go above and beyond the call of duty when they trust their environment. If they believe in the system, it will assist with the implementation of your safety programs greatly. Dr Mosher notes: "Trust has been shown to predict safety perceptions in the workplace... the influence of trust would extend to safety climate".

If work is an extension of our lifestyle as I'm promoting, then trusting, open communication may benefit other areas of our life too? Would introducing accountability to work task agreements have a flow on effect on our agreements at home? Would placing a high value on integrity at the daily pre-shift briefing, affect the accountability and levels of integrity for workers with their families? Leaders long for worker buy-in and commitment to the company's mission. But day-to-day activities must resonate with a worker's private life too, if they want that same level of commitment. Creating a higher level of trust in the workplace might promote the engagement and willingness to go the extra mile at home. But how much of a worker's personal sense of values are we prepared for? If we are going to acknowledge people's value systems at work, then personal issues, once a private domain, suddenly become more connected to the workplace. The repercussions may be that workers who are encouraged to build trust in the workplace may bring more of their private life into the fray. Asking people to be real may open up a Pandora's box.

Quite possibly the workplace might need to introduce social and relationship skills as part of its training. If someone reveals they are stressed at home, should employers provide stress relief or mental health support? Will we see some form of personal development and healing as part of the maturity process required to achieve inclusion and diversity? I don't want to seem alarmist, but I don't think anyone really knows what total worker commitment means. Would higher worker engagement and a trusting relationship introduce more complexity? Could this be one reason employers are hesitant to go the whole enchilada with their work crews? Food for thought perhaps.

Trust is built through actions not words. Leaders can model trust by being vulnerable and acknowledging their mistakes. When anyone owns that they didn't keep an agreement, they are taking full responsibility and control. Although trust is diminished because they broke the agreement, the opportunity exists to build the trust back immediately, by stepping into their power. From this perspective, it's how trust is maintained in the workplace. Everyone owning everything. To be frank, I experience resistance of introducing an all-encompassing accountability model across all levels of an organisation, from managers more than I do the shop floor. If I was to hazard a guess why, my sense is that managers fear being this transparent. It takes courage to be vulnerable. And some managers may not want workers to see they have blemishes too. I'm not being critical, it's just my observation.

In Section III, we'll uncover the perfect process for building trusting workplaces following a simple methodology. I said simple, not easy. Trust is not something you can switch on and off. Live by the sword, die by the sword. Getting Real means your words are backed by your deeds. Practising what you preach is not just an expression, it affects everything you do. Adopting the principles in this book will benefit the workplace, but it will impact other areas of your life too.

"I'm not upset that you lied to me, I'm upset
that from now on I can't believe you."
—*Friedrich Nietzsche*

BUY-IN

When I finished writing Get Real Theo asked, "How are you going to sell your message?" I hadn't really thought about this aspect. I just felt it needed to be written. However, what he was trying to say is that everything I'd written, all of the principles, all of the information would only appeal to certain readers. "How do you know it is what people want to read?" he repeated. I told him it didn't matter so much, that I was driven more by an urge to help others and offer our experience. That it might make a difference in the world. "Good answer," he replied. "People will know that it comes from your heart."

Self-Driven Workplace

Operational discipline, procedural compliance, accountability or any other program, needs to be branded and packaged into a product that provides good value to the 'customer', your workforce. The most important thing is the authenticity that goes into creating it. Were your workers involved? Was their welfare the primary driver? If leaders are the salespeople promoting any program, do they truly believe in the product? If the energy behind a program is genuine, it won't require any manipulation to implement. Manipulations are short term. Gaining buy-in means workers are in it for the long haul. Getting "real" buy-in isn't easy however. Especially if the process we use to secure buy-in is inherently flawed. In fact, in most situations it's not actually buying-in at all—but about "selling". We usually develop an idea, sell it to ourselves first, and then go about selling it to the workforce. We consider every objection and develop an air-tight defence before we roll it out. The problem is, how do you get others to be open to your ideas without using persuasion? Because if workers get a whiff that they are being *sold* to, they are more likely to resist or even totally ignore your communication. In a safety context this is not ideal. You may begrudgingly get compliance, but you won't get the kind of buy-in that motivates operational discipline. You may find yourself unwittingly resorting to pleading or manipulation. Not exactly how you imagined things when you first came up with your idea now was it.

Buy-in is critical for any organisational change. Even when change is obviously necessary. You must get people to care enough to support it. Sometimes they're happy with what they have. Or maybe you haven't addressed the "what's in it for me" question. Unless you get the support to create momentum for your ideas, big or small, they won't take hold or have the impact you want. Research has shown that 70% of all organisational change efforts fail. [49] And the main reason is leaders simply don't get enough buy-in, from enough people, nearly enough of the time.

Avoid Coercion

You could force workers to comply using the threat of disciplinary action or dismissal. But like taxes, even though we have to pay them, people still look for (legal) ways around it. The same applies to conventional modes of operational discipline and programs designed to reduce incidents. Even though logically we understand the benefits, if we haven't bought into them, there's something about being coerced that we resist. It's probably the word "discipline" that conjures a negative response. Personally I don't like it either. Even coupled as "operational discipline" to suggest structure and reliability. Although it is in everyone's best interests to embrace operational discipline in a positive light, it still takes a certain level of buy-in before a workforce will, or not. Let's take your own workplace for example. Is operational discipline inspired by the actions of your leaders and a clear company vision? Or enforced through written instructions and procedures? This is an important distinction. Most leaders complain that people won't follow procedures anyway. Whereas they will a worthwhile cause.

Recently I was asked to list what the military do better than most companies. I flippantly said, "Stay alive". Turns out I wasn't that far off. To stay alive the military boast: 1) Great equipment; 2) Superb training; and 3) Strong leadership. Operational discipline will emerge when this triad is intact. If we add a fourth dimension, "autonomy" or volunteering for tasks, then *voluntary* operational discipline emerges. The biggest hurdle for us civilian however, is that while we have access to good equipment, training and instruction, we probably fear the loss of control too much to encourage autonomy. Yet, we either let go of the reigns a little or miss out on people taking personal responsibility and ownership.

Ownership is intrinsically motivating. But it depends on the individual. Our job as leaders is to align people's individual values towards a common workplace goal. One that workers will embrace and want to pursue under their own volition. Without coercion.

I'm a big fan of Allan Jeans, a successful Australian Rules Football (AFL) coach. Jeans was big on discipline. But not the kind of discipline you might think. He would say, "The best form of discipline is players wanting to do the right thing to achieve a premiership or objective, a sort of self-imposed discipline." Like any sporting team pursuing a premiership or pennant, if a work crew does not have a clear sense of 'Why' beyond providing their product or service, then it won't connect with the Emotional brain. Communication becomes rhetoric (Rational brain). A 'Why', or sense of purpose, doesn't believe or trust in rhetoric. Your 'Why' becomes a BS meter and determines whether you will buy-in to the rhetoric or not. Then Leaders are reliant on manipulations, rules, punishment or rewards to get things done. Force or even pleading becomes the primary currency of communication. This won't create connection or trust in the workplace and the opportunity for learnings that a "buy-in culture" provides. Intrinsic motivation is borne out of inspiration, not rhetoric, not rules. Not blind faith in a system because it's always been done that way. Voluntary operational discipline is a workforce's decision, not the leaders.

A Sense of Purpose

Industry tends to rely on information, technology and catchy programs to alter behaviour and create buy-in. When simply it would pay to implement an idea that captures your workforce's imagination. Our basic human instinct is to seek for understanding and to belong to something greater than ourselves. It's what drives us at our core. Deep inside all of us is an innate sense of purpose and need to be valued for who we are and appreciated for what we can provide. When this need is not apparent in our work, we won't function at our most productive, or safest. In other words, people don't go to work just to survive, they want to believe in something worthwhile.

When a workforce doesn't buy in to rhetoric or the company has a patronising culture, you'll recognise it as compliance issues or poor operational discipline. Incidents will have no apparent cause and probably be attributed to traditional factors such as procedural breaches, insufficient risk management or human error. If workers smell impropriety or perceive management isn't walking the talk, operational discipline goes out the window. Indifference for the rules creates poor morale because the signs of indifference are hard to pinpoint. In fact, they may never be revealed. Signs of this nature are subtler than usual flagrant rule breaches. Indifference lurks culturally and rules have less significance.

Incident Fatigue
In creating today's management systems and much of our current safety, industry seems to draw its conclusions from subjective observations instead of traditional and proven branches of psychology. It appears that much of our operational safety stems from knee-jerk reactions to incidents and the frustrations of workplace noncompliance. We create concepts with the intention that workers will connect to an idealised notion of operational behaviour. Unfortunately, they

don't. Besides, creating a mutually beneficial goal that both a workforce and management buy into, is much easier and probably more satisfying than implementing programs in response to an incident.

Carl Ransom Rogers, one of the founding fathers of psychotherapy, warns us of relying on unrealistic goals to curb behaviour. Or the persistent use of concepts that seem out of reach. [50] His theory explains why zero safety programs create a standard in our worker's mind that can never be met. Rogers discovered that when we begin to compare the "I" if all goes well, with the "I failed" if notional standards aren't met, creates a gap between the real and the ideal. "I have to, Got to, Ought to, Should", eventually wears us down and a sense of fatigue from underperformance "renders us anxious and confused". [51] I venture to say that much of our workplace stress and fatigue can be attributed to unrealistic goals and targets. Either those we receive, or those we set for ourselves trying to meet the cycles of punishment and reward.

Things That Inspire Safety

Is there any evidence that catchphrases or safety slogans influence behaviour? Do workforces take them seriously? My experience is there are better strategies we could adopt to create a great safety culture. In Section III we will go over a technique for creating a 'Why'. It's a system Allan Jeans utilised to win the 1989 AFL Grand Final, and one I find work crew's respond to enthusiastically. Mainly because they are totally responsible for creating it. People resonate with a strategy if they are deeply involved in its conception. They don't warm to a list of rules which have been handed down and must be obeyed. Lifesaving rules, golden rules or whatever we call them, may be a great way to publicise important site standards or material risks. But we can't expect them to inspire safety and curb behaviour. We know this because cardinal rule breaches continue regardless, even under the threat of dismissal. When we dismiss people we lose a disciple who would have championed the cause if we educated them with a more inspiring strategy. Enforcing a set of rules will have little or no success compared with an ethos that includes everyone's values. And is a lot easier than reading workers the riot act. It certainly engages them on a much deeper and more personal level.

Although leaders and workers want the same things, they both have different views on how to achieve them. When a workplace embeds each individual's sense of values into a common goal, then daily communications start to reflect everyone's commitment to achieving it. It becomes a self-fulfilling prophecy. Having a "Why" helps people combat *conveniences*. They are more likely to roll up their sleeves and do what it takes to be safe. If we focus on statistics, facts, figures and data, it's a sign that a 'What'-styled workplace is in force. Operating from the level of the 'Why' ensures that the internal conversations workers have with themselves when making decisions, will include a little voice that says "do the right thing," not "just get it done". Having a 'Why' allows leaders to articulate safety requirements with a sense of purpose. Not out of necessity.

"From emotions to materials, it's
all about buying and selling."
—Mehnaz Ansari

VALUES

Theo was not ardently ambitious. Sure, he wanted to advance his career, but it was early days with his new crew and he was still getting a feel for what the company stood for. Perhaps if he had been there longer, it would have been easier to speak up about Skinny. But working with Skinny and the crew felt comfortable. They shared the same interests, liked the same sporting teams and loved Rugby. Theo felt more in line with the guys than he did with management's safety philosophies. Camaraderie is understandable, but what needed to happen so that Theo championed the company's safety stance too?

Have to, Got to, Ought to, Should

In his ground-breaking book the "Breakthrough Experience", Dr John Demartini discovered that when we live according to our highest values we are inspired from within and when we live according to our lower values we require continuous outside motivation. [52] Anything we perceive as supporting our highest values we label as good, anything we perceive as challenging our highest values we label as bad. Therefore, if our values are perceived to be supported, we will comply with directives. If they are challenged, we will outwardly be compliant, but secretly defiant and undisciplined. The art of communicating our values in terms of other people's values is how we influence people and make friends. Challenging people's values makes enemies. Those we perceive as living according to our highest values, we tend to praise and respect. Those we perceive as not living according to our highest values, we tend to despise and resist.

Demartini believes that when we hear ourselves saying, 'You've got to,' 'You ought to,' 'You're supposed to,' 'You need to,' you should,' this is our perception of having power over others. We are projecting our values onto them. Eventually they'll resist our efforts and rebel. Too many leaders expect the workforce to willingly adopt the company's stated values. It's not that workers don't want to, it's that company values aren't perceived as aligning with their own beliefs—even if they are great sounding values. No alignment means no buy-in. Alternatively, if we hear ourselves using imperatives such as 'I have to,' 'I've got to,' 'I ought to,' 'I'm supposed to,' 'I need to,' I should,' this is our perception of having lesser power than others. We are injecting other people's values. Eventually we'll secretly resist them and rebel, and our own values will prevail.

Underlying Values

I spoke earlier of secret values. This chapter aims to give you a further understanding of what values really are and how much they shape our workplace. Or more accurately, how much they shape our world and reality. Individual values conflict with company values all the time. Workplace secret and unspoken values shape our daily activities in direct conflict with publicly stated company values. Therefore, if you understand how values work, you can solve many of the issues that workplaces experience in this regard. Or possibly uncover those secret or unspoken values that simmer beneath the surface of everyday activities.

Our "characters" are forged upon deeply rooted values shaped from childhood. It's why we find it difficult to change our worldview as adults. It is the "who I am" to our core. It's how we judge what feels right, what drives our difficult decisions, what feels authentic and personal to us.

Our "persona" however, responds to the world very differently from our character. Persona is shaped by our coping mechanism. It wants to project we are in control, looking confident and capable, focused on what we do, not who we are. Persona is concerned with achievement, possessions and the external image. It is results-oriented, whereas character is values-oriented. Your persona is built upon other people's opinions, whereas your character is built upon self-belief. Character is the 'Why' while persona is the 'What'.

All values are learned through external sources. We are not born with a value system. It is taught to us. Yet our values influence the decisions we make every day. It is vital that our values align with safe work procedures. As this is the only way we will ever buy in to them. Values influence our decision to be disciplined or disruptive, safe or precarious. Inherently humans will only feel comfortable when they honour their own value system and will resist being forced to adopt other people's values. It's why dictatorships ultimately fail.

Suppression of other people's values is not sustainable and eventually they will mutiny. The world we experience is filtered through our value system. We will perceive the world much differently than the person next to us. Our values force us to believe they should be upheld by everyone else as well. These are core values like our personal sense of freedom, truth or justice ('Why'). Alternatively, some values are less important and fluctuate to the extent we will change our minds upon a persuasively articulated argument ('What').

Values fluctuate in importance when the environmental context shifts. As an example, picture you are about to give an important speech. You will be speaking about something that is close to your heart, aligned with your core values (character). All day you have been rehearsing in front of a mirror and nothing else has diverted your attention away from making it perfect. You're dressed and ready to leave home, but you can't find your car keys. All of a sudden, the single most important thing at that moment has changed. Now your punctuality is in question (persona) and finding your car keys is the single most important thing in your life.

If you were able to maintain focus on your core values, delivering your speech to the benefit of everyone at the function, would you handle things differently? Quite often if we maintained focus we might phone a friend and let them know they may be needed to drive you. Or book an Uber just in case. How many times do we subjugate our core values for immediately pressing issues at the drop of a hat? It's very human.

Values in Action

Some things challenge our values while other things support them. The same event may trigger different responses in two people because of the order of importance of their values. For instance, most of us may disapprove of bribery, but might approve of Oskar Schindler who bribed people to smuggle Jews out of Nazi Germany in 1944. [53] Even so, people may disapprove of bribery to the extent that integrity is much higher on their values, even if it were for a good cause. This is an example of a 'core' value.

Companies "perceived" to be simply giving their stated values lip service, will not get any buy-in from the workforce. In many cases, short of the threat of punishment or dismissal, most people won't adopt a company's stated set of values until there's been some sort of alignment process that links the company values to their own values. Every successful leader finds a way of aligning the workforce's values to the workplace, or they create new company stated values in alignment with the workforce. The scale to which a workforce will adopt voluntarily operational discipline is directly proportionate to how their values are aligned with that of the company.

When a company, its leaders, the workforce and associates align their values and beliefs, congruent communication and a connection to the same vision emerges. This is what is meant by purpose "and" direction. It's the ability to combine values with some sort of purpose or action, which creates intrinsic motivation. But it can never be forced. Either alignment of values is achieved amicably or secret values will emerge and friction will undermine the workplace.

"You never have to change anything you got up in the middle of the night to write."
—Saul Bellow

INTRINSIC

Theo lies hopelessly in hospital. Arms raised above his head, wrapped in a kilometre of bandages, he fights every moment to stay conscious. He dreams of seeing his daughter with a bunch of flowers, dancing around in her favourite dress. Watching his two sons play fight with each other. He imagines seeing his wife. These are powerful images and what gives him hope. His family is the highest value he holds on this earth. They give meaning to 'Why' he must stay alive. Except he swears if he ever survives this, he will also dedicate his life to making sure no one ever has to go through this living hell. Perhaps the ultimate motivation is survival itself. Theo begins to fight for his life. A force coming from somewhere deep inside, a place he's not felt before.

Morale

In his book "man's search for meaning", Victor Frankl discovered in the degradation and abject misery of life in a Nazi concentration camp, that those who had nothing to live for, those who lost hope, died first. [54] In life's extremes it seems Frankl was able to uncover its true essence. Without a sense of expectation or a desire to achieve, all hope is lost. High morale is the result of high hopes. Workplaces with low morale are fuelled by hopelessness and a sense of powerlessness. Workers will say things like, "Our workspace is cramped; our equipment is crap". I identify work environments that lack a sense of hope immediately. They are often consumed by issues which they "believe" they have no control.

Quite often I'll redefine their definition of control. By dividing things into those with which they have "direct" or "indirect" influence. By changing the implication of having no control to indirect control, it relieves their burden somewhat and revives hope of influencing the outcome via another (indirect) method. These workplaces believe they have no power, no autonomy or say, and thus absolutely no motivation to comply with company rules or requirements. Simple things like fastening seatbelts, wearing PPE, complying with signage or speed limits become an inconvenience.

Poor operational discipline is the result of poor self-evaluation. If a workforce believe they are underachieving, or they can't cope with workplace demands, it will create a sense of futility and hopelessness. Remuneration may be the only motivation left. Yet even a modicum of operational discipline requires more than remuneration.

Mission
Workplaces that feel a sense of reward for their efforts have a motive or belief that what they do counts for something. Without this you will never experience any form of job satisfaction—self evolved or otherwise. Quite the opposite is a purposeful organisation and equally important purposeful employee mindset. They will find the incentive to undertake activities based on the expected enjoyment of the activity itself. They don't expect any external benefits. The leader's role

morphs into a coaching role to assist the crew with uncovering their own purpose or intrinsic motivation. At this level a positive self-evaluation influences how people react to situations, how they accept instructions as well-meaning and draw positive conclusions about their work tasks. Which is directly proportionate to achieving a sense of satisfaction and pride.

The company mission statement or any other public statement on performance is not enough to motivate a workforce in this way. "Real" motivation comes from within the individual, not any external force and certainly not the words of a written statement. Successful leaders connect workers to a higher cause or the company's future. But these must support workers' individual values. It will be the process of engagement and participation, a sense of ownership and the inclusion and alignment of everyone's values built into any company mission that creates intrinsic motivation. Workforces are not motivated over the long term by wage incentives, even though workers may receive significant economic rewards. They aren't motivated by punishment and threats of dismissal either.

Motives

There are many examples where powerful motives were able to achieve great accomplishments. The Roman Conquests, the Great Wall of China, the Pyramids of Gaza, Angkor Wat for example. They all had one thing in common. The greater the motive—the greater the achievement. Recently it was discovered that the Great Pyramids were not built by slaves at all, but a willing workforce instilled with a powerful vision, the promise of an 'afterlife'.55

The Khmer royalty of Cambodia built Angkor Wat as a miniature replica of the universe, an earthly model of the cosmic world. The artisans of this amazingly intricate stonework were promised 'eternal-life' (reincarnation). If you've ever been to Angkor Wat, you will be astonished at the immensity of the stonework. I was dumbstruck at the scale of this accomplishment.

China's mystics immortalised constructors of the Great Wall with 'Shen Enlightenment'. And Augustus (Julius Caesar's successor) in the 1st century rewarded peasants who took up arms for his Auxilia (military) with 'Roman Citizenship', granting them lifetime access to "the greatest city on earth". At the time, definitely a motive any peasant would risk their life for. What is evident in these examples is how a single idea can carry such powerful meaning when it is articulated in terms of people's beliefs. A motive created with the right engagement and alignment will create the momentum for change. However, your success will be directly proportionate to how well your program aligns with workforce reality, how well it connects with their inner most beliefs. The simple facts are, if you want your workforce to value safety, they have to find it believable.

Be Prepared or Accepting?

OK. Time to get controversial. Most people are not going to like what they read next. But in an effort to be "Real", I want to throw it out there. If not simply to see the reaction. Workers aren't buying 'What' based safety rhetoric. They are screaming for more 'Why' inspired motivation to be safe. "But what's more inspiring than not getting hurt," I hear you say? I agree. But experience is showing us this is not motivation that works. Besides, what if there is 'Why' inspired motivation and there's still an accident? Is it possible our workplaces will still have accidents no matter what? Perhaps we may never see the total eradication of accidents altogether. I'm not saying this is good, I'm asking the question: Are we kidding ourselves? I don't have an answer. But blindly turning our backs on the idea that incidents might not be preventable, is certainly not the preparation Confucius was saying: *When all is orderly the superior man does not forget that disorder may come.* Is Confucius saying that order and disorder are both naturally occurring phenomena, and that we must accept it? Are we trying to tame that which cannot be tamed? If destruction and ruin are as intrinsic as structure and order, should we not factor this into our safety? Not "incident preparedness" which goes, *"In the unlikely event that we crash, please watch this life jacket demonstration (although we won't be flying over water today.)"* I'm talking about total incident acceptance. Which says near-misses and minor accidents are inevitable. It takes a brave soul to bring this up. But wouldn't it be nice if we could openly discuss it at least? It could radically change the way we approach things. More real. Less shaming. With more buy-in.

I know what I'm saying is hard to swallow. But please bear with me here. I said in the Introduction we'll get to the causes of accidents. But I didn't say we could eradicate them. My fear is that we miss out on more authentic responses when we sweep things under the carpet, ignoring what appears to be reality. Saying we can eradicate near-misses or minor incidents altogether, is like saying we can cure old age. Although we don't like it, we can't avoid growing old. So we don't create illusions about it. Embracing fantastical claims that we can achieve zero harm, is possibly dangerous in itself. Will we ever be prepared to drop the *all accidents are preventable* mantra and embrace more authentic beliefs? At what stage should we be challenging the efficacy of the most cherished beliefs we take for granted?

"What you resist not only persists, but will grow in size."
—Carl Jung

AGREEMENTS

When Theo reflects on his accident, he realises that if he had kept his agreements, he would not have had his accident. Like the agreement he made with his father before he left South Africa. They shook on it, "Promise me you'll look after yourself son." "Of course I will dad." Or the agreements he made with his wife and children. To always be there for them. He said if they move to Australia, he would give them a new life. Or the written and verbal agreements he made with the company. To maintain the PPE standards. But most of all the agreement he made with himself. To be reliable and do the right thing. Sometimes we slip up and maybe lose some trust. On this occasion however, Theo's agreements were written in blood.

The Price of Our Agreements

During early life our parents rewarded us when we did what they wanted and punished us when we didn't. We learned behaviours and habits from school, sport, other adults and children on the playground. The tools of reward and punishment were often emotional and sometimes physical. The impact of other people's opinions and reactions became a very strong force in the behaviours we created.

We learned to trust, and to be trustworthy. If trust was betrayed—our belief was shattered. In this process we created agreements in our mind of who we should trust, who we should not, who to believe, and who not to. In those developmental years we had an opportunity to learn the value of creating trust, by upholding agreements with each other, our parents, our friends and siblings. We learned to be accountable or betray the trust people placed in us. We learned there was an impact and a cost. We learned that in every agreement there was a price.

As a leader, how are you supposed to move towards a single objective and unified cause, with all of these different belief systems and behaviours swirling around your workforce psyche? The answer is, by forging commitments and agreements when issuing work instructions, and providing the opportunity for workers to create trustworthiness. By binding the activities to be carried out, with work crew goals, purpose and mission. By creating a game plan your workforce finds personally rewarding and intrinsically motivated to fulfil. These agreements can be reinforced daily at the pre-shift briefings. Combined with established consequences if the agreements aren't adhered to. In creating common ground and a desire that motivates crew members to keep their word, the term "agreement" is key here.

Agreements are a two-way street. Enforced by both leaders and workers. Both party's invite discussion around the proposed activity's goal's and a definition of success (no numerical goals remember). Also they are open to feedback. When that feedback is delivered within an effective and sincere accountability model, it carves out clear operating parameters and provides the "glue" which binds camaraderie, teamwork and support, otherwise known as trust.

Unfortunately, workplaces break agreements without realising the consequences all the time. Ignoring people who are late to meetings or turning a blind eye to minor infractions seem harmless enough. But there is an "energy" established that tears at the fabric of workplace integrity. It is so subtle, no one really notices the implications. Actually, that's not quite true. Workers notice something, and it creates an underlying tension whether to fully trust their environment or not. It's just that they can't quite put their finger on it. This affects their overall commitment to whether they will be totally congruent to the standards. Similar to whether you'd trust a politician who was fined for drunk driving. They might be stellar public servants, but it may nag at your senses whether to vote for them again at the next election.

The problem is people confuse accountability with some form of moral obligation. Like good or bad, right or wrong. But accountability is not an ethical question. Agreements are people aligning with an action or set of values and promising to respect them because it is close to their heart. They want to adhere to the agreed principles because it furthers their own cause or reinforces who they believe they are. Unfortunately, the art of keeping agreements is not a skill we learn in the workplace or even at home. But if we don't start teaching both workers and leaders these skills, how do we bring about the strict adherence to workplace minimum standards and requirements? More threats of punishment haven't worked and won't work in the future. The answer is to utilise the pride that is generated from within an individual who can be counted on for keeping their agreements. This is opposite to praising people get the job done. See the problem here?

Often, the impacts of broken agreements are outside of our comprehension. For instance, a guy caught speeding by police may seem less blameworthy if he was rushing his pregnant wife to hospital to give birth. Do you still trust him? But he broke the law, right? If you take the question of what is right or wrong out of the equation, what's left? Simply it's about upholding accountability to the speed limit. But that doesn't help his wife does it? What if he had killed someone on the road, or even his wife? Every agreement has a potential cost. Whether it's trust, property, people... someone's life. If this was the workplace, should he have made a contingency plan to call an ambulance if he couldn't make it to the hospital without speeding? I'm stretching things I know. The point I'm making is, when we make an agreement there must be awareness of the consequences for not keeping it. Blindly accepting an agreement will not create the commitment to uphold it. We may forget to plan for contingencies when we plan our work activities. For instance, what if Theo regularly reinforced his commitment to wear his PPE with a full appreciation of the consequences? His intention might sound something like:

"I have made an agreement with you my crew mates, that to achieve our objectives I will not remove my PPE. The long-term costs (consequences) of an accident may result in severe injury and may impact our goals dramatically. Therefore, we will lower the work platform down to the ground and discuss some other way of getting this tricky nut off."

OK, I'm joking. This is a bit far-fetched. I'm certain Theo wouldn't be so righteous in reality. But you get my drift. It's the underlying message I'm trying to get across. The ability to uphold and keep agreements is a personal responsibility. We can see from Theo's accident there are many layers of agreements that were broken: either personal, public, written, implied, spoken, unspoken, concise, vague or otherwise. When we have a 'Why' and an objective that encompasses more than just getting the job done, we overcome self-aggrandisation and catering to our desperate psychological needs. We'll do what furthers the cause instead. If Theo was invested in a team goal, and it was steeped in safe work systems, when Nico turned away Theo probably would not have taken off his gloves.

Remove subjectivity out of the equation and it is just the agreement. It's the Rational brain making decisions based on fact. It's the Emotional brain sticking with what it's good at, keeping agreements, maintaining belief in the mission, and being 'trustworthy' to the cause. By fusing everybody's ideas into a single goal or objective we create 'Why' to 'Why' connections amongst the work crew. Maintaining the commitments to safe work systems by holding each other's feet to the fire (accountability).

Workplaces can be subjective sometimes, full of values, judgements and opinions. We need to balance the subjectivity with reality to remain safe, to stay alive in our workplaces. If we want to maintain standards, then keeping agreements will generate the safe work ethic required. Keeping agreements will also build trust in the system. Both feed off each other. Keeping agreements creates consistent and credible communication because of the commitment to both safe work systems and a commitment to open discussions and keeping it real. Unfortunately, we don't teach skills of making and keeping agreements at schools, or our workplaces. It's a lost art form... until now!

Making Agreements

You are probably thinking, "What's so hard?" Well, the answer is nothing. Except if keeping agreements were easy, we'd be doing them already. The workplace would be reflecting congruent attitudes and conduct. There'd be no procedural breaches or short-cutting. If everyone had an understanding of the consequences of their safety agreements, through an embedded daily process at the pre-shift briefing, then the reliance on procedures would diminish. It is said that "Procedures are written in blood." Well I believe it's our agreements that are written in blood. Failure to keep our safety agreements can be catastrophic. Just ask Theo. We firmly believe agreements should be trained like any other work skill... and it can!

In Section III 'Why?', you'll learn a proven fun way to introduce an accountability model that reinforces agreements in your workplace. Getting Real may be a bit clunky at first, as the process might involve massaging everyone's values into one objective. But when every person in the team is accountable to each other to achieve a common goal, not just obeying the rules and procedures dictated by the leader, the foundation for voluntary operational discipline is laid. When implementing a safety program, agreements provide the conviction that it's the right plan, the right team and the right process. When you learn the technique in Section III, accountability sessions can take place during the pre-shift briefing and your workers learn to have fun exploring their newfound integrity. Without shaming or singling anyone out, so common in our current workplaces.

Of course, all of this accountability stuff sounds great in theory. If keeping agreements is all we need then we shouldn't have a problem, right? Except not everyone is going to be chipper about introducing a program that removes short-cuts and free rides. Not at first. But it soon feels uncomfortable to be the odd one out. Those few, will see that everyone else seems to be having fun with their newfound integrity, so they can too. This is what we see usually happening. Especially if we reward and acknowledge kept agreements. It's important that we don't just use agreements and accountability as a sword for control, or we fall back into old habits. Easily done. But that we can bask in the triumphs everyone "walking the talk" can achieve.

Walk the Talk

When you introduce the Agreements model, those little incongruities you once accepted as part of the culture will suddenly get cleaned up. For instance, smokers who stray from designated areas; unapproved caps worn beneath hard hats; the middle passenger seatbelts left unfastened, etc. Grey areas soon become black and white. It's much easier though if the agreements we wish to make in the workplace match everyone's values. You wouldn't have any problem creating voluntary operational discipline. Except, rarely will everyone's values be moving towards the same goals. There will be some people who do not want to comply with various workplace agreements.

Fortunately, the bottom line is that regulatory authority regulations and company corporate governance are the deal breakers. They are non-negotiable. We all know that. Namely, adherence to speed limits, the wearing of seatbelts, smoke free zones or mobile phone restrictions. So these should become the foundations of your workplace agreements initially. These types of accountabilities need to be reinforced face-to-face with work crews repeatedly. And personal commitments must be established with new employees and visitors too. So that the consequences of breaking those agreements are set in stone and crystal clear. Because rarely is our letter of employment or written procedures an adequate accountability tool. These are 'What' styled commitments and avoid the sense of response-bility that 'Why' styled agreements generate.

Problems with agreed commitments can arise when conflicting unspoken values override company stated rules. For instance, these are the casual agreements we let ride. Such as wearing jewellery around moving machinery, rolled up sleeves around jagged edges, etc. When leaders arbitrarily enforce certain rules when it seems convenient, or ignore them if the consequences seem minor, it creates inconsistency. Inconsistency is the enemy of accountability. Arbitrary responses to minor infractions will influence more seemingly major ones to occur. Not only did Theo remove his hands from his gloves, but they had to surgically remove his metal watchband that had melted around his wrist. Doh! Jewellery and high voltage!!?

Find a Motive

Take a PPE standard. One that says shirts must be tucked in and sleeves rolled down and buttoned up. And people are not adhering to it 100%. Some do, some don't. Either the standard must be changed to be more specific, or total accountability to the standard must be maintained. Some of these grey areas are larger than others. The issue however, is that when there's an incident, and suddenly leaders enforce the standard, implementing such discipline will be seen as two-faced and trust goes out the window. The motive must be the act of accountability, not the adherence to rules. Think about that one for a bit. Agreements such as bins being emptied, or vehicles cleaned up at the end of each shift are often not high on people's values. Therefore, a motive must be connected to completing those tasks, a (connection to a goal) and clear concise agreements on how these tasks are to be handled (accountability). A supervisor who simply says, "I want the bins cleaned by the end of shift," rarely gets what he wants their growing frustration decreases trust. Ensuring a specific person has volunteered (or been nominated) for the job and to which they've agreed and understand the consequences, means the chances of success is increased a thousand-fold.

This clarity increases trust in that if the task was not completed before the end of shift, the accountability rests with one individual. No need to allude to the whole crew. If there's a process where that person can get back into integrity by owning their action or inaction, making a new commitment is an opportunity to reignite trust and the journey towards continuous improvement resumes. This "psycho-technology", the art of communicating workplace accountability in terms of keeping agreements, and the ability to provide support, will allow workers to fumble through their commitments daily until they become second nature (habit). The goal is to replace the urge to make convenient choices and replace them with safer ones, purely because of the satisfaction it provides.

*"Unless commitment is made, there are only
promises and hopes... but no plans."*
—*Peter Drucker*

ACCOUNTABILITY

One moment Nico is staring out at the horizon taking in the scenery, when he hears the familiar ⚡ZAP⚡ of a live link disconnection. But how can that be? They are not doing a live link disconnection today!!? Then thud. Theo lands contorted at his feet, smoke and burning flesh. Nico immediately lowers the basket, years of training kick in. He's shaking on the inside but calm and collected as he yells down to prepare water and first aid. He knows he can be counted on when it's required. It's the unspoken agreement. So is never putting each other at risk. However, somehow, Theo has broken that agreement.

No Expectations

When Theo is taken away by ambulance, Nico has a chance to reflect and try to unravel what happened. He looks into the work platform and sees Theo's gloves unscathed on the floor. That's when the anguish wells up inside, "Domkop Theo, he's taken off his gloves." It was the ultimate consequence that only Theo had the power to control. Perhaps if Theo's workplace reminded workers to always wear their PPE, things would have been different, right? Except of course, they are reminded all the time. So that's not it. Some people shrug their shoulders and say, "Well, workers are supposed to be accountable to the PPE standards as part of their job?" Except if these expectations were valid, then people would not bypass the standards. But they do. All the time. So simply expecting accountability doesn't work either. I used to be convinced that if workplaces just adopted a sense of accountability to their daily activities, such as reinforcing the most basic PPE requirements, that this would solve everything. That promising to wear PPE would somehow be at the forefront of everyone's mind. Until I discovered it's NOT accountability to the standards that will ensure people follow them.

> *People are only accountable to their OWN sense of values, standards or authority.*

It's difficult to understand this disposition at first, but imperative that you do. So let me break it down for you.

Foundation of trust

Our own values create the buy-in to keep agreements. As I mentioned in the "Values" chapter. Yet it's the agreements people make with themselves, about who they believe they are, which they will uphold before any company standards or procedures. Theo's value was: "I am the *Go-to man*, the *Fix-it guy*. I get things done." And look where that got him. In the *heat of the moment* the PPE standards meant nothing to him. His choices to meet his own values were detrimental to his health and wellbeing. They are great values mind you, but with the wrong sense of purpose. It was "ego" and nothing about the greater good. It was an inwardly concentric world view, not outwardly caring and thoughtful. When faced with 'Procedural Breaches', you may be tempted to ask, "Why didn't the dude just follow procedures?" Or, "How can I get people to be more engaged in safety?" You might think you can solve your safety problems by telling people to be more careful, by reprimanding them, written warnings, zero tolerance or by issuing a new rule or procedure and demanding compliance. But it doesn't work and doesn't address the real underlying problem. Thinking that punishment will make procedures more important is a false sense of security and why people are still hurting themselves. You don't want people dropping their guard because they are told to follow procedures and trust the process is safe.

If you think your system is sound and if it were not for those few unreliable misfits that nothing would go wrong, think again. Nothing could be further from the truth. Relying on procedures as a method to control behaviour, and resisting human nature, will lead to even more problems. What you resist will not only persist, it will grow (Carl Jung). Why do we call things a procedural breach anyway? It's the perception that people are naughty for not following the rules. Our language is saying this. "Breach", "Zero Tolerance", "Poor Behaviour". This is how we talk to children. Our frustrations are manifesting themselves in punitive terms. What if the procedures are flawed? Otherwise we'd simply follow them, right? Think about it! There are a hundred other procedures people are following just fine, and don't have an issue. Maybe we are trying to bang square pegs into round holes. What procedural breaches are showing us, is that the existing procedural methodology has competing goals. It might be time constraints, it might be resource limitations, it could be boredom and a sense of repetition. Whatever it is, it is a "human" problem and we need to entertain a human solution. It's not a procedural problem.

Trying to turn humans into robots won't work. Perhaps if there was a relationship built on a foundation of trust, not enforced through punishment and written warnings, we could ask work crews how we could do things better. Perhaps underlying the problem is there's no foundation of trust that will expose the 'real' issues. Maybe it has nothing to do with procedures at all. The point is this... in my experience procedure breaches are really a cry for help. If you ask the "offender" what changes they'd make, and involve them in the remedial process, it might create the buy-in your looking for.

Tweak It, Don't Enforce It

When I was a kid my dad scolded me if I was late for dinner, or gave me a hiding if I didn't wheel my bike around the back out of the rain. But going around my mate's house after school made it hard to be home for dinner by 5:00 pm. I'd skid onto the front lawn, drop my bike, race inside and be seated by 4:59. Of course, after dinner I would forget to bring my bike in, and copped the hiding anyway. After a while, it would happen all over again. One day my Dad asked me, "Son, why don't you just follow the rules." I said. "I've tried." He suggested I leave my buddy's house 5 minutes earlier. But I couldn't leave 5 minutes of fun on the table (human nature). Despairingly he probed, "What are we gonna do?" I offered that if I didn't have to take my bike around the back I'd be fine. So one day he installed a garden shed out the front. We made a new agreement that if I didn't use it, he'd sell my bike to pay for it. From that day on, I was never late for dinner and my bike was never left out in the rain. Dad installed a shed (installed new equipment), changed the agreement (tweaked the procedure), and I avoided hidings (improved safety).

Consequences

Even the ancients contemplated the subject of accountability, tracing back to Aristotle and Plato. Aristotle said choice is voluntary and deliberate, therefore connected to consequence. The connection to consequence has alluded much of our current workplaces, if not simply ignored. Lost perhaps to the demands for more profits, production and increasingly onerous corporate liability. Nonetheless, everything has a consequence. Commonly, supervisors will issue directives with no clear consequences if the agreement is not upheld. Sometimes we imagine that accountability will simply emerge from corporate governance or procedures. But it won't. Workers will only absorb instructions and commit to agreements when they understand how the consequences will affect their own values. Even so, the most basic agreement is to employ the personal protective devices given to us for our safety, right? Yet people violate this agreement every day. It's why I don't advocate that more procedures will improve safety. Instead, consequences attached to agreements to adhere to procedures... will. We may just need to tweak the procedures to include consequences. Like my Dad did.

Honour Workers' Value Systems, Not Procedures

Originally, procedures were simply operating manuals. But now they include legislation, regulatory authority references, national standards, codes of practice, etc. They've become so arduous to read; they cannot be learned in their entirety without complete dedication. So people hardly learn them. Others, not even armed with the same amount of information or access to procedures, are very proficient at operating within the rules. In fact, they "value" the idea of wearing as much PPE as they possibly can. Then some people think procedures are bunk. This demonstrates that commitment to procedures is determined by one's own personal values, not the idea that the procedures are available. How do we hold people accountable to even these most basic agreements? Truth is, you can't hold anyone accountable to anything. That is, you can only truly hold yourself to account. The idea that someone else can hold others accountable is a fallacy. Yes, it takes two parties to make an agreement, but what you essentially abide by is, "I hereby agree to be bound by the consequences of my own actions in this agreement".

It is human nature to place our own values above all others or other things. It is part of the Habitual brain's plan for our survival. Some people will disagree with me and say things like empathy or altruism places other people's values first. However, people show empathy or are altruistic because of the benefits to their own identity. It's still a self-identity concept they uphold above all else. And another great example of how values influence our behaviour. Procedures don't influence behaviour at all. "Values alignment" does. Making agreements outside of our own value system will have the least probability of them being maintained. Our own values must be aligned with the goals and objectives of the workplace if we are to maintain even the simplest forms of accountability to uphold them. It's a key reason why people violate commitments to the rules. We know people should follow procedures, but it's not enough that we "should" do anything.

IOS and Accountability

When leaders and workers experience the ability to create and maintain clear and concise lines of agreement, there is clarity of direction and the emergence of trust. Yet, the ability as a leader to say, "OK team, what was the agreement? Did you keep it, yes or no?" is not a technique normally handed to us when we accept leadership roles. Instilled with this capability however, and a leader carves out very clear expectations both up and down organisational lines. Remember that accountability is a competence, not a behaviour. Facilitating accountability must be accompanied by some form of training. Otherwise things drift back into an ethical argument and become a blame game again. Right back where we started. Pure accountability is not a process which workplace's have had much experience or opportunity to learn. I didn't learn it in the workplace.

Over the past twenty years I've facilitated personal development workshops and weekly men's group meetings for the Mankind Project™, instituting principles of integrity, authenticity and accountability as a mission of service. The "Accountability Model" we employed binds these principles together. Over one hundred thousand men, women and their families have adopted this model around the world. Radically enhancing their lives. Teaching this model has provided me with invaluable insights into how people live, work and interact. Their hopes and dreams, their attitudes toward life, their views of the world; the past, present and future. The ideals they set for themselves and the way they interact with their families, friends and colleagues. The Get Real philosophy is basically a combination of these principles and how workplaces would benefit. If accountability works in the real world, why not at work? I've been fortunate enough to work alongside workforces across Australia and in South East Asia. Canvassing them on their workplaces and relationships with leaders. What I discovered was that whatever judgements leaders and workers project onto each other, they are only seeing reflections of their own dissatisfaction. The old saying holds true, when you point at others there are always three fingers pointing back at you. One finger is Blame, one is Excuse and the other is Denial. So, how do we build trust in the workplace with all these judgements flying around? One word: Accountability.

With any agreements model, there must be a way of managing the consequences if agreements aren't being upheld. But it must be done with respect and dignity. Pointing the finger at someone and saying, "You broke your agreement to wear your PPE" is the exact opposite of what I'm proposing. That's where "real" accountability comes in. The first rule of accountability is that it is not about being right or wrong. It's not about meeting a perceived standard. It is simply the ability to commit to agreements and steadfastly upholding them, with a process of correction that isn't about behaviour. That's it. No morals, no ethics, no judgement. No blame. It goes without saying that the model relies on people being prepared to take full responsibility for their actions. You can't police accountability. In Section III, we'll discuss this further in the chapter called OAR BED.

But in the meantime, the idea is to avoid personality conflicts during the process. This leaves ego at the door.

Allowing ownership to emerge that is self-regulating, empowering and remedial. This is a sure-fire way that safe workplaces are cultivated. By instilling a program where safety agreements support your initiatives and a model of accountability is incorporated to reinforce them. I suggest at every pre-shift meeting (all meetings really), you implement a way of recording your workplace agreements. A whiteboard will do. A place where you can tweak your 'Why', also written in big letters across the top. It lists the important agreements, who they are between, and what the consequences are for not keeping them.

Simple Accountability Steps

The Diagram below shows how accountability follows the same vector as the IOS Model, starting with "Why".

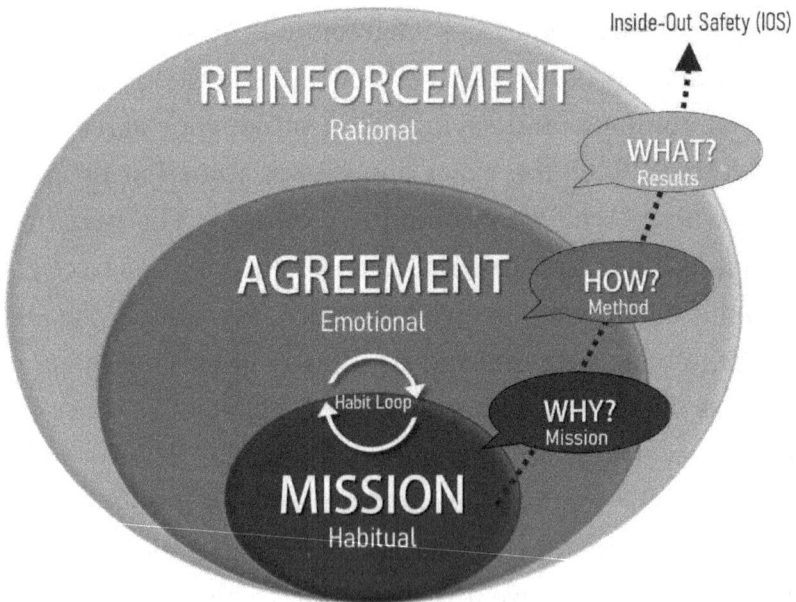

Diagram 2—Accountability Steps in Terms of the IOS Model

Step 1: THE WHY—Does the **Mission** fit the workforce's objectives? Or does it need tweaking? Always ensure it "fits".

Step 2: THE HOW—Negotiate the **Agreement**. Resolve ambiguity. Clarify the consequences for not keeping it.

Step 3: THE WHAT—Constantly **Reinforce** all agreements at every pre-shift meeting and support each other to stay on track. Utilise OAR BED (and have fun).

On this level, accountability is a learned skill and should be modelled until it becomes habitual. It is a process that work crews and supervisors can learn easily enough. There are simple steps that make workplace agreements fun and empowering. Accountability is a definable process which must be embraced before "extreme ownership" can become a reality in your workplace. Otherwise agreements simply become "lip service" and the same old blame game will re-emerge. By the way, notice *Diagram 2* on the previous page. If you operate outside-in and incorrectly START with *"Reinforcement"*, be careful what you are reinforcing. The Rational brain will reinforce the results, and override anything which isn't getting the job done. The mission must be established FIRST. Inside-out... always! In following chapters, we will lay out the Agreements model, OAR BED and other key processes that Theo and I implement in our workshops. You can start using them in your own workplace immediately. But what's most important, is that you begin with defining your 'Why' first. So that Agreements are made against a sense of purpose and conviction. Something worthwhile. This is an extremely important ingredient. Without a 'Why' there is nothing to bind your agreements to. I'll go through this process with you soon.

"Honesty is the fastest way to prevent a mistake from turning into a failure."
—James Altucher

SECTION III

WHY

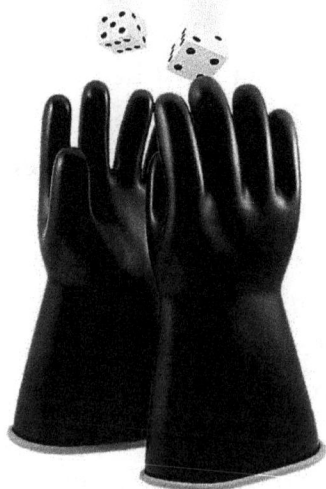

Now it's time for the rubber to meet the road. We will put the principles of human nature we've just discussed into action. Section III 'Why', is about unlocking the secrets of creating intrinsic motivation and learning the processes that create job satisfaction and fulfilment for your work crews. Continuous improvement and workforce autonomy are possible when there's a foundation of trust and a belief in the leadership. Only then will voluntary operational discipline and a self-driven workforce emerge.

THEO'S STORY

LIFE GOES ON

There was a momentary lull in Theo's emergency ward. It became eerily quiet. The initial hurry to treat his injuries had been attended to. There were other people who needed attention now. Theo imagined hospital staff were simply waiting for him to die. He lay there in a semi-unconscious state, alone. Contemplating deeply what his life really means. Tears well up in his eyes. It was those dearest to him that meant everything. It wasn't his job; his home, possessions. It was being fully alive. Playing with the kids, a round of golf, driving his car. Will he ever be able to do those things again? Theo thought about his car. There it is, this magnificent piece of engineering. Yet, if you lose the keys it is useless. A pile of junk. You might be able to sleep in it, or brag about it, but it will never fulfil its function. He wonders if he will ever fulfil his function too. He considers what will become of him if he can't use his hands.

As he drifts in and out of consciousness, perhaps for the last time, he wonders what his family will think of him if he can't look after them, or himself. Eventually these thoughts would become a reality. Although his recovery included many, many operations and procedures, the impact is more than physical. Once home, the voices in his head become all-consuming and his will-to-live disappears. It will take something extraordinary to come back from here, as he tackles a massive depression head on. The enticement of suicide loomed daily like a dark cloud.

The biggest challenge for Theo was the state of his spirit, his mental and emotional wellbeing. He struggled to accept the agreements he broke with his family, his work, the crew... his dad. A healthy spirit knows no bounds. Disabled people will tell you it's more than willpower that moves them to achieve the things they do. It's coming to terms with reality, accepting their disability, and finding something worthwhile to live for. In contrast, a wounded soul is more debilitating than disabilities. Theo's soul was unwilling to come to terms with his situation. He owned his mistake and accepted the accident was of his own making. That wasn't so hard. What he couldn't face was the effect his actions had on the world around him. The tragic toll it had on his loved ones, the effect on his company, his colleagues, friends, neighbours, acquaintances.

The ripple effect was far reaching. To this day, Nico and Theo are still good friends. But Nico had only come to terms with everything recently, after all these years. Before that, he would not talk about the accident. It affected him too much. He just wanted to find a way to let it go. He became addicted to painkillers. He's recovered now. A changed man. But Theo still feels the guilt. They have both acknowledged that life must go on. When you are at rock bottom, the sun still comes up each day. The children still need a father.

What finally gave Theo some hope, was when he could eventually go to the toilet by himself. It wasn't pretty at first, but it was a massive victory. It gave him back some sense of independence. Such an undignified burden it placed on everyone around him. He started to re-learn the everyday tasks which we take for granted. Making breakfast, washing your teeth, buttoning a shirt. His left arm and hand will always have limited capacity, but his right hand has learned to compensate.

After many, many months of painstakingly frustrating rehabilitation, Theo begins to feel life re-enter his body again. There is light at the end of the tunnel. He finally passes a special driving licence after failing twice. The assessment didn't even leave the parking lot. He couldn't fasten his seatbelt. The intolerant instructor saying, "You can't fasten your seatbelt mate. What am I supposed to do?"

Theo went back to work, under a program that would ease him into the workplace. Gradually, slowly, he worked three hours a week. Then four, and more. Retraining in the field of health and safety. He's now a very determined advocate for change. Focusing on workers' attitudes towards upholding workplace agreements. He firmly believes PPE is useless if what's going on between the ears is in conflict with site requirements.

Public speaking came naturally to Theoi. Initially he was asked to talk to a crew of Liney's. Then to a group of leaders. Then a seminar, a conference, and eventually across entire organisations. Theo's mission grew to encompass much more than what he wanted for himself. It's a global mission to change the world, with himself as proof 'Why' things need to change.

Has he forgiven himself? Well, he still wakes up at least once a week in a cold sweat, reliving the accident. He can hear it, feel it, smell it, all over again. Perhaps not until his message is making a difference, where it is needed most out in the field, will he ever start to feel a sense of ease. The idea that his mission of service will have a positive impact on anyone who will listen to him, is the 'Why' that drives him now.

Theo's audiences are overcome with both emotion and inspiration when he speaks. After he finishes people rush to the exits and their phones. An instant need to call loved ones, to hear their voice. Yet he knows he still has a lot of work to do. Because workplaces are no closer to authentic, open communication than before his accident. He wants more than to simply be an inspiration. He wants transformative change. "Everyone needs to know that my biggest revelation, and my biggest regret, is that both me and my workplace didn't know how to be honest about what was going on." "We didn't promote openness or learnings as our highest value, so that speaking up felt safe, let alone how we were going about things."

Theo returned to Royal Perth Hospital to thank the

surgeons and the burns unit. Especially the physios who were angels in disguise. Relentlessly, they instilled a vision of normalcy back into his thinking. They taught him the power of 'Yes, I can do this', and to be thankful that he is alive. To be able to see his children's successes, be there for their failures.

When you see Theo speak, he relives every second of pain. Every moment of heartache. Total accountability and ownership. He has dedicated himself to changing workplace culture by not shying away from the truth. But not providing managers and leaders exactly what they want to hear either. Instead, he offers his own story as living proof that much of how we operate our workplaces today, means his accident WILL happen again. Amazingly, he preaches to the converted. It seems most managers fear the same thing will happen too, as oddly as it sounds.

What Theo tries to convey most is that life is a series of agreements and commitments. Made over and over again. If we keep them, we move forward. If we break them, we will have to learn the lessons before we can move on. By recommitting to new agreements after any infraction, it rewires neural pathways to form positive habits. Building affirming connections between work-teams, allowing people to support each other so to stick with the safety mission.

Theo is lucky. He survived his injuries and the severe depression. He began to reap the rewards from more empowering decisions. Ones that produced a different set of consequences. He started to make a difference in his own life and in other people's lives too. But at what cost? Would you go through what Theo did to get where you are today? Of course not. But you can achieve the same results by thinking in terms of consequences when you plan your work activities.

Everything in life hinges on our carrying through with our commitments. We either renegotiate them if things change or complete them as agreed. This one keystone habit changed Theo's life forever. It took him from the depths of the abyss to the pinnacle of understanding. Theo believes that today's workplaces will be transformed if leaders and work crews would be clearer with their agreements, and if a simple fun process of accountability was introduced. Mixed in with some well-defined 'Whys'. Something to stem the mental anguish that seems to be fuelling the disenchantment we experience in our workplaces. Many people identify with Theo's depression. They often talk with him about their own demons after his presentation. A need to express themselves and their own frustrations after seeing him do it. It's a growing trend that more people are speaking about their demons more.

Another clue that people want to say more, is the advent of social media. It reveals the importance society now places on personal recognition as a human trait. Theo's Facebook and Linkedin pages have become an emotional release for many people. A social 'Why' screaming to be fulfilled.

We all want a fair day's pay for a fair day's toil. Yet there is a growing sense that there's more to life than simply turning up to work and sticking out our hand for a pay cheque. People are also seeking:

- *A sense that their work is making a difference.*

- *Autonomy and a say in decision making.*
- *Recognition and a feeling of being valued for their contribution.*

In coming pages, you will discover how to pursue these universal aspirations and inspiration. Theo finishes his presentations with his own. While he was recuperating, there was a day at the "physios" that went particularly well. Closing his eyes and concentrating with all his might, he managed to reach into a bucket pick up a 12mm nut between with his thumb and forefinger (yes the physios had a sick sense of humour). At last his fingers were coming back to life. In celebrating this massive achievement, Theo promptly tells his kids they will go to the park today. Summer is in the air. As Theo sits on a bench with the sunlight glistening through the trees, he enjoys a slight breeze and watches the children play.

Suddenly, he realises the picture of his most cherished dream is happening right before his eyes. The image he clung to and valued more than anything in the world. The one that gave him hope. He barely holds back the tears as he recalls:

"I'm sitting on the bench and I am overcome with appreciation. My beautiful little princess is dancing around in her favourite dress, smelling the flowers. While my two sons are play-fighting in the grass the way loving brothers do. It was exactly as I had dreamed. The image that kept me alive... and now it was real."

"But in the end, one needs more courage to live than to kill himself."
—Albert Camus

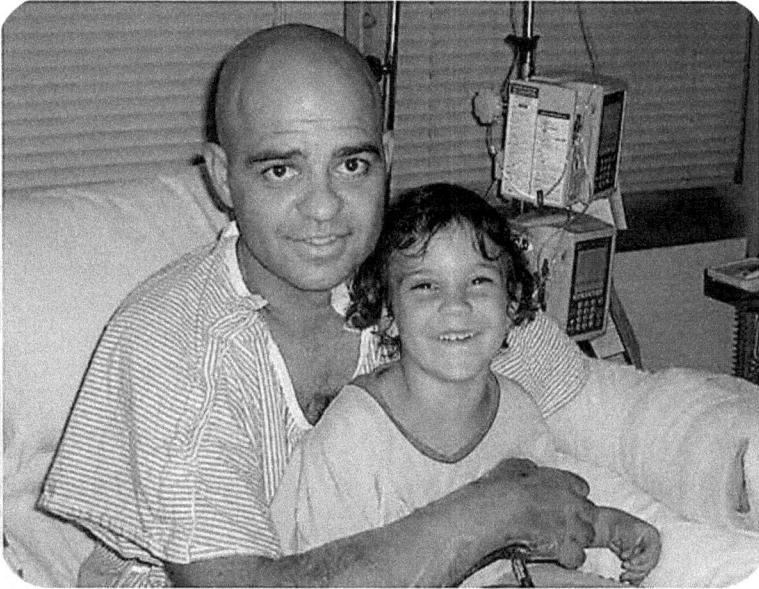

*After four months in hospital it's time to go home. Theo had lost a
lot of weight and would need his family's full support.*

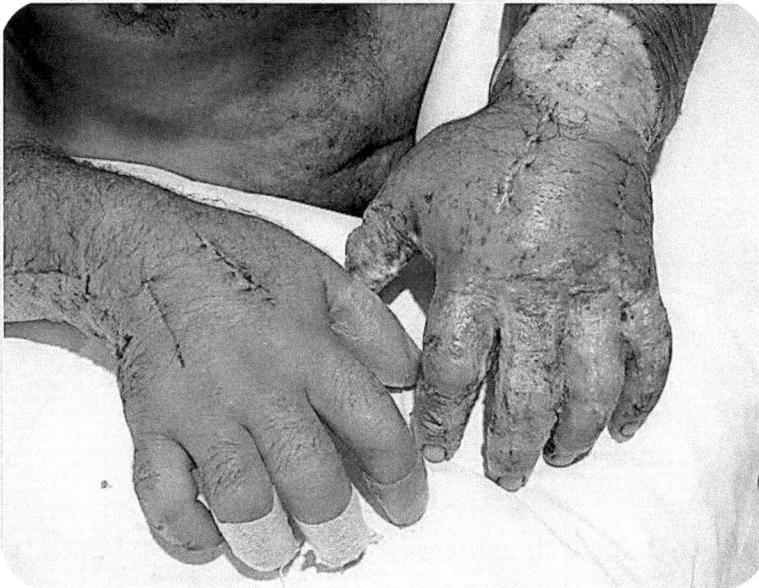

*At home, Theo's left hand was still badly damaged and required
further medical treatment. His right hand couldn't clutch anything
yet. That would take years of painstaking rehabilitation.*

WHY-POWER

When Theo reflects on that fateful day, he often recalls the feeling of temptation to remove his gloves. "If only I had more 'will'-power," he laments. Of course, PPE is really only a last line of defence. But in Theo's case, gloves are a "have-to" non-negotiable safety device. Putting logic aside, something more fundamentally vexing is at play here. Why do workers take matters in their own hands (excuse the pun) when things heat up? And why do leaders need to plead with their people to follow safety procedures? There's a tension between what people "want to" do and what they "have to" do. It's how most workplaces operate. Yet neither of these are conducive to a safer more fulfilling workplace. So what is?

Temptation

When we think of something that requires our will power, most of us remember new year resolutions and how often we failed to achieve them. When people say, "I have no will-power" what they really mean is, "I can't seem to resist temptation". When facing temptation, what's really happening is, you have limited your alternatives with an "I want". But which honestly, is not that high on your values. You want to lose weight for example, but you're not keen on exercise, or you can't say no to ice-cream. There's really no such thing as temptation, or even things like procrastination. It's simply a case where you commit to something that is not high on your values. Will-power or its alter-ego 'won't-power', means forcing yourself to do something that you have committed to. When really, you don't *want* to.

Seen in a safety light, leaders want their workforce to exhibit a more will-power or won't-power. In other words, more self-control. Yet will-power and won't-power are only two aspects of self-control. They alone don't constitute your true capacity to follow safety procedures. There is something far more powerful than saying yes when you really need to say yes. Or no when you really need to say no. Will-power and won't-power isn't enough when we *need* to do something—even if a part of us doesn't *want* to. You need a higher power.

A more successful technique is called "Why-Power". As a leader, communicating what you "want", must come from this higher realm. Otherwise it won't instil self (intrinsic) motivation. You will have more success inspiring your workforce to carry out work practices safely, than strong-arming them. The idea is that achieving safety should provide a sense of satisfaction.

Why-Power (intrinsic motivation) doesn't require discipline or punishment or pleading to achieve. It's a way of harnessing everyone's values and attitudes towards a single vision or goal. Otherwise, what's going to stop people from following their own immediate impulses, or look for convenient options or short-cuts, in the *heat of the moment*. Punishment, dismissal? These won't work. For a worker to exert the self-control needed when it matters most, they really convert *I will, I won't,* and *I want* into "Why-Power". Why Power is about harnessing all of these "power muscles", to help you achieve your workplace goals. Ones that "naturally" steer people away from trouble and harm.

Self-Control

Human beings possess unique capabilities when we combine *I will, I won't,* and *I want.* It separates us from the animal kingdom. In fact, the development of these three powers defines what it means to be human. Thousands of years ago, your responsibilities, living in a closely-knit tribe was dependant on others for your survival. Communities required cooperation and sharing of resources. You couldn't just take what you wanted or steal another person's food. You'd be exiled from the group—or even killed. Moreover, you may have needed your tribal companions to care for you if you got sick or injured. Even in the stone age, there were rules for how to cooperate with your neighbour. You needed to share your cave and food, even if you were cramped or hungry.

In other words, you needed to exhibit some self-control. It's not just your own life on the line, the whole tribe depended on your ability to get along. Even being selective about who you share your interest in genetic diversity with. You would need to learn to leave that cave-guy's cave-woman alone. Or risk becoming his cave decoration. This was just the beginning of the need to exhibit will/won't-power. Fast forward to today's increasingly complex world and there is an even greater need for self-control. Big equipment and machinery have replaced

Jurassic animals. Just like dinosaurs are always seemingly out to get us. Our brains have evolved, but we still require the ability to control the impulses that helped us become fully human. In modern day l`ife, will-power has gone from being the thing that distinguishes us from animals, to the thing that distinguishes us from each other.

In Two Minds

We may all have been born with the capacity for free-will, but some of us use it more than others. People who have better control over their attention, emotions and actions, have a better chance of finding more employment, fulfilment and satisfaction. Even maintain a safer work environment. The answer appears to be our ability to stay focused and pay attention to what we want, even when after a long day, there are things that distract us.

Will-power, won't-power and want-power reside in three different sections of the Rational brain, and are designed to help you cope with various tasks. Like stopping the job if it's unsafe or assessing changes in condition when you'd rather push on through and get the job done. Why-Power wrestles control away from the Rational brain and allows the Emotional and Habitual brains to find a purpose or cause. Making it easier to go and get that safety device when you really want to turn a blind eye. It's Why-Power that motivates you to open the procedures and start ticking off the checklist of safety controls, when it's easier to put off doing a risk assessment.

Why-Power holds you back from following impulses that change your focus. To resist the temptation to speed, or read a text message while you drive. Keeping your eyes on the speedometer instead. Why Power is about developing and keeping track of your goals and your desires in the workplace. It's the ability to maintain team focus on what's really important. Not necessarily safety. Safety is the natural by-product of a workforce with attention on a higher purpose, a 'Why'. Remember that safety is the "What" not the "Why'. It is a RESULT, not the GOAL.

Without Why-Power it's kind of like having two minds. Or even two people living inside our mind. There's one identity that acts on impulse and seeks immediate gratification, and another one that controls our impulses and delays gratification to protect our long-term goals. They're both still us, but we switch back and forth between them. Sometimes we identify with the person who wants to wear the correct PPE and use the appropriate safety devices, and sometimes we identify with the person who just wants to get the job done.

Unfortunately, a snapshot of our current safety model demonstrates a reliance on will power or won't-power exclusively. Why-power is missing. Relying on only these two parts of ourselves will exhibit conflicting goals. One part of us wants one thing while the other part wants something else. Perhaps the present-self wants to do the right thing, but our future-self thinks it would be better off if we took a shortcut. When these two selves disagree with each other, one of them has to win and override the other. The part of you that wants to take a shortcut isn't bad, it simply has a different point of view about what matters most in any given moment. Thousands of years of evolution have created our need to conserve energy and do the quickest easiest thing. Which is not always the safest. Seeking convenience defines the human condition but also endangers it.

Every incident I ever investigated is the result of will power/won't-power challenges and the conflict between these two parts of ourselves. This constant inner conflict distracts us and it's not always achievable to make the right choice. Our workplaces have to stop relying on will power and won't-power for our safety. We need to rely on a higher power, a Why-Power. When we find a 'Why' for what we want, aligned with our values, we will find the "Power" to overcome these conflicting impulses. We'll stop activating out of our primitive functions and start to utilise the most modern of our human capabilities. Our ability to dream and manifest what we want. In other words, Why-Power.

"A big part of willpower is having something to aspire to, something to live for."
—*Mark Shuttleworth*

FIND MEANING

Reliving his story time and again, Theo's presentations engage the audience at the deepest level. To admit his mistake over and over takes fortitude. He never moves to hide it or fade it or fix it. Normally when people make a mistake of this enormity it's natural to sweep it under the carpet. But for Theo there's a determination to be earnest, to be real. Walking the talk means the willingness to be responsible for the damage he caused. To be held accountable for the agreements he broke. He lost people's trust, lost the use of his hands, lost his wife... he even lost hope. He survived his injuries but how did he survive his own soul? How do you come back from that?

The Truth About Linking Safety with Family

Workplaces who dream up safety campaigns targeting the family are misguided. They challenge their workforce to place as much value on their own wellbeing, as they do their love of family. Except there's a problem when you relate to safety from this perspective. What if today, you are arguing with your spouse? Or going through a divorce. Will this lack of love translate into a lack of safety too? Of course it will. Furthermore, using family ties to create intrinsic safety motivation is arguably the worst thing you can do. It will create just as much angst as it does warm-heartedness. Some workplaces, and I see it a lot, have a distorted sense of motivation. They believe anger, punishment, warnings and constant pressure will keep a workforce in check. As sad as this sounds, in many ways this is a reflection of many people's true family dynamics. Yet we don't go to work to be treated like children and we certainly don't expect our superiors to lose their cool when things go wrong. What these workplaces overlook, is that their high incident rates are actually a result of poor family experiences. It's not always rosy at home, yes or no? Be honest.

The truth is, attaching warm and fuzzies to your family life will have little bearing on whether you act safely or not. Because this concept appeals to a part of your brain that does not believe anything bad will happen to you today. Family arguments or otherwise. This part of your brain has no determination on you being safe—unless there's an emotional connection to you acting safely, not to your family. The reality is that we are more likely to take short-cuts to get home to our loved ones quicker. Confused? Welcome to 'real' safety.

Half Your Life

Have you ever thought about the impact work has on your life? Not just the means it provides but how much actual time it consumes and affects your attitude at home. If you enjoy family and lifestyle one third, go to work one third, and sleep the other third, then you're splitting HALF of your waking, conscious life between home and work. Half! That's a huge chunk of time dedicated to making a living. Therefore, the question is, do you work to live—or live to work? From this standpoint, it appears that work is even more significant than your lifestyle. Would there be any lifestyle without the means to sustain it? Whether you're at home or work, you're seeking the same satisfaction and durable fulfilment. We need to shift the conversation.

Perhaps the question is not why people take risks? But, why do we skate the thin ice of probabilities? This is a huge distinction. No one believes they are taking "risks" when I interview them after an incident. They deny it. In every case they say, "I didn't think it was risky" or "I knew what I was doing." I always get this same response. ALWAYS! Take a look around you when you're on the road. People speed, they run red lights, sneak text messages or talk on their phones while they drive. Even when they know it's illegal. It happens every day. Riskiness is not just a workplace phenomenon. People have an inbuilt need to "get the job done". It's a desire to be efficient, effective, capable, competent. It's an inherent yearning to express prowess and skill, to be masters of our physical world. Then we reward ourselves if we pull it off. Beating the odds makes us feel proud, alive... dare I say human. How do we harness these inherent desires, safely?

Forget Control

We all know that if you get injured you won't be able to fend for yourself or family. Yet this doesn't appear to change people's behaviour. We seem to be fighting against instinct, human nature. Problem is, even though we like to be adventurous, we all know it is not possible to flirt with the laws of probability at work. Certainly not from within the confines of our dangerous workplaces. As leaders what can we do to control risk taking? At the same time, as workers, how do we control the urge to take risks. How do we find that edge we are looking for, safely? Well, what if we didn't focus on control at all? What if the real question is, "What meaning should we find in our work?" Imagine if we had a higher meaning in what we do as an expression of our purpose, would tasks take on more significance than simply putting food on the table, or not getting hurt? It's too clichéd to say your safety and staying alive is paramount to you and your family's survival. What about saying, it's paramount to your soul's need for a sense of fulfilment and achievement? Or the need to feel valued for who you are and appreciated for your contribution.

We don't go to work and switch this aspect of our lives off. We can't. Our work 'IS' our life. The workplace is a shrine to our dedication and toil. It's where we spend half our waking conscious life, interacting with other people and working as a team. Hallmarks of our humanity. Workplaces would do well to focus more on our mental, emotional and dare I say spiritual wellbeing. Then safety might be a natural by-product.

Truthfully, Get Real is not really about safety. Although it reveals why people have accidents. It's more to do with finding out 'Why' you go to work and do the things you do. It's about finding your own motivation from within. Intrinsic motivation.

A New Way of ~~Working~~ Living

Given the amount of time and resources we dedicate to our work; we should be treating work the same as our lifestyle. After all, work is our second home, right? Perhaps we should find as much 'meaning' in our work like we are trying to find at home. The last part of this book, the 'Why', will take you down a path of finding more meaning in your work. Combined with some key understandings in the field of leadership, ownership and fulfilling agreements. To get what you 'really' want from work, we aim to establish the idea that safety is not a set of rules and procedures... but a mindset, an attitude and a way of being. A way of life. The pursuit of happiness. Is it even possible?

You bet. I've never met a great safety culture operating from the level of low morale. I've never worked in a company with great relationships and teamwork, who comes from the standpoint of excuses and denial. I've never seen anyone go home at the end of the day with a smile on their face and feeling good about themselves—who didn't care about their workplace, have pride in their work, and belief that what they were doing— meant something greater than just putting food on the table.

There's a formula for durable fulfilment and achieving a sense of satisfaction at home. And it's the same formula for achieving great safety and less accidents at work. Finding meaning in your work, bringing about a sense of fun and buy-in, is not just a catchcry, it's absolutely possible. Workplaces with a 'Why' improve quality, increase production and eliminate accidents. We are going to show you a simple technique we use that embeds enjoyment and satisfaction into your daily work tasks. But let's quickly look at the difference between leadership and stewardship and see where you are along that journey. Stewardship promotes autonomy and self-empowerment. Leadership is just one step along the path to stewardship.

"It is very difficult to have a meaningful life
without meaningful work."
—Jim Collins

STEWARDSHIP

When Theo's manager asks if there is anything the team knows of that needs immediate attention, Theo is faced with a massive test of his leadership. Yet he is stuck. Overcome by a fear of speaking out. A 'Rabbit in the headlight' scenario. In what seems like an eternity, Theo's manager eventually backs down. Theo breathes a sigh of relief as he is let off the hook. But he feels like a coward and questions his commitment to safety. What would his father have done he wonders? A veteran liney. His mentor? How might a man with all that experience have helped Theo assess the situation better? Whereas the manager is a leader, his father is more like a steward. What is the difference?

Duty of Care Vs. Entrusted with Care

What is good leadership? Is it the confidence, experience and training to do the right thing when it's required? Is it the courage to speak up when you are called to? Should it ever get to a point where you need courage to speak up if it will save a life? If Theo spoke up at the wheelchair presentation, would it have changed the course of history and the way things were done by future work crews? Would the 12-millimetre nut problem be resolved for every other liney too? Help the entire industry? Would Theo have had his accident at all?

Consideration of the work crew is a leadership question. However, consideration of "future" work crews is a stewardship question. There is a difference in the way stewards approach their leadership. Stewardship expands the magnitude of the timeframe to also include a generative quality. To include decisions now that affect future generations.

The term stewardship used to be a job description, denoting the office of a steward, or the manager of a large household. In recent years, the "management" sense of stewardship has evolved into a caring connotation. As in the "careful and responsible management of something entrusted into one's care". [56]

I really like this analogy. Entrusted into one's care. It puts a new spin on the idea of "Duty of care". Rather than a liability it becomes an honour. If you were asked to supervise a work crew, or have them entrusted into your care, which one has more meaning? What type of attitude might you adopt if you were entrusted with someone's care? I would love to ditch "Duty of Care" and replace it with "Entrusted With Care".

The Stewardship Hypotheticals

There is a mountain of literature on the subject of leadership. Suffice to say, there is far less material available on the idea of stewardship. Therefore, if you want to test your leadership for stewardship qualities, perhaps you might contemplate the following challenge. In a quiet space I suggest you reflect on these two hypothetical questions that you might ask of your leadership:

'Where am I going?' and 'Who will go with me?'

In his book "Fire In The Belly", Sam Keen asks us these two very important questions. They snapped me out of a mid-life crisis twenty years ago. I think they are as powerful today as they were when he wrote them. If you assume a leadership role, you would do well to reflect upon these questions until you get the right answers. That's how powerful they are.

If you are not asking yourself these questions, or worse still, get them in the wrong order, it's a fair chance you will experience many challenges and frustration as a leader. Far worse, symptoms may include poor workplace compliance, low morale, a rise in incidents and accidents, waning operational discipline and a general mistrust in you the leader, or path set by management.

Regardless of whether the answer is evident to you or not right now, to understand their significance, allow me to ask the questions again. But answer them for you this time: 1) 'Where am I going?' Answer: "To follow my calling and path in life". 2) 'Who will go with me?' Answer: "Those who trust and believe in me". You will have your own answers of course, but the order in which you answer them is so crucial. How will you know who will go with you—without first determining where you are going?

'Who will go with me?' is a question borne out of, 'Who am I?' You must know who you are before you can ask anyone else to go with you. Or more to the point, are people going with you because they want to—or because they have to? Leaders tell people to follow them all the time. But, *"Stewards guide people to follow themselves"*. Knowing who you are will determine which one of these styles is the best fit for you. I suggest you seriously consider the stewardship question.

Too often, the question companies ask of their leaders is more about their capacity to give directions and instructions, and less about stewardship. There's a big difference between *follow* and *force*. Carrot and stick leadership will restrict your capacity to cultivate a healthy safety climate. Guiding workers to discover their own intrinsic motivation is the fine art of stewardship.

Creating Autonomy

A safe and productive workplace evolves when a leader conveys the company's business objectives in terms of the workforce's values. This is primarily a stewardship function. Consistently achieving high satisfaction levels in a workplace means workers feel valued for their contribution, are connected to a common goal and have a sense of ownership of their work tasks.

It suggests a steward might guide them along this journey, to find the intrinsic motivation which inspires the level of voluntary operational discipline they crave. You may be thinking how distant voluntary operational discipline seems from your current situation, or if it is even possible. Truth is, I've had my doubts too. I've run workshops where morale was so low people walked up to me afterwards and said, "Thank you for today, I was ready to quit until now". I spent a couple of hours helping them redefine their situation and create an objective aligned with their own values over the long term, and it turned things around quickly.

It's never the company's values that inspire a workforce.

However, the company's values are usually met when the workforce's values are met too. Once you realise what motivates a workforce, it will change your leadership style to include stewardship. Unearthing self-determination, autonomy and intrinsic motivation requires that your time is spent productively assisting work crews in solving their own problems. If your work crews aren't shown how to solve their own problems, you'll always be having to solve their problems for them. Does this ring true for you in your current situation?

Following are some examples of how you can cultivate stewardship into your leadership style, and help you get those hypotheticals in the right order.

Extreme Ownership

In their book 'Extreme Ownership,' Jocko Willink and Leif Babin believe leaders must own 'everything', that there is no one else to blame. [57] In battle, decisions have immediate consequence. Everything is at stake. The "right" decision, even when all seems lost, can snatch victory from the jaws of defeat. Imagine if Theo abandoned the 'nut' conundrum and lowered the work basket to the ground, to rethink the situation. What a victory that would've been.

Alternatively, the "wrong" decision, even when victory seems certain, can result in catastrophic failure. For instance, when Theo celebrated removing the nut, the insulator started to fall. Instinctively he reached out to grab it and BANG! Or consider the guy who sped his pregnant wife to hospital. What if he caused an accident or harmed his wife and unborn child, let alone others? In the *heat of the moment*, ownership provides a moral compass to guide you through the minefield of leadership responsibilities in any given day. Ownership is fundamental to the accountability principle. Accountability breeds trust. Trust breeds belief in your leadership.

Voluntary Operational Discipline

Admiral Hyman G. Rickover was known as the "Father of the US Nuclear Navy". He dreamed of a fleet of nuclear-powered submarines and ships before there was even a commercial nuclear power plant on land. [58] Forget the engineering challenges, what about putting something as complex as a nuclear reactor onto a vessel, under the sea, and run it with a crew of inexperienced sailors.

Rickover threw out centuries of traditional military dogma: follow orders; do what you're told; don't ask questions. Instead he successfully created a culture founded on integrity, a questioning attitude and uncompromising open communication. Experts agree, the Nuclear Navy is one of the greatest examples of voluntary operational discipline on the planet. What Rickover taught us is that operational discipline cannot be instilled. It must be cultivated. Rickover was a steward in the true sense of the word. He had a vision where individuals would be led by their own leadership.

Identify and Empower Leaders

Sporting teams rely on self-discipline and on-field leadership as the hallmark of overall team success. Although athletes who exemplify these traits are often chosen as captains, individual performances also inspire the team. Obviously, a coach who understands how motivation works will convey the team's ethos through the identified 'leaders' within the group, because this perpetuates discipline and the desired attitude amongst other players. In the workplace you will inspire autonomy and greater problem-solving capacity by giving those who show initiative the reins. You can just sit back and watch the show. Offering your experience when it's needed. A true coach.

Set the Example
During the Great War, discipline among the troops reflected a leader's competence. The Australian Light Horse infantry chose their own leaders based on savvy, not education or class. Discipline, loyalty and trust were inspired by a leader's "fine conduct under fire". Not by King's regulation or arduous hours on the drill square. As a result, the infantry performed their duties voluntarily and without orders. [59]

This type of self-regulation set the tone well into the next century and beyond. Admittedly, it's a far cry from the battlefield to our workplaces, but a leader's conduct under pressure is scrutinised by the work crews and they'll respond accordingly. Fine conduct under fire is a stewardship quality and one your work crew will respect and admire.

Inspire Teamwork
Innovation and input comes from everyone, including the most junior personnel contributing to decisions. Therefore, inspiring the team to work together will require a leader guiding his team to find and believe in a cause. If not, the workforce will not buy-in to instructions because there's no reason to. Leaders inspire teamwork with the "end goal" as the incentive, not trinkets and treasures, or punishment and reward.

Working collaboratively leads to increased motivation,

due to the accountability that will emerge from within the group. [60] Pulling together a diverse team of people, in various groups, executing complex tasks in order to achieve strategic goals is no easy feat. Therefore, utilising the team to help shoulder the load, asking for their help, is inspiring on its own. But it also shows that you have mastered delegation. However, to delegate is to entrust a task or responsibility to others and a leader usually thinks "spread the load". Whereas a steward will think "bestow empowerment". Consider the difference.

Believe to Be Believed

Your workforce does not robotically and blindly follow orders like most people think. On the contrary, they are smart, creative and freethinking people like anyone else. For foot-soldiers on the front line to risk life and limb for the mission, they must believe in the cause for which they are fighting. They must believe in the plan they are asked to execute, and most importantly, "they must believe in and trust the leader they are asked to follow". [61] Your work crews are no different.

If we want workers to buy in to our safety programs, they'll need a sense of purpose in what they do. If the leader conveys a cause, work crews will be eager to embrace anything that raises job satisfaction. A leader who articulates the mission, believes in it wholeheartedly, and "leaves no one behind", is displaying the stewardship qualities that creates an inspiring workplace.

Recruit Volunteers

Remember the movie Mission Impossible? It used to be an old black and white TV show. Every episode opened with a tape recording, "Your mission, should you choose to accept it..." The mission was explained and then the tape would self-destruct. Pffssstttt! Those scriptwriters knew more about human nature than just a compelling TV show. It wasn't that the agents always accepted the mission, it was that they had a "choice".

Military operations, secret forces or any elite organisation where team members are required to take on life threatening missions, always ask for volunteers. This is no accident. People are more committed to a path they choose for themselves over one that is assigned to them, due to a very basic principle of psychology. People view their own choices as superior over others and are more committed to choices they make for themselves. Cultivating the 'volunteer' in your workforce relies on their response to your actions, not your instructions. Your actions, not instructions, determine the workforce's willingness to comply and respond to your safety instructions. Asking them for their views will increase responsiveness tenfold.

Summary

I quote military examples because they are the oldest hierarchical leadership structures in the world, only amplified and intensified to the extreme. We can learn a lot from the amplification. Although the military environment seems a far cry from the workplace, they do offer magnification of the problems we see so prevalent in our industry. So that we can examine them closer.

Stewardship is a generative quality and revolves around your legacy. How will your leadership style influence future leaders? What will you leave behind long after you've gone?

This places a lot more emphasis on your conduct because the implications have far more importance than tomorrow's work tasks. Stewards are well aware of the impact their decisions will have years from now... be it positive or negative. It's up to you which one you choose.

  In the next chapter we will discuss what some texts call the maturity curve of a business or company. It's the level of responsibility an entity assumes. Or as some say, the level of response-ability. Suggesting some sort of progression akin to reaching adulthood in company terms. Stewardship can only emerge when a company's leaders are able to respond to situations in an adult-like manner. Let's see if you can identify where your company is at, in this regard. Or more importantly, you might be able to gauge where YOU are at in this regard. That is if you're willing to. Ownership is an adult concept, and necessarily so. If you truly espouse that you want a safe workplace, then learning the fine art of response-ability is the first step to being a safety steward.

"A society grows great when old men plant trees whose shade they know they shall never sit in."
—Greek Proverb

RESPONSE-ABILITY

Theo notices a line has been drawn around the bandages on his left arm. Awkwardly, Surgeons present him with an amputation release form. There are placeholders for four signatures plus Theo's. "No Way!" Theo holds firm, refusing to endorse it. They decide Theo is impaired and approach his family. Despairingly they sign. Theo's is shattered. He feels so "powerless". One Surgeon's signature remains. Before the next operation Theo begs the surgeon, "Please don't take my arm" as he succumbs to the anaesthesia. After the surgery Theo slowly awakens. The surgeon is seated beside him. Theo murmurs groggily, "Did you take my arm?" The surgeon smiles, "No problem Theo, let's shake on it," reaching out his hand.

There's No Common Sense!!?

There's a quirk in our system where we are told in company safety inductions that we shouldn't use our *common sense*. This is worrisome. Not so much whether common sense is a valid function or not, but that we are told not to think for ourselves. That all we need is to follow procedures and everything will work out fine. The implication is people may disown taking personal responsibility for their work tasks. Or resist speaking out about safety, if they are seen to be showing common sense. Sheesh! In these instances' workers feel like they are being treated like children. Of course, if you treat people like children some of those bad habits learned growing up will emerge. Children create strategies to shield themselves from getting hurt. They develop self-protection mechanisms through the cycles of pleasure and pain. These coping strategies served us great when we were young, but as adults they don't work out so well. Especially when we plead our innocence if something goes wrong. Let's take a look at why innocence is disempowering.

The Cost of Innocence

Fred Kofman, founder and president of the Conscious Business Center, defines "Response-ability" as being able to choose your response to any situation, by focusing on aspects of reality you can influence. Instead of feeling victimised by circumstances you cannot. [62] He uses a really great analogy that I think you will identify with. Imagine someone arrives late for work. Of course, we might view this as a defect. Something bad, not desired. What is the normal excuse many people use to shield themselves from blame? Traffic, right? Let's use that one. It works everywhere. Let's assume that traffic was heavy, and if you did not encounter traffic, you would not have been late. Some people might lie, and they would have been late without bad traffic, but let's assume that this time it is true.

What is good about this? There is something comforting in relying on traffic. Why does this come to mind so easily? The answer is, because it's not our "fault", right? It's out of our control. Traffic gives us something to hang our hat on. It means we get to be "innocent". But when we choose a story that makes us innocent, there's a cost. We have to earn that innocence. And the unfortunate cost of innocence is "powerlessness". So let's look at the shortcomings of this strategy.

What makes you late? Think like a computer. If the variable is traffic, then *traffic = late*. What needs to happen for me to correct this defect? Less traffic, right? You can't say *"I should have left early,"* or now you're changing the story. You might have to "own" something (scary!). If you stick with traffic, is it something you can control? No way. It's outside of our sphere of influence. So the price of innocence is being "powerless". It means you have no control. Innocence is what you buy—being powerless is the cost. If you choose innocence, you have to acknowledge that you ARE powerless. Because if you acknowledge power, and you say, *"Well I'm late because my departure time was inadequate",* then that's *powerful.* But then you change everything. You've "owned" it. And with ownership comes responsibility. Let's continue down either of these paths and see where they lead.

The Pain of the defect

With ownership comes its own dilemma because now you're stuck. All of a sudden, it's your fault, your responsibility. It's much nicer to say, "Well, you know, traffic was terrible." But traffic is always terrible. Therefore, any excuse you use that is not plausible, erodes faith in your trustworthiness.

What about this one, "Sorry, I was in a meeting and it ran over." The meeting ran over like there's no choice. *"I didn't choose to stay; I couldn't leave; it was the meeting's fault."* Again, the price of innocence is your powerlessness. It's the perspective of the "victim". The victim perspective says, *"Life just occurs, I'm a spectator, things go on around me and I don't have much control over it. Shit happens."* This is one way we defend ourselves from the "pain of the defect". Instead of having a look at the defect with a spirit of, *"What is going on here, what is my role in all of this?"* We look at the defect in a way that seeks to protect the story we hold about ourselves. Which is, *"I am good; I am right; I didn't do anything wrong; it's somebody else's fault."* Unfortunately, this is a childlike response. Take *slips, trips and falls* for instance. *"It's not my fault, the ground is uneven, cables are in the way, it's rocky."* This is how we hide from responsibility, through the stories of choiceless-ness. Except having no choice also takes away "response-ability", the ability to "respond". 63

Traffic; the meeting ran over; slips, trips and falls. We blame these external experiences as a natural defence mechanism, like children do. Except, when we do that, we've polarised ourselves. Some things we can see, but most things get blindsided through ignorance. As a victim we miss the opportunities for growth and expansion. What immediately surfaces for the victim is, *"It's not my fault"*. The Victim's penchant for avoiding blame is deep within our psyche. It's very difficult to grow out of. Especially when society sucks us in with scapegoating so prevalent in our bureaucracies. Victim and blame is probably leading to more accidents globally than we can imagine.

Choose How to Respond

The alternative on the other hand, is to say, "No, it wasn't traffic that made me late. It was the time of my departure. I didn't give

myself enough time and I didn't call to let you know I'd be late."
What being honest gives you is the power to change things
because it is now back under YOUR control. When you own
things and bring them under your control, you become
accountable for your actions. Signalling some higher authority
is influencing your choices. You stand tall in the face of
circumstance. Response-Able. I invite you to practice this level
of ownership in your own workplace. Although, there's also
another subtle influence at play here. The difference between
acting *responsibly* and being *response-able* in the "face" of
adversity. It is the capacity to choose how to respond to any
event, whether you think is completely out of your control or
not. Let me explain.

For instance, are you responsible for world hunger? Did
it start with you, is it your fault? Of course not. Are you
response-able in the face of world hunger? Can you do
something in the face of it? Yes, you can. In fact, there is no way
that you don't do something. You could ignore it, you could
donate money, or you could devote your entire life to it. But
whatever you do, you cannot avoid responding whatever arises.
So why not own something instead of shrugging your
shoulders. Even acknowledging that you simply understand it
exists is a response. Admitting you have a choice, no matter
what, increases your personal power base. Both consciously
and unconsciously. Even if you don't know it.

In Victor Frankl's book, "Man's Search for Meaning" he
basically says, "I'm in a concentration camp, I've lost
everything, I have absolutely no power. What is my last human
dignity?" His reply is, "Well, I can choose how to respond in the
face of this situation. Nobody can take that away from me. I can

be killed, but I cannot be forced to change my attitude or the way I respond to any circumstances."

If our workplaces were taught this simple principle, that they can choose to respond with "power" or "innocence" to any situation, how might that influence the ownership of our work tasks? When Theo was faced with getting the difficult 12-millimetre nut off, did he choose power or innocence? In the "face" of the situation he had options. A convenient choice (gloves off) or the power not to take things personally (allowing Mr. Fix-it to admit defeat). He could have been response-able. Which was, *"I am faced with a challenge and have the power to choose my response wisely."* Unfortunately, without a 'Why' that encompasses safe work systems, choices fall into the arms of convenience. Convenience and innocence are bedfellows. It's in your power to respond. Which way will you choose?

Response-ability is the source of power and
integrity, the power to influence your situation and
the integrity to do so in alignment with your values.
—Fred Kofman

OAR BED

In the years since the accident Theo has spent many hours considering his actions. For a long time, he blamed himself for the agony he put everyone through. But there's a big difference between owning something and blaming yourself for something. It's the difference between victor and victim. Clearly it wasn't until he decided to pursue his life and stop using blame as an excuse, that the depression and suicidal thoughts resided. Nowadays he clearly owns his mistakes and has the courage to relive his accident over and over again. To save others from having to go through his ordeal. Having experienced both sides of the coin, he will forever choose ownership, over blame.

Choices

We all make mistakes. However, we can choose to maintain our power or give it away afterwards. One way we give it away is to say we had no choice in the mistake. It was something or someone else's fault. As we previously discussed, this is the powerless perspective of the victim. But the fact is, everyone has choice. When we decide to maintain control, by accepting our part in any situation, the perspective of ownership emerges. It is our ability to own any given moment, the capacity to own our role rather than play the victim, that builds trust. It allows us to change things in the direction we want them to go, not fall into a comfort zone without options.

Sorry Doesn't Work

Excuses never work out well. Especially saying sorry. Anything I apologise for, sort of gives me an out-clause of my responsibilities. If I can say sorry whenever I break an agreement, I have no incentive to uphold it. The link in the chain of responsibility is broken. Here's why.

If someone agreed to fill the water tank and they say, "I'm sorry, I had to pick up my kids". Suddenly it's the kids' fault. What they are not owning is the insufficient preparation given that their kids needed picking up. It means they are trying to claim their innocence through something outside of their control, when actually it was only ever in their control from the beginning. In this case the cost of innocence was trustworthiness. Everyone's internal BS meter is on high alert for people who use *sorry* instead of taking ownership. Quite often they'll nod in acceptance of an apology, but secretly harbour mistrust and resentment. No trust, means no sense of teamwork or camaraderie can emerge. A workplace may lose faith in one another, or in the system for that matter.

For a sense of trust to emerge in a workplace, it's fair to assume that people can be counted on to be *real*. They don't make promises they can't keep. They recognise the consequences for the choices they make. They understand there are no out-clauses, no excuses, nothing or no one to blame. If everyone considers the impact of their choices more seriously before they make them, they wouldn't rely on sorry as an excuse. If I am connected to the impacts and the consequences of me not keeping my agreements, I am much more inclined to uphold them. So, in the interests of empowerment, *sorry* is simply not an option.

We should banish *sorry* from the workplace altogether. Some of you won't agree because saying sorry has been ingrained in us from birth. As children we used sorry as an excuse, and the adults took it as an agreement that we'd change. Our parents expected that somehow if we said sorry, we'd never do it again. From where they got this reasoning is a little unclear. Hopeful thinking perhaps. Yet the remnants of these parental expectations still infiltrate all corners of our workplace today.

Leaders expect that if you are sorry you will somehow change what you do or even who you are... but you won't. Consider this: whoever you say sorry to you will do it to them again. And whoever you forgive for saying sorry, they will do it to you again. Because the underlying principle of sorry is the avoidance of ownership, and the avoidance of pain. Saying "I'm sorry it was my fault," is not ownership. It's ownership of guilt. True ownership does not say sorry, it says "I promised to fill the parts bin and I didn't. What I made more convenient was chatting on the phone. What I own about that is that I don't prioritise my commitments and I often let others down." OK, so would someone say it like this? Well, yes. Why not? The point I'm making is, what will you trust more? I'm sorry, or I own it? Remember: no trust means no sense of purpose can emerge.

For some reason, leaders still expect that if someone hasn't operated within the requirements of our lifesaving rules, we should punish them until they are sorry. We threaten them with dismissal and stand them down. If they are on a remote mine site or construction camp, they will be banished to their accommodation room as punishment. Made to sit alone. Until we determine whether they can come back to site, or be sent home. It's true. I've seen it many times. An extremely immature model. Akin to sending our kids to their bedroom. I know one site who make's "offenders" write a letter to the boss as to why they shouldn't be sacked. My fear is one day they'll go to their room and find a suicide letter instead. We should not be ignorant of the effects that deep shaming has on people. Not in today's mental health crisis.

Meanwhile back on site, everyone has an opinion as to why they didn't do this, or how they should have done that. And not one person is prepared to put up their hand and own their part in the overall dilemma, nothing. As far as they are concerned it was all the worker's fault. The leadership style and decisions that created the work environment had absolutely nothing to do with it. *"I will not accept any part of your poor behaviour,"* is the usual stance. Unfortunately, when we take this approach, when we don't consider the ripple effect our leadership has on every aspect of the workplace, we miss out on an enormous opportunity to lead by example. When we can't even own a tiny fragment of responsibility for the whole drama, there is no way safety has any chance of evolving.

Ownership, Accountability, Responsibility

Human beings have an inbuilt instinct to survive. Our Habitual brain is programmed to warn us of any perceived threats or danger. When it senses fear, it releases a chemical cocktail throughout our bodies to make us become alert. It's an awesome example of how we are designed to ensure our physical survival. Unfortunately, it can't tell the difference between a threat to our survival or a threat to our ego or identity. That's why we must take ego out of the equation.

Because it makes us run when we need to stand and fight. We get defensive when we experience a threat to our ego. It's a major reason why workers don't speak out about safety or have a fear of public speaking. It's akin to a threat of survival as far as the Habitual brain is concerned.

When I run the Agreement Process on site, it disarms this fear. It even makes people proud to own their stuff. When I work with crews in any capacity, I always use the OAR BED model. It's a great way of helping people understand their power base through Ownership. I usually print off a diagram and pin it to the wall in training rooms, the workplace and especially meeting rooms. Then it can be easily referred to in any situation. The catchphrase is, 'row the OARs and stay afloat' (above the line) or 'you've made your BED, now lie in it'.

OAR BED

Row the oar and stay afloat

- **O**wnership   *Proactive*
- **A**ccountability
- **R**esponsibity   Above the line

- **B**lame   Below the line
- **E**xcuse
- **D**enial   *Reactive*

You've made your bed now lie in it

Are You Living Above or Below the Line?
Living "above the line" means taking Ownership, being Accountable and personally Responsible. Living "below the Line" means looking elsewhere for Blame, running Excuses and

living in Denial. In the next chapter, we will harness the ownership philosophy further and use OAR BED as the glue which holds our commitments to agreements together. Before we can do that however, an understanding is required of the impact the OAR BED model will have on your workplace.

When I'm working with crews to create their 'Why' I allow them to voice their problems and any disenchantment in the system. I often experience a lot of BED if not flat out anger. It depends on the morale of the crew I'm working with.

If they have low morale it quite often means they have no faith or trust in the company or their leadership. They often have no sense of hope that their situation will improve and no sense of connection to the idea they can change their own destiny. When I experience this it's because workers blame management or external causes for their sense of dissatis-faction. I'm not going to deny that sometimes management or a company is the source of the negative situation. However, the way workers can climb out of the hole they're in, is to take back control of those things they think they have no influence over.

When "Things" Happen

We all know that shit happens. But it is our response to those events that determine whether the outcome will be within our control or not. BED is the convenient choice. It takes much more effort to stay above the line in OAR. But worth it of course. Often, we can't control what happens. But certainly, we can control how we react, we can choose how we respond. By consciously being aware of the source of our judgements, whether they are above or below the line, we choose to stand in our power base. If you compare "below the line thinkers" to crew members who adopt ownership, the latter thrive on being accountable for any mistakes they produce. The way people perceive their situation has a major influence on whether intrinsic motivation will emerge. Until work teams start playing above the line, you are never going to achieve any of your goals voluntarily, let alone create an open and transparent workplace so essential for accident prevention.

The Self-Driven Workforce

Living above the line means having a victor's mindset. If you're below the line, you have a victim's mindset. Living above the line means producing results. Living below the line avoids progress. The Agreement Process that we will discuss in an upcoming chapter, uses OAR BED as an evaluation tool to gauge where a self-driven workforce is along the journey to self-determination and autonomy. This process allows work teams to compare where they want to be (objectives) against daily performance (progress). Operating below the line means blame, excuse and denial will fritter away any opportunities to achieve personal satisfaction. The big question is where do you want your work teams to be operating from, above or below the line? More importantly, where do YOU yourself operate from? Because this will have a big impact on how successful you run the OAR BED model. Don't worry, if you are NOT operating above the line, your crew will be pointing anxiously towards the OAR BED poster to let you know. That's why it works.

*"When things are going bad there's going
to be some good that comes from it."*
—Jocko Willink

SAFETY MISSION

Theo's life operates on another level since the accident. He's more determined, more focused, and has an innate drive to make a difference. He wants to share his message and the things he feels most passionate about with the world. It's a greater cause now that doesn't focus inwardly on himself. Which he did necessarily for so long during his rehabilitation. Having an outwardly concentric view now, allows him to achieve the most change. He doesn't know how all the pieces will come together, but he has faith in the idea that his mission, his life's work and his destiny will take care of that. And what of his game plan? Theo's mantra has become: "Change the world's workplaces by inspiring cultural awareness".

Why Create A 'Why'?

We've said throughout this book that "Safety is NOT your goal, it's a result. The way you think, act and communicate is a much better target. We've insisted that numerical goals are really anticipating results, and not much in the way of motivation. Because they are largely out of our control. But let's take this philosophy to the next level. It would be foolish to abolish metrics altogether. This is NOT what we are saying. Metrics are powerful "gauges" of success. Although quantitative targets won't *predicate* attitudes, they will record how we've been functioning. The key here is measurability, not predictability. The Problem is when we don't achieve numerical targets, they can be quite DE-motivating. Metrics are a Rational brain function ('What). So when can we use metrics to could effect? The answer is when they can be used as a Habitual brain function ('Why') to influence behaviours and routines.

The things we often think matter most—salaries and job titles—actually only account for 15% of our motivation at work. The other 85% is about how we belong and feeling like we make a difference. That we serve a purpose larger than ourselves. Transformation is about helping workers feel connected to "their" own mission or purpose, while discovering the core beliefs of your business. Creating change in workplace culture requires an incentive that makes change desirable. It's a cause or purpose that's more inspiring than simply going to work to earn a living, or producing products and services.

If most workplaces know 'What' they do: make stuff/sell things/help people etc., do they know 'Why' they do it? If some workplaces know 'How' they go about things: marketing/ supply and demand or good old-fashion luck, do they know 'Why' they do it? By 'Why', I don't mean to satisfy shareholder value or to make a profit. That is always a RESULT. By why, I mean what is your work crew's purpose? What is their cause? What is their belief? Why do they even come to work at all? If your answer is to earn a living, or to produce your product or service, you've reverted back to your 'What'. We need to reassign key motivations to the right parts of the brain. Especially if we want to inspire the self-discipline required for voluntary safe work decision making. One way we can do that is by making the workplace enjoyable and inspiring.

Operation Tackle – A Great Workplace 'Why' Model

One of my favourite sports is Australian Rules football (AFL). My favourite game of all time is the 1989 Grand Final between Hawthorn and Geelong. The record books will show that Hawthorn coach Allan Jeans orchestrated one of the most remarkable game plans in history, winning by a slender six-point margin against all odds. A retired policeman, Jeans formulated "Operation Tackle" along the lines of a tactical police mission. It was a stroke of genius. Operation Tackle's game plan was written on the whiteboard in the player's room before the game. The aim was to foil Geelong's formidable offence with a record-breaking forty tackles. Their average number of tackles per game was twenty-five, so setting a task of forty tackles was not going to be easy, but achievable with the right focus and attention.

OPERATION TACKLE [40]

SITUATION:	*Geelong are a very offensive team but vulnerable in defence.*
EXECUTION:	*Apply ferocious, relentless tackling and score from turnovers.*
MISSION:	*To create history by winning back to back flags.*

Now, before confusion sets in, let me explain the number "40" after the title. Because I can already hear you say, "But Ken and Theo, you said never to set numerical targets as your goal." So let's be clear. "Operation Tackle [40]" is not a goal. Nor is it a target or even the objective. It is the name of the "Tactical Operation". The *Situation, Execution* and *Mission* are the real goals. They state the real motivations. Operation Tackle contains the essential S.M.A.R.T processes. **S**pecific (ferocious tackling). **M**easurable (40 tackles). **A**ctionable (scoring from turnovers). **R**ealistic (core skills). **T**imely (final whistle). It's why I love using Operation Tackle to explain succinctly how important it is to distinguish GOALS from your RESULTS, and combines both of them beautifully into an all-encompassing ethos and philosophy. Truthfully, we need to champion both goals and results. But in a way that's inspiring. And balanced.

The forty tackles metric is like setting a value for three accountability processes every pre-shift meeting. Is it doable. Absolutely. If we don't get to do them because of pressing production matters, will it change the world? Of course not. But will including time for three accountability processes a day improve safety. Absolutely! In contrast, LTIFR's create a sense of failure when we don't achieve them. And this is the distinction I really want to get across:

Key Distinction:

> *Motivation vs. De-Motivation.* Who cares if Hawthorn makes forty tackles or twenty? It is a motivational tactic only. Not success or failure oriented. Whereas, who cares if you achieve an LTIFR of 5 or 15? Whoops, different expectations, right? LTIFR's are either success or failure—not motivational.

It's OK to monitor injury frequency rates for comparison purposes. "Results" are how you gauge progress. But if the workplace mission is called "Operation Zero", it creates a conflict when the metric is nothing? Wouldn't you want as many Zero Harms as possible? It should be Zero Harm 100%, right? What's confusing is when a workplace creates a "0" LTIFR target. Zero is unrealistic. I've never seen it achieved in forty years. Even setting a low LTIFR target doesn't make sense, and is hardly inspiring. As in reality, most LTIFR's are in double figures. In contrast, could forty tackles be achieved with intensity and focus? You bet. It's within our control. It's not uncommon for a team to lay one hundred tackles today. So was it inspiring and motivational back then? The players thought so. And that's the point. Tackles weren't the average game plan in '89, kicking Goals were (how befitting). Forty tackles reflected the attitude required, not the ability. Taking a metric that is inspiring and doable is the opposite of measuring one's success by it. No one would be disappointed if they didn't reach 40 tackles. And they may still have won the game.

If you want less injuries, would you encourage more targets that created safe work practices? Why would you use an LITFR as the objective? Why not use: "Operation Buy-In [100]" (100% support)". "Operation Unity [4]" (4 shifts working as one). Setting unrealistic expectations doesn't achieve anything. Using a metric in your Headline knowing that it's inspiring and doable, is fine. Setting an LTIFR as your Mission is not. It's about what you can control, not what you can't. **Enough said!**

Numbers Game

The original concept of voluntary operational discipline was developed by the United States Nuclear Navy. So, what of our workplaces then? Will they ever have the same motivational incentive as the Nuclear Navy? Probably not. So we can't follow that model, right? Or can we? Some might say high risk workplaces should naturally create this military level style of motivation. Well, they do. I know a crack team of rope access maintenance technicians who love scaling almost any impossible structure. You'd think they were military the way they conducted their activities. They check all their equipment as if they were going into battle. PPE, check! Shackles, check... On the other hand, the underground miners at the same operation were un-inspired and had miserably low morale. How can that be? Two departments, same company, opposite attitudes. Which department do you think had pride in their work and a sense of accomplishment in their tasks? Which department used the threat of dismissal or other types of punishment to instil discipline? Using deterrents as motivation is not sustainable. Pride is. The rope technicians were driven by pride. They prided themselves on their communication and teamwork. Consequently, the supervisor walked the talk and empowered the crew. The crew made their own decisions about how they were going to set up the job. The supervisor trusted them implicitly and supported them. The levels of congruence throughout all lines of their operation was tangible. Their motivation was called "Do it right the 1st time".

This apparently struck a chord. 'Do it right' was the vision ('Why') and '1st time' was the action ('How'). These are Feeling/Habitual brain functions with a metric thrown in as motivation (1st). No results to be found, just inspiration. Just the number of rappels completed without a hitch (1st time). Or maybe the number of projects completed on budget and schedule, so they could TRACK performance. The "correct" use of numerical results. "Do it Right the 1st Time" determined what they said; how they said it; their use of time; planning; the mission and purpose. These are goals that improved their actions and behaviours. They are the only valid goals, because they are the only ones that control their activities. They might have used "Operation Verify 100" meaning they checked their rope access equipment for 100% quality and condition. The slightest fray in a rope and it was replaced immediately. But they didn't need to, because "Do it right the 1st time" uncannily had all the motivation they needed. Remember, metrics are worthwhile only when you use them to "motivate actions and behaviours". Otherwise, numerical values should remain where they belong... used to record your progress as results, not used as goals. results

Setting a target of forty tackles was definitely not out of Hawthorn's control. In the week leading up to that *last game in September,* Jeans had Channel 7 make a highlights reel of the best tackles Hawthorn made during that year. Against the musical backdrop of "Eye of the Tiger" and the "Rocky" movie theme song. Jeans played the video before and after every training session at full blast. And especially before they ran out onto the MCG Grand Final day. They focused on tackling all week. Training the mechanics of a good tackle, how to approach one, when to lay one. Hawthorn became obsessed with tackling.

Imagine if your workplace were obsessed too. What if you had a tactical objective called "Operation Autonomy [100]". Which gave workers 100% control over their workplace for 100 days. They were given the resources to improve any concern or troublesome process that restricted their performance. They were totally responsible for budget, quality and safety. Leaders would act like coaches and provide support. Major expenditure needed to go through the usual channels. But if it could be shown to increase value for the company and the workforce, as good return on investment, they would go through the necessary capital expenditure processes as normal.

At the end of 100 days, each team gave a presentation to management and the board, showcasing their initiatives. These types of concerted efforts provide enormous value, emotionally and financially. They're actually easier for leaders to manage.

Create Your Why with IOS in Mind

Before I explain how Jeans created Operation Tackle in the next chapter, let me show you how it aligns perfectly with the three elements of the IOS Brain. The Mission is the 'Why', the Execution is the 'How' and the Situation is the 'What'. It's another remarkable coincidence, or is it? The *Mission* inspires the *Execution* plan. Which in turn creates a great *Situation* for the team, and you win the game. Creating desire to pursue goals and objectives require a team effort from all parts of the IOS Brain. That's why Operation Tackle integrates so well with IOS. Operation Tackle styled game plans, superimposed on the IOS model inspires team effort because it harnesses everyone's individual 'Whys' in the process. The breakthrough is that before you create your *Mission,* you have to thoroughly understand your *Situation.* You discover what the "real" problem is that's hampering your progress.

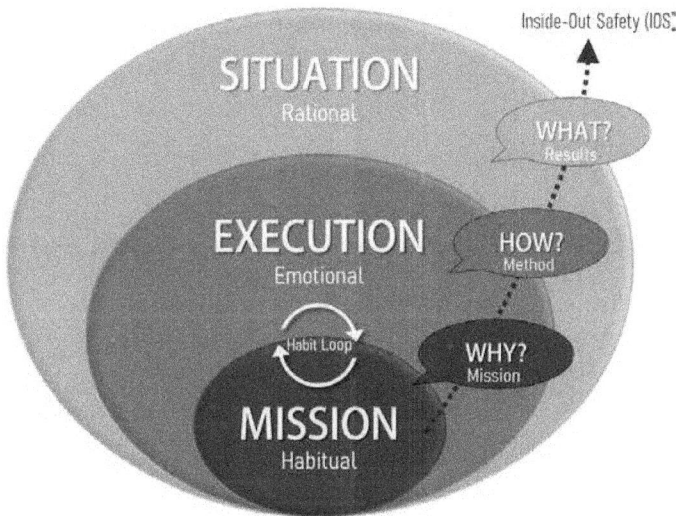

Diagram 3—Game Plan Process in Terms of IOS

In the next chapter we will go through each phase of the Game Plan process as if you were conducting it with a work crew.

"Because we focused on the snake, we missed the scorpion."
—*Egyptian Proverb*

OPERATION TACKLE

OPERATION TACKLE [40]

SITUATION: Geelong are a very offensive
team but vulnerable in defence

EXECUTION: Apply ferocious, relentless
tackling and score from turnovers

MISSION: To create history by winning
back to back flags

*Download a comprehensive guide to the Game Plan Process here:
www.getreal.net.au/operation_tackle.pdf

How to Create Your Game Plan?

Your overall task with this process is to guide the crew to discover intrinsic motivation from within their own resources. To capture their values in such a way that it injects meaning and purpose into their work tasks. The Operation Tackle game plan technique, is one method. There are probably countless.

But it's one that works well for me and Theo. The idea is that you have a blueprint you can refer back to when you create a mission for your workplace. You can compare your own *Situation* with Hawthorn's for succinctness. You can check that your *Execution* is the appropriate remedy and solution like theirs. And that your *Mission* has a *vision* and an *action*. That's how Theo and I do it. Below are the exact steps I employ when doing this process. The *Situation* is your starting point because it's the crew's immediate reactions and responses to their current environmental conditions. It's about identifying the collective disenchantment in your workplace or that that one big issue. Trust me, your crew have one. Hawthorn identified Geelong's devastating goal scoring power. Let's discover yours.

Step 1 – Define the Existing Situation

To know what you want, you must be aware of what challenges you face to get it. Hawthorn would not have beaten Geelong in '89, if they didn't identify their greatest threat. There were many. But identifying one key issue will in all likelihood address the others. Hawthorn could have got caught up in their own celebrity. They were a powerful offensive team too. Jason Dunstall (Full-forward) was a three-time Coleman Medallist (League's leading goal kicker). Instead, their *Situation* identified that they should change direction. And focus on defence instead. It was a good call in the end. I believe they would have lost otherwise.

The aim is to arrive at some bedrock of truth during this first step. To reveal the honest perceptions the crew have of their workplace. Your success will reflect how well you can facilitate the crew to discover for themselves a core issue. Careful though, it *ain't pretty*. Facilitated well, it can get quite heated. But you must gauge any disenchantment the crew harbour. Are they perceiving double standards or policies that are in conflict with company stated values? During this process people will often centre on a perceived lack of communication with management, or the desire to improve conditions, or training or equipment. Great, it's all good. Ask them to translate their feelings into words. Words that describe their current situation. The idea is to write these up on a whiteboard or flipchart, it doesn't have to be neat, just authentic.

I call this getting your 'Ya-yas' out, after a Rolling Stones music record. I call it *blowing off steam*. Encouraging open honest judgements. Is it 'Poor' communication, 'lack' of equipment, 'bad' supervision'? I can't stress how important this step is. These are judgement words. We have to get them out so people can see where they are living on the OAR BED model. Above or below the line? Words such as "poor", "lack" or "bad" infers there's a solution required. Great, that's what defining the *Situation* is about. But that's all. No solutions yet. Just problems, challenges and judgements. Solutions will come.

I've tried to create a game plan before, without everybody getting the 'stuff' off their chest. And the end result was a disaster. It wasn't real. So it didn't get to the foundational issues. Everything is hinged on how well you capture everybody's honesty. Don't stop until the group is exhausted. You want a wall/whiteboard/flipchart full of nasty adjectives scrawled all across it. The dirtier the better.

Now we put those words into a phrase. We are not trying to solve anything yet. But we do need to be more specific. For example, 'Work teams and leadership aren't communicating clearly', 'Our equipment is in poor condition'. These are great

Situation sentences. Out of the many offerings scribed up on the wall there will emerge a single clear message. Don't have any preconceptions about what you think the message is or it will taint the next *Execution* process. You may be surprised what emerges. There may be many, but we'll only need one.

The key here is that it is a combination of everyone's input. It is not management telling the work crew what the situation is, but vice versa. This is important because it's key to creating buy-in. Remember, this step is more about creating openness and honesty than it is about capturing the message. The *Situation's* significance and meaning will take care of itself. When I facilitate this step there is never any lack of perceived shortfalls in the workplace. I've never met a work group who say, "All good, nothing to bitch about here". Quite the opposite. Therefore, you should now have a concise description of the biggest problem that's behind all the other smaller problems in your workplace. Don't worry about the smaller issues, they'll be taken care of once a keystone habit is established. Write the problem in a concise sentence:

"Our Situation is..."

How does your sentence shape up against Operation Tackle? Check that it's captured in the same succinct way.

Step 2 – Define the Execution

The *Execution* process is a tactic to counter the *Situation*. Creating it takes a bit of skill. Hawthorn's *Execution* was two-pronged: 'Apply ferocious, relentless tackling' and 'score heavily from turnovers'. The most important thing to remember is to create a target that is laser focused. "Ferocious" and "Relentless" are hypnotic words. Use similar adjectives and spice up the *Execution* with some feeling. Ask the group to come up with grand ideas. If they had a magic wand, what would they like to see happen in their workplace, that is the exact opposite of the *Situation*? What will it take to achieve it? Ask for everyone's suggestions and workshop everyone's ideas until it feels good.

Write key phrases and words on another whiteboard or flipchart. If the crew mentioned "Supervision" in the *Situation*, what is it about the supervision that they mean? What is it about "bad communication", "better equipment", "management's lack of involvement"? What do the crew really mean? Keep asking, keep writing. How will you approach the *Situation* to resolve it? It's ALWAYS the exact opposite.

Watch for reactions when you read the first *Execution* drafts out loud. Look for cues that there's some passion flowing. The *Execution* is the benchmark to which you will set the accountability standards later in the pre-shift briefings. When someone is doing an accountability piece, they are measuring their performance against a commitment to the *Execution*. This is the whole premise of your game plan. Something to be accountable to. I imagine Allan Jeans yelling at a player during the quarter time breaks, "Are you applying ferocious and relentless tackling laddie?" It is about setting a benchmark you can keep referring to that sets the momentum for change.

NOTE: Avoid a benchmark set on production targets or zero statistic targets. And definitely don't include a safety goal, unless your activities are specifically safety related and that is your objective. Why? Because safety will take care of itself during the daily agreement/accountability processes, I promise. The *Execution* is a strategy for things you have direct control over, and it must always be something that is within your sphere of capability and influence. New and expensive equipment or building an extension to the mobile workshop is too vague. That's like Zero Harm. You can achieve them by focusing on the actions your team can conduct daily, where equipment and extensions are the 'indirect' result. Funding decisions are outside your control, unless your game plan is to create the funds for your goal. You should now have a concise description of your *Execution* plan, written in a sentence:

"Our Execution strategy is..."

How does your sentence shape up against Operation Tackle? Check that it's captured in the same succinct way.

Step 3 – Create the Mission

This is the meat and potatoes. The *Mission* process has a very specific structure. A combination of Vision (values) + Actions (behaviour) and is overarching. Vision is how we see the future ('Why') and Action is what we do to get there ('How').

Wikipedia states that finding "meaning" in any activity can be defined as a connection linking two presumably independent entities together. [64] The biological reality of life (action), to a symbolic interpretation or meaning (vision). The *Mission* process is a fairly serious game and must be facilitated with proficiency. The first part of the entire process is the work crew getting their ya-yas out (Situation), then defining what can be done about it (Execution). Once they have flipped the negative energy into a sense of hope, inspiration will emerge. The *Mission* will take the *Execution* and create a sense of triumph and victory from it. To the victor go the spoils. It's a long-term vision the team can define themselves by.

The *Mission* is not only the doing, it's also the receiving. However, it must contain "two" very important elements: A **Vision** phrase, followed with a *"by/through"*, then an **Action** phrase. Here are some real-life examples:

• *"Our crew creates harmony and satisfaction <u>through</u> positive communication and engagement."*

• *"Our destiny as industry leaders relies on teamwork <u>through</u> camaraderie and setting an example for each other."*

Warning: This is a tricky manoeuvre when there are both management and workers creating the game plan together, and Managers want to create a benchmark set on production or zero incident targets. They might lean towards wanting a "safety first" or "zero" statement. You know I recommend against it. Refer to my summary at the end of this chapter on page 225: *"Important Notes on the Game Plan Process"* for further clarity. You should have a concise description of your Mission now, written in a sentence:

"Our Mission is ...*(vision)*... by/through ...*(action)*..."

How does your sentence shape up against Operation Tackle? Check that it's captured in the same succinct way.

Step 4 – Create a Headline (Operation....?)

The headline of your game plan is a catchphrase that work teams throw around for good measure, because it's catchy and sounds fun. 'Operation Tackle' is reminiscent of a military operation—it has a ring of certainty about it. It sounds important enough that it requires your attention. What sounds more inspiring: *Operation Tackle* or the *Tackle Plan*? Get my drift here? The game plan's title connects the workforce's imagination to what's possible. Here's a title from an underground drill maintenance work crew: *'Operation Handled'*. This crew needed to focus on the things they 'did' have control over. 'It's Handled' became the catchcry at pre-shift briefings when the supervisor distributed daily tasks. "Are the bins emptied?" "Handled". "Parts shelf filled?" "Handled." It became fun to have safety *handled* too. "PPE?" "Handled." "Risk Assessment?" "Handled."

Use your imagination and find an alternative to the word Operation if you want. Consider these other examples such as 'Target Purity', 'Destination Africa', 'Medical Discovery' or 'Do It Right the 1st Time'. It's about connecting 'meaning' to the game plan through the Title. Though I recommend for the first one you use the word "Operation" until creating and achieving game plans becomes second nature.

Step 5 – Define The Metric

Now, the most controversial step. But not really. The metric of 40 tackles next to Hawthorn's headline was a stroke of genius, and an important aspect of the overall game plan. '89 was probably the ageing Allan Jeans' last chance at another premiership. He had to find a meaningful way to win just one more time. Even though Hawthorn were already the reigning premiers. So it would mean winning back-to-back grand finals for the first time in the club's history. Hawthorn were already the most successful team of the 80's. It's not as if they were desperate for another premiership. But it's one tag that alluded them, "Back-to-back Premiers". By adding '40' to the title of Operation Tackle, Jeans invented something quite remarkable, and a promising discovery for those of us who want to understand the secrets of motivation. Or how to imbue a work crew with a metric that is a target or goal, not a "result". There's a difference. If you understand this, you will understand motivation. And how a metric can be inspiring, not de-motivational. Seeing the number '40' as inspiration, sparks the synaptic impulses in the Rational brain with an imaginative intensity for the symbolic meaning of the number 40. It equates ferocity, hard work and effort with the Emotional brain's passion. Although forty tackles were rare in a game, it was well within the realms of possibility. Here we have a symbol, that combines with a goal, which incorporates both hemispheres of the cerebral cortices of the brain. The left hemisphere functions like a serial processor (systems, logic), the right hemisphere functions like a parallel processor (creativity, symbolism). Anytime we charge both sides of the brain with a task, and it is achievable, we are creating a very powerful unconscious cerebral partnership... that works! Just to reiterate. If your confused by the distinction between a goal and a result in terms of motivation, go back to the highlighted text on page 210.

A Game Plan Example

On the following page is an example of "Operation Handled", a game plan derived from a workshop I conducted for a drill maintenance crew. We created it in a meeting room undergr-ound. The (100) means 100% accountability. It is a great example because it had an immediate impact on morale and overall job satisfaction. The most important thing about a game plan, using Operation Handled 100 as an example, is the work crew didn't have to focus on the specifics of the *Mission*. They just had to ensure their agreements were 100% handled.

Job satisfaction, quality, work ethic and positive communication were all maintained by focusing on 100% accountability. Everything else basically took care of itself after that. The
idea in any workplace environment is that, if you achieve your
Execution, the rest will follow. Safety is a natural winner. This
is important, and why production targets are counterproductive. Sometimes having the opposite effect when they aren't
achieved. 95% accountability can be corrected, improved and
then on you go. Once a production target has failed, it's
impossible to fix. You have to start all over again. No correction.

OPERATION HANDLED (100)

SITUATION: We function well as a team but are
influenced by things outside our control.

EXECUTION: To be efficient and effective with
a positive attitude and being accountable for
what we have control over (not fret over what we
don't).

MISSION: Job satisfaction through demonstrating a quality work ethic and continuing positive
communication.

Hawthorn's focus on '40' tackles did not preclude them
from scoring goals. In the end both teams kicked twenty-one
goals apiece. So imagine the discipline to average ten tackles
per quarter as well. Forty tackles would break the league record.
In the end the final tackle count was... wait for it... "47". The
players and coaching staff were amazed. Not only did they meet

their target—they crushed it. Imagine if a work crew were 100% accountable. Not 100% perfect, but doing their best *warts and all.* Owning mistakes 100%. They'd crush it too.

When I worked in Laos, I had the honour of inspecting a coveted CAT 5—Star workshop. The highest distinction a workshop can achieve anywhere in the world, as offered by the Caterpillar equipment company. And this was in a developing nation mind you. It would be the jewel in the crown of any western society's mobile equipment workshop. Let alone in a developing country. So how did they do it? They had the 'Why'. "Operation CAT 5—Star". It took the Laotian's two and a half years to achieve, with none of the resources like we have in the west. What they couldn't order they made, all from scrap metal. They had the best safety record, the highest morale and longest retention rates of any department in the company. This mobile workshop was the flagship of the business and had the best operational discipline by far. It was "Why-Power" in action.

Important Notes on the Game Plan Process

One of the challenges I receive from managers is that the game plan doesn't include business or safety objectives. Yet clearly, the whole process is about creating an attitude where safety goals and production targets are the easy winners. A 'Why' is the means of creating the spirit which allows a work crew's values to align with any goal and be proud to achieve them. I specifically do not include production or zero safety targets.

Here's why:

1. What if the company goal was to be the #1 copper business in the world? The Mission would be: *Supply low cost, consistent high-quality copper (vision) through a motivated and eng-aged workforce (action).* So the question is how will you engage them? Would the following, really motivate anyone?

Engagement through surveys and gauging absenteeism, safety performance and adherence to the training schedule. Focus on customer requirements, supplier performance, produc-tion recovery rates, tonnes mined, kg's shipped, liqueur concent-ration, reserve definitions, development strategies, budget varia-nce, revenue generation, share-holder contribution and etc. etc.

Absolutely necessary yes. But hardly inspiring as motivation. Do you get what I'm trying to say here? These are all 'What's', there's no 'Why' amongst them.

Company 'results' used as goals are largely lost on work crews as far as intrinsic motivation goes. These important functions are for the leadership team to implement as needed. In that context I fully agree with managers. Put these into the business plan for sure, but the work crew game plan is reserved for creating attitude and engagement in the hearts of the workforce. It's a KPA (Key Performance "Attitude") not a KPI. Business process metrics will only work in a game plan if it can be translated into meaningful inspiring *human* metrics.

2. Don't confuse 'business plan' metrics for the game plan target. Standing on the steps of the Lincoln Memorial, Dr Martin Luther King spoke to an audience of a quarter million people and said, "I have a dream!" He left the planning for his team to organise. He could only effect buy-in and lasting change through 'Why' inspiration. "I have a dream" overrides "I have a plan" hands down. Business plans are a 'What' tool and used exclusively for those purposes, and necessarily so. Whereas, a game plan is used as a "value alignment tool". It's not really a plan per se. It's a mindset.

3. Ensure the metric in the game plan title is not production oriented. For Hawthorn, although (40) tackles is technically a production target, it stood more for the grit and tenacity it would take to win the game. It would create history for the

Hawthorn faithful. It had nothing to do with shareholder's value. Targets where work crews bust their gut for a tonnage record does not feel like a triumphant victory for them. For most workers, record production targets mean long hours and backbreaking work, for little personal value. They might even perceive production targets as lining the pockets of shareholders—and it will backfire.

Breaking records month in/month out is unsustainable. Whereas maintaining 93% of target variance creates equilibrium and resilience. Perhaps annual records would fall anyway. Besides, "Operation Equilibrium 93%" is far more inspiring and conceivable than "Operation Ore Production 20KT".

4. Avoid using safety objectives that influence the metric. Operation Zero Incidents (0) is not a realistic game plan title. Besides, if there was an accident, the game plan is shot to pieces. It's too finite and constrictive, whereas 'sky's the limit' if you are inspired by the title. Aiming for a LTIFR of 2.5 is not going to inspire maintenance output targets for a workshop. Whereas "Operation Quality (90)", targeting 90% of equipment availability and quality of work, would have a much better chance.

We are trying to meet a higher standard, be grander, excel, expand, grow, evolve. Zero or 2.5 is small, narrow, diminishing and creates downward pressure. It will affect a worker's interest and buy-in negatively.

5. Leave safety targets and objectives for the right forum, for instance during safety committee meetings and statistical briefings. 'Relentless and ferocious tackling' is an attitude and practiced skill. "Zero Harm" is clichéd and uninspiring. It's like 'Do it safely'. Akin to the 'What' brain trying to inspire us—when that's the 'Why's' responsibility. If the objective is related to an operating standard, and workers hold themselves accountable daily, and carry out open dialogue and

maintain each other's care and wellbeing, safety will take care of itself, and be the big winner. I promise.

6. I firmly agree with management that "what gets measured gets done". But these are the results, not the goal. The game plan metric is not that kind of metric. If Allan Jeans had said, 'Tackle hard guys", and focused mainly on scoring goals, Geelong might have kicked more because of their highly offensive game. As it was, they both kicked the same amount of goals (21). But hawthorn won by a slender six points. It wasn't record 'tonnes of ore' (goals) that won them the game, it was the spirit with which they went about their business (40 relentless tackles). It wasn't the goals that won them the game, it was the points scored from the goals they missed! It was those one-percenters that came from deep within.

   No one really understands what "Be safe" feels like. But "Be free and easy" speaks to the 'Why'. The metric must define the target number in terms of personal goals, not tonnes or sales numbers or meters and tonnes. These are seen to be boosting shareholder profits. The metric and the *Execution* is about defining what the end state looks like as a "feeling". A great example is where Operation Summit 5, 000 is not about how high the summit is in metres, but the euphoria you feel after trekking and reaching the peak of a 5,000m climb. If you were looking for fish-bait and one shop said, "Prawns for sale", but another said "The Fish Are Biting on Fresh Squid today", which bait will you buy?

   The metric, as far as the game plan is concerned, must be 'Why' are we going there, not 'When' will we know we are there? This is imperative. It wasn't important if Hawthorn won the game, as much as it was if they lost because they didn't follow the game plan. Team character is forged in the journey. If the game plan was the wrong tactic, they live to play another day. Heads held high. Geelong strayed from their game plan and it haunts them to this day.

7. Sales and performance goals in numerical terms are the 'What'. The reason why you want 93% schedule variance is because it provides sustainability and balance, a 'Why'. It's about the journey. The reason 'Why' you want things 100% handled is because of the teamwork it inspires. Why would you climb a 5,000 metre summit? It's not to reach the peak, it's the sense of what you overcame to get there?

8. The last but most important advice is this: make sure the game plan doesn't set the team up for failure. If Hawthorn tried to make 80 tackles, they would not have won the game. No belief in the mission. Unfortunately, using a tonnage or metres target "IS" the game. If you don't make it, you lose. If you don't meet 93% variance of schedule on the other hand, or less than 100% of jobs 'handled', the game's not over yet. There's room for tweaking. Tonnage/metres/sales are finite and require a complete reset. Too deflating and uninspiring.

Summary

Why I say concentrate on what the workers want and capture their values, more than creating a "safety" goal, is because the safety climate is developed in the agreements we make in the pre-shift briefings and other meetings. Once the standards are moulded into the *Execution*, and the metric symbolises the level of motivation required, feedback from the work crews during the Agreements Process sessions will calibrate where safety is at. Most people can't define what *safety* is, only what it isn't. For leaders during the pre-shift briefings, they must discuss where the crew *IS* in terms of achieving the *Mission*. Basically, are they meeting their agreements? It's accountability. Either they achieve their goals, or it isn't safe. They aren't waiting for a result or an incident to say so. The bar just went up ten notches.

The game plan is the wrong instrument for making

business targets. Business plans and targets are the 'What'. Of course, they are imperative, but not in this environment. To 'create history' (the vision) and 'back to back flags' (the action), the 'Why' and 'How' comprehend and champion them emotionally. The vision is creating a feeling and inspiration and the action is creating safe actions steps, and habits to get there. The *Mission* is 'Why' you do it (sense of purpose). The *Execution* is 'How' you do it (operating boundaries and standards) and the *Situation* is 'What' needs to be overcome to get there (the status quo). How do you "cut" through the myriad of daily communications and instructions with one single inspiring message? A Game Plan of course. So that activities include a concrete commitment to safe work agreements. With so many conflicting messages with varying degrees of importance in the workplace, or even a general awareness that they exist, a 'Why' cuts through. Without one, Mr. 'What' leading Mr. 'How' astray, will have a field day. Does this sound familiar?

One word of caution. If you don't feel that you have the facilitation skills to run this process it may pay to have it facilitated by someone who can. The reason I say this is because of two things: If you can't hold the space during the *Situation* process it could get away on you. Secondly, if you create a game plan and by mistake it turned out to be another 'What'—based goal, you may in fact perpetuate your problems.

"A young boy went into a shoe store to buy a pair of shoes. He had a choice between buying a cheap pair or an expensive pair. He settled on the cheap pair and made his purchase. Within hours, he regretted his decision, wishing that he had paid the price for a better pair of shoes. Are you willing to pay the price lads? Right now... today?"
—Allan Jeans half-time speech, '89 Grand Final

HOW TO MAKE AGREEMENTS

Theo rubs shoulders with some of the most progressive companies in the world. They are usually No.1 when it comes to their product or service, or they are changing the face of industry. Other companies carry out their activities without much fanfare at all. But they all hire Theo for the same thing. Incident and accident issues. Theo prepares his clients by asking them what is the one thing they want to change above all else? The response is always the same: "We just want our people to stop and think about what they are doing before they put themselves at risk." Theo wonders if these companies are prepared for the level of integrity it requires throughout all levels of their organisation to achieve this. When it appears one main ingredient is missing... Accountability.

Agreements Will Transform Your Workplace

The power behind agreements is that you want to cultivate intrinsic motivation. The idea is to implement a model of accountability that augments existing meetings, pre-shift briefings or any team gatherings. To increase belief, trust and buy in of your safety. It is common for workplaces to kick off meetings with a "safety share". This is usually some observation of a hazard or a safely executed work task people have conducted or witnessed. But honestly, it patronises workers and comes off as condescending. I might as well just say it.

However, an Agreement Process is a much different approach. It creates better participation and involvement. It's structured so that judgements or opinions aren't required. Only frankness and commitment. There's no punishment, no praise. No *carrot and stick* mentality. No prizes for being compliant. Leave your ego at the door. It's time to get down to the serious business of personal responsibility and integrity. The Agreements process itself is the prize. The art of making and keeping agreements is more powerful than the results it aims to provide. It's the "How" in full flight. It's a continuously improving safety culture with trusting leader/worker relationships. How might that be a workplace worth experiencing?

For it to work though, a work crew must already have clear objectives and a mission or game plan (a 'Why') in place, before the agreement process makes sense. Refer to the previous chapter 'Operation Tackle' and follow the game plan process for best results. Whichever way you arrive at your mission is fine. As long as it was facilitated to encompass a combination of everyone's values. And as long as everyone has thoroughly bought into it. Existing company missions or kist of company values won't necessarily work unless the workforce genuinely buy-in to them. In my experience this is rare. It's your call, but just know that not having a common goal will mean there's no 'Why', and undermines the whole purpose of this next process. You telling your work crew, "This is our mission," is not the same as them defining the mission around their own sense of values.

The following steps will guide you through running the

Agreements Process. I usually pin these steps on pre-shift meeting notice boards, board rooms or wherever meetings are held. The Agreements Process is meant to augment your existing meetings except it will transform the safety share into something much more invigorating and worthwhile. By implementing this process whenever there is a pre-shift meeting, safety meeting, production meeting or any meeting at all, you'll discover a method where everyone is supported and reminded of their agreements to keep them on track with their mission (game plan), their 'Why'. The meeting kicks off with a mission-tracking check-in. "How are we all doing, is everyone on track with the mission?" This one sentence is about to transform your whole workplace, if not your entire life!

Follow the Bouncing Ball

Whenever someone volunteers that there's a hitch or challenging situation, it's an opportunity for the work crew to find a solution. If someone advises that they've committed to something they can't complete, or they've failed to meet an agreement or obligation, a facilitator walks them through a process with the whole crew's support. Remembering that any commitments people make are for the mission's success. Not because anyone was "told" to do something. This is the birth of voluntary operational discipline. It not only straightens out responsibilities, but it builds camaraderie as well. Huge trust emerges when people proudly OWN their "stuff".

The process is a set piece written down on a form. It works so well that nobody has to stray from the format or offer their opinions or judgements. Especially about someone's character or conduct. What better way to build trust and confidence in the idea that people can speak up when something is "wrong"? It gives a new meaning to the word wrong. It makes wrong RIGHT, and encourages speaking up.

During the Agreements Process an individual simply follows the steps they've learned (off-by-heart) or it can be facilitated. When it's new, I help crew members by modelling it. Very quickly they pick it up themselves and self-process. The key is:

Accountability means keeping your agreements. Or if you can't, then re-negotiate a new one before it's due.

That's it. It's not complicated. The agreement can be anything the work crew or leader needs to create more clarity around. It could be to agree that everyone will adhere to the PPE standards. Either 100% today or every day. This is usually assumed, right? But PPE is flouted every day without continual reinforcement or agreement. Maybe choose something around the activities that keep work areas tidy. It might be compliance, procedural, governance or whatever. The idea is that commitment to the mission means keeping our agreements, or the mission derails. Imagine if a navy seal team were preparing a mission and an operative in charge of the ammunition didn't keep their agreement. It's life or death, right? Ask Theo if keeping a PPE agreement is life or death! If there was an agreement in place that no one removes any part of their PPE today, and there was 100% commitment from the crew with clear consequences established up front, would Theo have removed his insulated gloves? I agree in hindsight it's easy to say this now. But if every instruction given in the pre-shift meeting was reinforced with a clear verbal agreement and an awareness of the consequences should they break that agreement, how might that clean up workplace integrity over the long term? Once accountability becomes a habit, and I asked you that question, you will know what I mean.

    During the pre-shift meeting, to kick things off, there are

two rounds to the process. The first round asks if anyone needs support with their accountabilities and allows ownership to emerge. The second round is to support those who are either not aware they have let an agreement slip, or they don't think that they have. You only run the Agreement Process if a commitment to an agreement is in question. If everyone is on track with the integrity of their agreements, you simply move on with your pre-shift meeting.

But what if there was an incident yesterday? What if a work crew agreed with their supervisor that they would adhere to the Working at Heights Procedure 100%? Except a crew member stepped onto a handrail in contravention of the procedure's guidelines. The consequence was the whole crew was stood down pending an investigation. The next pre-shift meeting is usually akin to walking into a morgue. Because everyone is expecting some sort of discipline. The problem is, the real root cause of the problem will never be revealed in this scenario. Because no one wants to open up for fear of being punished.

However, using an Agreements model will have a different response. Instead of blame and shame (below the line) we encourage ownership (above the line). Allowing people to be mature and work through their issue in the spirit of continuous improvement. In this instance, the crew member is encouraged to see how the prize, the "mission", is ultimately the goal. We take personalities out of it. Shaming someone has never created lasting change. It never worked on you as a child and it doesn't work on you as an adult. Voluntary Operational Discipline is borne out of mature self-accountability and ownership. So this is what we aim to establish here. We simply ask the crew member if they still believe in the mission or what support they need to get back on track. The idea is that before the task was issued, there was already a clearly pre-determined consequence in place if the agreement lapsed. Was it to stand down for a day, to be re-trained? Was it to transition to another part of the team until a firm commitment to the procedures can be maintained? Any expectations must be pre-determined at the time of the agreement, not after an incident. This is imperative.

The Agreement Process Goes Like This...

The outcome of any Agreement Process is not to shame or question a person's behaviour, it's to discover how they can be relied upon to meet any new agreements in the future. If you shame people, they will never buy in to your overtures for workplace accountability. They will withdraw instead and not believe in the mission.

Accountability really means keeping agreements that reinforce belief in the mission's success. It doesn't need to be personal, just methodical. Worse, it could lead to an accident if egos are crushed. Agreements are your equivalent of wanting to achieve *40 tackles*. If everyone's values have been infused into the mission, they will have bought in to its accomplishment.

Thus, safety becomes the by-product. So instead of blaming, we offer support in name of the mission. It's a completely different paradigm than what we are used to in our workplaces today. We wrongly think that punishment is the answer. But it never is. Therefore, the Agreement Process might go like this:

Q: *What was the agreement?* A: *"To follow the Working at Heights Procedure 100%."*

Q: *Were you able to keep the agreement* (*Use OAR BED, no excuses, no story. Just yes or no.*) A: *"No, I didn't."*

Q. *So what did you do that was more Convenient?*
A. *"I stepped onto a handrail without fall arrest equipment."*

Q. *What's the impact of not keeping your agreement?*
A: *"I could have fallen. There's now an investigation."*

Q. **What was the pre-determined consequence?**
A. *"I was to get re-trained if I broke the agreement."*

Q. *"Do you still believe in the mission?* (*Does it need tweaking?*) *Answer?*

Q. *What's the new agreement? What will be the consequences for not meeting it this time?* *Answer?*

Choosing a convenient option means the crew member may not have bought into the mission or they were distracted. Obviously, this needs to be resolved. Because it has become a serious safety issue. Quite often people are so focused on getting the job done they'll take short-cuts without thinking. Now we are discovering a deeper root cause. Underneath a person's behaviour is quite often production targets, schedule overruns, management pressure, or a self-identity complex. *Ah la* Mr. fix-it. If we discover that the mission is not so desirable, we must tweak it as a team until we are back on track and it is high on our values. Then the crew member can get back into integrity with themselves. For ultimately, we can only ever truly be with integrity to ourselves. We can only ever make a new agreement confidently believing in a 'Why' if we believe in ourselves. But if the pre-determined consequences are clear from the start, then not keeping that agreement must result in it being carried out. This is imperative. So in this case, off they go to be re-trained, and a chance to get back into integrity.

The Agreement Process can be learned by anyone. They

either follow the format from a handout or they can be facilitated by someone who is trained in the process. Or train everyone in the process is even better. I usually have a poster on the pre-shift notice board or print off handouts for people to follow themselves. If it's on a poster, it's a constant reminder. You don't have to be all "Captain America" about it. My experience is that it's fun and light-hearted, but with a sincere undertone. Especially when there's been a deviation from a procedure or minimum site standard. Remember to allow the person to self-facilitate where they can. It's about Ownership! In the long run, supporting a person to re-commit to an agreement, fully aware of the consequences, will have far more success than shunning someone or shaming them after an incident. Shame doesn't create buy in; pride does.

THE AGREEMENT PROCESS

Step 1 Agreement: 'WHAT' was the Agreement?

Q. Did you keep it (or change it) yes or no?

  Remember that "Sorry" doesn't cut it. That's an excuse!

Step 2 Values Check: 'HOW' did this affect the mission?

Q. What was more convenient than keeping the agreement?

Q. What was the impact/pre-agreed consequence?

Step 3 Renegotiation: A new 'Why'?

Q. Does the mission need tweaking?

Q. What's the new Agreement?

Q. What are the new Consequences of not keeping it?

Q. What support from the crew do you need to keep it?

Oppositely, what do we usually experience when an incident occurs? We investigate it, put the (presumed) root cause down to behaviour then apply some form of discipline to change it. But punishment doesn't change behaviour, it creates resentment. We often use the incident at the next pre-shift meeting like a weapon, reading it out loudly like breaking news, presuming it will change people's behaviour. But it doesn't. Often nothing is ever done to address the real underlying cause or truly curb the potential for it to happen again. Not corrective actions borne from the 'Why' anyway. Instead we apply disciplinary action or sometimes dismissal. Whereas the Agreement Process enables a workplace to focus on the real issue—a lack of Accountability!

Let's go beneath what the Agreement Process achieves. It's about creating focus on a cause, with a team orientation. Not the instructions from any particular leader or person. In this way, the ability to self-regulate workplace standards emerges out of a sense of pride in the goal. It will take courage for leaders to let go of the reins a little, and allow this process to develop, but it is imperative if intrinsic motivation is to emerge. Let's use a game plan as an example and follow along.

The *Mission* is: *'To create satisfaction through working as a team and using positive communication".*

The *Execution* is: *"To meet the project's milestones in a consistent manner."* Now, because the game plan has been infused with everyone's values, there will be a high degree of emotional investment to see these goals achieved. Leaders and team members make agreements at pre-shift briefings in support of the game plan and mission, daily, or over the longer term. In this way it is not beholden of the supervisor or other crew members personally to enforce accountability. They don't have to make it about themselves. Agreements are made to further the team's mission, purpose and cause. It removes personalities from the equation.

Here's an Example

Let's imagine that everyone agrees to arrive at the daily pre-shift meeting by 6:00 am. In this way a timely approach is agreed upon by each crew member to meet their pre-shift attendance schedule. The commitment is, if someone can't make it by 6:00 am they agree to contact the meeting organiser and change their arrival time. But let's say a worker has arrived at 6:10 and they didn't change the agreement. This might hold up the meeting or they will miss important safety information.

Arriving after the agreed time creates a dynamic that might challenge the mission's objective. So the pre-shift meeting will follow round one—the 'Agreement Round'—as part of its agenda. Someone with facilitation experience engages the crew member and helps them get back into integrity with the game plan (mission).

Step 1: DATA CHECK: Facilitator asks: "Did you make an agreement to arrive at 6:00 am?" ("Yes"). "Were you in a position to change the agreement?" ("Yes"). Did you? ("No"). "What impact does this have on you and the others?"

> If they were NOT able to change the agreement (which is rare), allow them to map whether they are living above or below the line using the OAR BED model. This usually weeds out any excuses or denial.

Step 2: MISSION CHECK: Facilitator asks: "What was the convenience trap?" "Does the mission still fit?

> What this implies is that something is more convenient than keeping their agreement to the mission. A values conflict. In this case the "teamwork" and "communication" part of the mission has broken down. Which leads to the possibility of the crew not meeting the "project milestones". Asking

if they still believe in the mission, ensures everyone is back on board with the same intention. Otherwise tweak the mission until they are.

Step 3: AGREEMENT: "Would you like to make a new Agreement and be aligned with the mission?

They affirm wanting to get back into integrity with the mission—NOT with other crew members, or the supervisor. This is about mission focus. Not 'people' focus. Personalising things leads to shaming, achieves nothing.

Step 3 notes an important distinction and central to the theme of self-accountability. Pledging devotion to a cause is strong motivation. More powerful than a promise made to a leader. Devotion to a leader is about agreeing with the leader's cause, subjugating their own. Unconsciously this is a problem. Take the subjectivity out of it and remove problems that arise around self-identity concepts and egos. Focus on the mission instead.

How the IOS Model Fits In

The power of maintaining agreements is to recommit to them in the name of the crew's mission. The message the crew receive is that maintaining agreements furthers the chance of meeting desired objectives, which enhances the prospects for overall personal satisfaction. Ownership and accountability create trust and raise the prospects of open safety discussions.

When accountability is in action, voluntary operational discipline has an opportunity to emerge, particularly when accountability processes are accompanied by extreme owner-ship using the OAR BED principles. IOS workplaces beginning with 'Why', foster ownership and increase the likelihood of openness and disclosure. Creating greater opportunities for learning and discussion. Individuals can self-process and find their own feet amongst the team, who in return will support them through the processes. Crew's learn trustworthiness and the ability to be trusted. Accountability ensures a team can begin to trust each other from within a 'Why' inspired safety system. One they can believe in. It's imperative, as mentioned before, that the work crew have a clearly defined game plan and mission, a 'Why'.

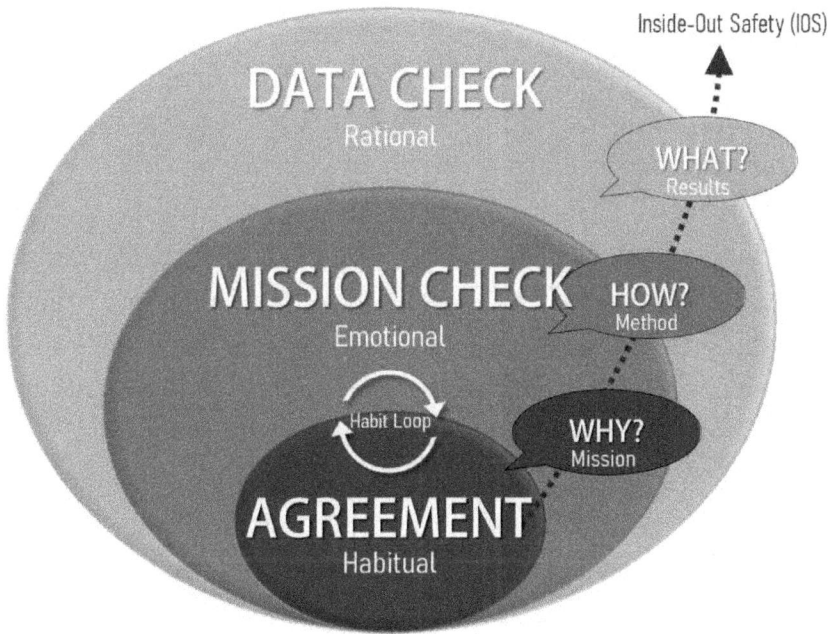

Diagram 4—Agreement Process in Terms of the IOS Model

Systems that embed intrinsic motivation will have a well-defined 'Why'. How many workplaces do you know, which have crystal clear direction? I don't mean instructions; I mean a distinctly clear benchmark that everyone measures their levels of satisfaction and durable fulfilment against. All in the name of a greater cause. Not many, right? Well, there will be soon. This process has legs. Every time I introduce it in the workplace everyone enjoys it. It's the best way I know, by experience, to finally achieve some authenticity and genuine accountability.

Self-Accountability

If I can hold myself accountable to the self-imposed standards of the 'Why', and follow workplace protocol willingly, I don't need to endure the embarrassment that breaching standards and procedures brings or try to conceal them if I do. It avoids unnecessary personality conflicts between the crew and leaders. But only if the crew's game plan is something worth buying into. If nobody cares about upholding the game plan, then it hasn't captured the crew's true essence and values. The 'Why' becomes a 'What' and you're back where you started.

Let's consider a latecomer who says, "Oh, I stopped on the side of the road to help an old lady with a flat tyre". Perhaps performing this good deed was the essence of the work crew's game plan, i.e. "to support others". This issue could be resolved quickly by reaffirming a commitment to the game plan and sorting out why a phone call to change the agreement didn't occur (that's the accountability right there). There was no bloodletting, no accusations, no feelings of guilt or shame. Just a 'Why' solution and further commitment to the team's cause.

When you hold yourself accountable (you're the only one who can), you're saying 'You can count on me' to be there for the game plan, for the team. So it largely takes personalities out of it, or the need to accuse and isolate people. It creates inclusion and support instead. If there is a procedure breach or incident because of a broken agreement, extreme ownership is an opportunity to identify the real root cause. This self-accountability is the only true way of dealing with incidents. That is if you want an authentic result. For agreements that someone hasn't upheld, instead of letting them slide if they haven't owned it, we can support that person to revisit their commitment in the spirit of continuous improvement. But you can only support others when you are proficient with your own self-accountabilities. Then you can graciously support others during this round, the "Agreement Support" round. But volunteering someone else to own their integrity is hypocritical if you can't own your own integrity first.

Agreement Support In Action

It can go like this, "Hey John, did you make an agreement to have the skip bin emptied yesterday?" This reminds John that he needs to clean up his commitments. Agreement Support only works however, if you have not missed your own accountabilities. You'll be reminded sure enough if you haven't. Work crews usually enjoy throwing their newfound integrity around.

So leaders beware, either you walk the talk, or your crew will want you to do the process as well. Which you must do of course. If there are newcomers, they learn quickly what their expectations are because the Agreement Process takes place before every engagement/meeting/briefing. If anyone simply makes a mistake or a breach of procedure because they are new, they are supported to re-commit with their newfound understanding, avoiding shame or embarrassment.

It doesn't take much to imagine how a fully engaged workforce might enjoy self-accountability and ownership principles more than carrot and stick safety. I've seen work crews on the brink of quitting, then create a vision and mission in line with principles and values they hold dear—and completely turn their workplace around. Workers have walked up and thanked me months after I spent as little as three pre-shift meetings teaching them accountability. Their supervisor was still issuing clear agreements and an understanding of the consequences embedded with their daily instructions.

Safety is only one winner here. Quality and productivity are equal winners too. But more importantly, the biggest winners are the workers and their families. Not only does the breadwinner come home with a smile on their face, but interactions with their family have more clarity as the agreement and accountability principles cascade through all aspects of their lives. Make no mistake, this one process alone has the potential to create empowering new habits right across your organisation. The impact of a workforce making and keeping agreements is a powerful one. But importantly it creates so many other benefits because of the concise nature of the interactions. No more ambiguity, no more guesswork or letting things slide. Keeping agreements is why the saying "walk the talk" was invented.

One last thing. If you are reading this and have some apprehension or sense that the Agreements Process wouldn't work for you. Or that your work crews are such that they would never adhere to being held accountable, I can only offer you that I have run this process to the roughest and toughest of mining and construction crews you could imagine. Even I was afraid of what might happen. But there is something to be said for authentic communication and being "real". Genuine commitment to a higher cause runs inherently deep within all of us. Given the right opportunity and facilitation, you will be amazed at how people want more truth and integrity in their workplace, if not their entire lives.

"Planning Is Everything. The Plan Is Nothing."
—Dwight Eisenhower

PRE-SHIFT MAGIC

When I first met Theo, and we discovered we both had upcoming assignments at the same mine, it took us both by surprise. It was incredible when we caught up. We hit it off immediately. What gripped us both was the common vision we had for the workplace. To change the way people go about their tasks so they can find meaning in their work. This was safety. "Real" safety. We were two people from opposite walks of life, but it was a game changing moment to discover how aligned we were. When people meet and they find common ground—it can be pure magic.

Won in the Locker Room.

Imagine a football game, a basketball game, a soccer match, a game of volleyball or a netball game—where there was no communication from the coach. No game plan communicated or no team goals. How strong will the team's performance be without any direction or feedback? Basketball legend Michael Jordan was a huge fan of pre-game player meetings and team briefings. He said, "The game is won in the locker room."

If you don't run some sort of communication session

with your team before a shift, the shift will run you. And if you don't reinforce the team's goals before every shift, your work crew and team members will presume there aren't any. And will substitute their own. Not a good way to focus the team on overarching principles that might keep them out of harm's way, right?

Now, if you're in construction, the heavy industrial sector or mining, pre-shift meetings and briefings have become a way of life. It never used to be like that, but as regulatory authorities have instilled more and more rules and regulations, pre-shift briefings are mandatory. Good thing too. If you're not running pre-shift meetings, guess what? You soon will be.

Pre-shift briefings are exactly the place you can tackle the cause of incidents and accidents head on. In fact, if you're not running pre-shift briefings or you're not running them correctly, chances are your accident and incidents levels will be abnormally high. Is that true for you? That's why I agree with the regulator on this one. Pre-shift briefings, toolbox talks, pre-starts, whatever you like to call them, should be mandatory. Not optional. Every day, not just the busy shifts. Here are the key reasons why.

Agreements ARE the Game-Changer

Pre-shifts have enormous power when you swap the safety-share moment for an Accountability round, which is a safety share anyway. I've witnessed massive transformation from this process. I believe every pre-shift meeting should give the work crew an opportunity to track their satisfaction levels against a benchmark, such as the game plan or a mission. If you don't, how can you tell what has the potential to derail the team or impede their progress. What will indicate in terms of mindset, whether they will have a fulfilling and meaningful day? How will we know if people need support around their commitments and agreements? If someone can't meet an agreement, what better place to offer support and provide alternatives to removing your insulated gloves. Get it? Provided there is a trusting atmosphere and camaraderie, there's no reason why people can't share everything. Especially if they know it's in the spirit of flushing out convenience traps. Not a blame game.

Keep your pre-shifts short and sweet. I think fifteen minutes Max. Pre-shifts should be interchanging dialogue and inspiring. Not monologues and complaint sessions. Distribute production goals and targets wrapped around the Agreement Process. And always issue instructions with an understanding of the consequences should the agreement not be met. Ensure you execute one-on-one agreements with team members who come late. Incorporating concise agreements around everything you do will see a marked improvement in morale and becomes the foundation for voluntary operational discipline. Just watch the difference it makes.

Use the Agreement Process to kick off any and every meeting on site. From the board room to the shop floor. Practice making agreements with one another at every opportunity. I.E. Manager meetings, safety committees, toolbox topics, anywhere, anytime. Why not share accountability success stories, set topics around integrity and support, and definitely practice appreciation, recognition and encouragement at every opportunity. I've never heard of anyone being inspired and performing at their best from the perspective of shame and blame.

There's a phrase that goes 'plan your work—work your plan'. I like to say, "Plan your work to have fun—have fun planning your work." No matter the intention of the 'Why' Process or Agreement Process, one thing above all else is how much fun you have. Watch the smiles on the faces of your crew when someone steps into their power and owns something. Or the laughter when you catch someone out who forgot to keep their agreement. It's actually fun to do an Accountability piece.

Workplaces have been trying forever to get workers to support each other to wear their PPE. But No one wants to say to their work mate, *"Hey Phil, shouldn't you have worn your PPE?"* It's just not in our nature to be a PPE cop. But work crews will banter, *"Hey Phil, accountability dude"*. This really happens. Workers say *"Oi, accountability"* as if to poke fun at each other. There isn't the fear of coming across as a puritan when it's fun. It's one of those benefits I didn't anticipate. Turning an otherwise awkward moment into a game. It's a great by-product of the Agreement Process and really solves a problem in getting people to speak up, or remind others about safety. When used in a light-hearted fun way, safety becomes a joy, not a burden.

I have a dream. That one day every workplace will have a brief Accountability round before they head off to their work tasks. This one keystone habit would encompass governments, board rooms, all of society. Even prisons. Anywhere people meet and rely on each other to keep their word. When it comes to high risk workplaces, keeping our word is paramount, and vital for our survival. Persistency will get you there, consistency will KEEP you there. We can change the world in less than fifteen minutes a day with some Pre-Shift Magic. We have to play the game, we might as well play to win.

"Start by doing what's necessary; then what's possible; suddenly you are doing the Impossible."
—*Francis of Assisi*

TIME TO GET REAL

Get Real is the only program in the world which can proudly say you will slash your incident and accident rates—with just 15 minutes of Safety Mission tracking per day. Hands down, there is no other program that we know of which can boast that. The Get Real model guarantees that if your workplace doesn't reduce incident and accident rates virtually overnight, with improved morale and a positive mindset, me and Theo will work with your teams one-on-one until you do. Absolutely no question. You either transform your workplace culture through empowerment and autonomy (implicitly following our system) or we'll personally show you how. If you are totally committed to an accountable workplace, then so are we!

Intrinsic Belief

We believe wholeheartedly that workers will perform at their best if they trust 100% in their workplace. When there's a 'Why' guiding their decisions. It's no small feat for sure. But very doable and happening every day. Training just a handful of your staff to facilitate the Agreements Process will embed the accountability model and maximise your daily stand-up performance meetings.

We estimate that introducing the Get Real Accountability Model into pre-shift meetings, inductions, safety shares and other selected trainings and meetings, would reduce incident and accident rates virtually overnight. Plus, it infuses integrity as the foundation of your workplace culture and embeds accountability as its most basic function. It allows your workforce to uncover intrinsic safety values and support each other to maintain commitment to safety agreements. This is a far cry from today's workplaces where punishment and disciplinary measures are so prevalent. It's no wonder there's no "intrinsic motivation" encouraging workforces to be safe.

When a workplace pursues safe work practices purely for the satisfaction it provides, they do so because they are intrinsically motivated. Intrinsic safety motivation emerges from within an individual rather than any system of external incentives or rewards. Intrinsic safety creates safe work practices because of the sense of satisfaction and durable fulfilment being safe provides. It's a completely different approach to a carrot and stick mentality and one you will have great success with. Intrinsic safety motivation is a proven technique which creates voluntary operational discipline through layers of commitments to safety agreements. It's the foundation upon which an accountability model can be overlaid. It means you step back and allow ownership and responsibility to prevail, freeing you from the mundane chore of using governance or constant coercion or persuasion as motivation. No more conformance issues, no more manipulation or pleading. Just flick the switch and your work crews willingly adopt full ownership and responsibility. The only problem we see is your total commitment to a complete company transformation. Most companies we work with are stubbornly hesitant to release themselves from the control-based systems that they run. For sure, the Get Real model requires skilful facilitation, but even the basic core of the program will have an immediate effect on morale and buy-n.

What's the Secret?

How it works is that instead of you enforcing standards and procedures, you teach your Trainers and Supervisors how to mentor work crews into finding meaning and satisfaction in their work. This unique process addresses mental health and mindset issues too, through the use of vision and goal setting techniques unique to Get Real. Work crews will actually create and buy in to their own safety 'mission' and 'objectives' before they'd follow the safety rhetoric we tend to preach. The Get Real model relieves you from the burden of carrot and stick tactics. Instead you have a way of dealing with things openly. Solving workplace mental illness and accidents/injuries caused from low morale, or a lack of conviction in your safety system. The best part is, it's a simple system to apply and you can select who learns the technique of self-managed continuous safety improvement, based on people's position of trust and standing in your company.

When you begin the Get Real journey, those who are selected as facilitators should get together and create their own group mission. "We facilitators create...." Then they'd begin implementing the benefits of their own mission at the same time. The idea is that you have a sustainable model that empowers your workforce long into the future. So that you have within your own resources the ability to facilitate your workforce into discovering personal fulfilment and job satisfaction, eliminating careless incidents and accidents caused through the lack of buy-in and disbelief in your systems. Following are some principles that Get Real espouses.

The 7 Get Real Principles

1. Buy-in of a company's safety values is achieved when there is more to work than simply earning a living. People not only believe in a fair day's work for a fair day's pay, they desire durable fulfilment and job satisfaction as a matter of course.

2. Self-driven safety will evolve when a workforce discovers its own intrinsic safety motivation and voluntary operational discipline.

3. Improved work environments built upon accountability create improved mental health and retention. This creates a workforce who care about their workplace and who will support their colleagues through difficulties and challenges.

4. Safety is a by-product of maintaining firm commitments to workplace agreements and an understanding there are consequences for not keeping them. This invites self-accountability, personal responsibility and extreme ownership as a workplace's highest value.

5. People buy in to safety when they connect with the company's vision, combine their own sense of values with that of the company's and when a workplace has a 'Why' and they believe in the cause. Then they will become more vocal and involved in eliminating unsafe work habits. Because it is personally satisfying to be part of the camaraderie and feeling of success to do so.

6. The reduction of incidents and accidents increases quality and production and perpetuates a continuously improving

self-sustaining workplace culture.

7. Approaching safety from the perspective that every individual deserves fulfilment in what they do, whatever your industry, will slash your incident and accident rates. By following the 3 core principles below, your ultimate goal is to ensure that everyone feels a sense they are:

- Satisfied and fulfilled that their job/work tasks have meaning,
- Valued and appreciated for who they are and their contribution,
- Receiving a sense of pride and purpose in their workplace.

About You

If you are willing to change your approach, follow a proven system, and take responsibility for your success, then you might invite Theo and I to transform your workplace. You can be assured your key message will be delivered with a powerful delivery. Theo's Get Real presentation called "Just Another Day, delivers a message of extreme ownership and accountability followed by a Safety Mission process. All tied in with your company's predominant key safety strategy.

The Get Real Accountability Model is changing the way industry thinks and talks about safety. Instead of drumming standards and procedures into your workforce, Get Real allows the workforce to discover their own 'intrinsic safety motivation'. When you stop forcing safety as the primary focus and start promoting personal values and durable fulfilment, safety will take care of itself in ways you could never imagine. And it solves mental health issues and builds resilience.

Making a difference. The A-Team at Christmas Creek WA (FMG Iron Ore) 2019. From left: Theo, Trevor Lake, Deon Wessels, Ken.

Delivering the "Safety Mission Process" to AusGroup (AGC) April 2021. Theo and Nico presented together for the first time since that fateful day. From left: John Pica (AGC), Ken, Nico, Theo.

CONCLUSION

So, What Now?

Well, that's the end of the book: The 'What', The 'How' and the 'Why' in all its glory. The following segments are about how Get Real evolved, how I came across the principles and theories, and how you can seek more assistance from Theo and I. We are available to come out to your workplace for one to two-hour presentations or a full-blown company transformation. I know of no other tool on the planet that will have the same effect as the Get Real accountability process. Contact us or follow us on LinkedIn or Facebook. Search for "Get Real Book" or "Just Another Day" on social media. Let us know what you think and share your ideas. It will help others if you do. At the front of the book are our contact details and we would relish the opportunity to discuss with you how to empower your workplace, and begin the journey of voluntary operational discipline. Drop us a line or give us a call (getreal@email.com).

https://getreal.net.au
https://theoventer.com.au
https://au.linkedin.com/in/theo-venter
https://au.linkedin.com/in/thekenroberts
https://www.facebook.com/KenAndTheo

How Get Real Philosophies Evolved

Get Real was actually conceived in 2016 after I had been working in Laos for three years. When I returned to Australia, there was a distinct disenchantment on the work sites I visited. Which I sensed before I left, but couldn't put my finger on it at the time. I guess there had been a global recession, a downturn in the industry, and the levels of disbelief and mistrust in the system may have emerged from that. Nobody would say anything publicly, only in lunchrooms or behind closed doors, or when I got to know people better and delved a little deeper.

I've always conducted the Operation Tackle game plan sessions wherever I could as part of my roles. They've always been a big hit. I learned Operation Tackle from Ken Judge, ex-Hawthorn player and coach. Before he passed away in 2015. Allan Jeans passed away in 2011. So I felt it was important to continue their legacy. They always made it about the players and their wellbeing. Focusing on getting the best out of each person, creating a sense of "team". It seemed such a natural winning formula to me. So I began to work on a system that followed this belief. To get the most out of players (workers):

- Create trust, and then openness will emerge.
- Openness encourages dialogue.
- Dialogue leads to empowerment.

I had hoped in the past that this was all I'd need, a total solution for getting people to speak up about safety. Allowing them to reveal the truth about their disbelief in the system. That they might discuss issues authentically, so we can discover what they needed to achieve more durable fulfilment. But when I met Theo. things transformed. We knew instantly that combining our passions would have fantastic results. But I wasn't expecting the amazing things we discovered writing this book.

Then I introduced Theo to my long-term mentors:

- Anton Fouche (www.armourplus.com) who knows more about mining and heavy industrial safety than anyone I've ever met. He taught me a lot about how big mining companies operate and many operational tactics.
- Larry Dawson I've known for over twenty years. What he doesn't know about relationships, group dynamics and personal development is not worth knowing. He brought the Mankind Project to Australia and helped me start the Western Australian community.

I've had long discussions with each of my mentors on how Get Real, the ethos and philosophy might have a real impact globally. They, Theo and I put our heads and hearts together and voila... "Get Real" the book was born.

Writing the Book

After Theo and I started exploring his accident closely, Get Real became, well—*real.* I wrote everything down zealously. The principles were mostly developed, as I'd been using them in various capacities for years. But Theo's story was the catalyst, as it succinctly demonstrated them perfectly. I remember explaining to Theo what "came" to me when I first saw him speak. The epiphany I had as to why I thought his accident occurred. He agreed with me emphatically. It was like a light bulb above his head. "Yes, exactly, you've nailed it," he said. "Those were exactly the voices in my head. I took the convenient option so easily." When I first asked him if I could write my theories around his story, there was no hesitation.

We see Get Real as a game-changer. Injecting work-places with an ethos of extreme ownership via the "Why Process". With a top to bottom approach. It's proven that honesty, openness and disclosure will promote safety and that learnings communicated openly in this environment will ensure that a safe work culture will emerge. It really works.

As trainers and consultants, Theo and I get to cover a large cross section of industry. We meet and talk with all types of operatives, from management to the workers on the shop floor. Canvassing them on their experiences, gauging their sentiments, their attitudes, even their emotional states. We firmly believe deep inside every person is a profound need to be safe, a primordial sense of mortality. It's counterintuitive to imagine that anyone would act in a way that exposes themselves to injury deliberately. Yet it happens every day.

Coaching Philosophy

Einstein said you can't solve a problem at the level it was created. So we flipped the idea of workplace injuries on its head. Instead of creating more procedures and enforcing new rules, we wanted to un-complicate the situation and meet the workforce right where they were, always trying to meet mandatory daily minimum standards and requirements. We decided to turn a chore into intrinsic motivation. We wanted to turn something workers thought they HAD to do; into something they WANT to do.

Get Real promotes the idea that any solution requires workers and leaders to be absolutely real about everything that happens in their workplace, and to resolve issues using everyone's combined values and input. It's the idea that a workforce becomes part of their own solution. This shift means 90% of the work is cultural and does not confound workers with more paperwork, procedures or systems.

The biggest problem companies' face with any program

is trying to implement "change". Without across-the-board buy-in at all levels, any implementation of a program is doomed. So we suggest you don't implement change. Work with what you've got. Get Real conveys a level of authenticity and openness that brings an organisation closer together, so learnings pass freely into the culture and workers feel they have helped create it.

One of the main endorsements for adopting a Get Real culture is the idea of continuous improvement. Personnel at any level, who learn to facilitate the Agreement Process or run the 'Why' Process (game plan), is bestowed the skills to consolidate the program throughout their organisation. There's no prerequisite to be a leader or be proficient in any discipline or profession. Learning to facilitate the Get Real processes is available to anyone. It's right here in this book. I urge you to try it.

It's not about giving instructions. It's about coaching the workforce, not training them. Popular perception is that coaching is a form of training or mentoring. Think tennis coach. This misunderstanding means leaders think they are coaching when really, they are providing instruction and direction. To create a workplace that is truly autonomous and self-improving, coaching is quite the opposite.

The fundamental principle behind Get Real as a coaching technique is that the workforce is creative, resourceful and holders of the keys to their own empowerment. If a work team needs direction to complete a complex task, or staff need to resolve a problem or meet personal challenges, Get Real provides leaders the skills to guide them towards discovering their own solutions and creating the self-accountability to carry them out.

The program is a structured process of discovery and correction, connecting workers to a deeper sense of commitment to company standards. It reinforces the existing programs by understanding the human elements that require them to succeed. Get Real monitors daily performance through a model of self-accountability and offers shame avoiding solutions for addressing behaviour. Get Real is delivered by stripping back the barriers to authentic communication and interaction, through which a degree of trust develops and aligns work teams to personal and company goals. It facilitates an environment where people speak out comfortably on safety issues and opportunities.

The Get Real approach may be the most purposeful and rewarding journey a company will ever take. Following are some of the ways that Get Real may benefit your organisation.

Resilience, Inclusion and Diversity

Get Real solves a huge problem for companies coping with a rapidly changing demographic and the difficulties associated with an increasingly diverse workforce. Race, age, gender, sexual preference, ethnicity, skill base, background, personality, cognitive style, tenure and culture can often marginalise a workplace rapidly. Subtle interactions between workers unaware of their power and privilege can have a devastating effect on a company aiming for inclusion and diversity.

The value of developing a Get Real culture beyond basic skills training, is it enhances employee engagement and interaction, and people learn the value of diversity. Leaders can embrace inclusion and diversity, equal opportunity and other staff development strategies as a monument to their workforce's potential. Developing agreements and an accountable and personally responsible culture across all levels of your organisation creates tolerance and understanding.

There's been a lot of discussion lately regarding the benefits of a resilient workforce. Unfortunately, work crew's that lack resilience will experience: a loss of self-confidence, depressed mood or a difficulty in managing emotions, difficulty in decision making. Their outlook may change, optimists become pessimists, pessimists lose their counterbalancing perspective, reduced creativity, reduced desire for social contact.

Resilience is sometimes misunderstood as having a shield against difficulty. Or that it means perseverance. Except persevering with a detrimental cause is at your peril. Resilience is the capacity to maintain equilibrium and remain flexible. Flexible in thoughts, behaviours and emotions when under stress. Stress can arrive from a one-off event or an accumulation of demands over a period of time.

Pulling traditional levers to solve these issues may not be the answer. Other operating model redesigns rely on small, incremental changes in process to improve efficiency and quality. They can take a significant amount of time to implement before you realise the benefits. A people focused approach is often what is needed.

Get Real is a program that provides staff with a prompt solution and pathway through their challenges, right from the first encounter. It promotes capacity and capability-building mechanisms that drive new behaviours and increases effectiveness within days of implementation. A workforce's resilience, engagement, desire to succeed and confidence in its leaders can be measured by psychometrics. Which means a workplace's well-being has a value which can be gauged during the processes.

Sifting through absentee rates, training attendances or injury statistics assume people will act the same way in every situation. If you score high on self-confidence, will you always be self-confident? Trained facilitators who understand how people can be measured in terms of their resilience capabilities, offer a comforting solution.

COVID-19 Edition

The 2021 edition of Get Real comes at a time of great change. They say the world has changed forever. However, there's been no real changes in safety philosophy or the way we carry out our activities. Other than the added protections required to shield us against contracting this deadly virus. The difference between what was then when I first wrote Get Real, and what is now post global epidemic, hasn't changed the basic principles in regards to human nature and how we manage safety. So there's not a lot to say about COVID-19 that would increase the value Get Real might provide. So I won't. ☺

One Last Thing...

At the beginning of the book I wrote that Theo confirmed a theory of mine that all workplace incident and accident sources are traceable to the same origin. Essentially, that origin is our "Humanness". Human nature unavoidably provides us with the many challenges we experience when we work with other people. Sometimes we have a full complement of tools from within our own resources to cope, at other times we need help. Whether we ask for help or not is another question.

An open communicative culture is the best solution to

equip managers and leaders in understanding the intricate dynamics of a 'human' workforce. Creating and keeping agreements is the only infallible process I know that addresses the actual real problems we face in our workplace.

Acceptance and understanding of everyone's values as a leader is often considered a specialised skill. The Get Real approach does not require a manager or leader to have any special abilities, or superior understanding of people's values or personalities. Get Real is inherently other-oriented and work crews assist each other with workplace challenges. The benefits leaders are open communication, integrity and accountability. Therefore, resolving mental health issues, absenteeism, inclusion and diversity challenges, is a natural flow on effect from these attitudes. With the cultivation of a workforce's full trust and cooperation, the fostering of a culture of care, openness, disclosure and learning—becomes a reality.

I guarantee if you only follow half the principles in in this book, it will still provide the most effective way of approaching incidents and accidents in your workplace. It is the development of a culture which captures everyone's combined values, so that both company and individual goals create the intrinsic motivation for personal satisfaction and a common vision for team success. Get Real is the tool of a thousand uses. It solves many, many problems. Not just safety. I know of no other program that will turn a workforce around in the quick time that Get Real will. The transformation literally occurs overnight. Trust is a powerful force. Good luck in your endeavours and bye for now.

"You can't change the world, but
you can change yourself."
—Madeleine Bunting

KEN'S STORY

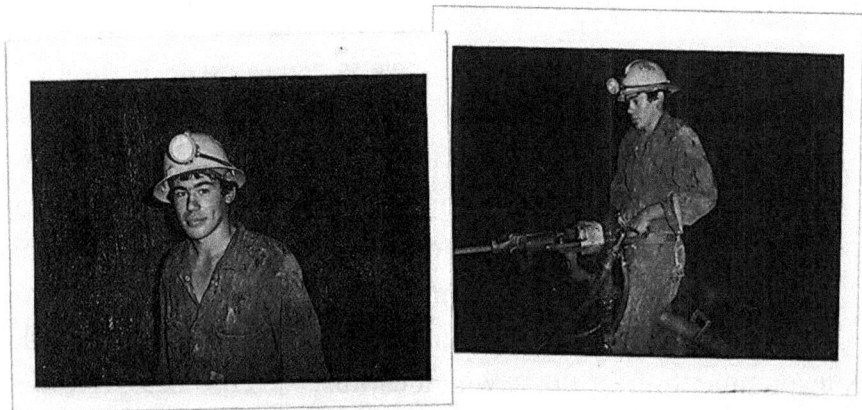

Marvel Loch Underground Gold Mine, WA 1982 (17yo)

I stumbled into the skip shoulder-to-shoulder with the men. Cap-lamp on, waiting to zoom down into the darkness. I was a little nervous but excited. Ol' Doc Snell, the shift boss, walks over and inspects the kid with the oversized boots and baggy overalls. "Just a minute Robbo," he suddenly realises. "You can't go down the hole. You're not eighteen yet?" Despondent, I started to step out of the skip. But suddenly, Doc's index finger stops me in my tracks, and pushes me back into the skip. "OK" he smiled wryly, "You can go down the hole. But if you hurt yourself—*I'll Bloody Kill Ya!*"

Welcome to my first ever safety lesson. If you could call it that. Being underground for the first time, I had to learn the fine art of fending for myself and staying out of trouble. The small-gauge rail locomotive I was supposed to drive, had flat batteries. So I hand-trucked twenty-seven one-ton side tippers through several hundred metres of winding tunnels. I would jump on and ride them downhill to the ore-pass, tip them out and push them all the way back as fast as could run. It was hard work, but awesome. There were no self-rescuers or underground refuge chambers back then. No two-way radios, no machinery safeguarding. The ore-pass was wide open, waiting to get you. No grizzly bars (mesh) to catch you if you fell. Next stop... 100 feet down to the next level. The word 'safety' didn't exist. It just wasn't something we ever mentioned or spoke about.

I have many amazing stories like that. Like asking the winder driver (hoist) if I could jump into a fully laden skip heading for the surface. So I could have some dinner (crib). Or sitting on a plank of 4-by-2 strapped across the roller brackets of a conveyor belt. Plucking sticks and debris from between my legs. I've built houses wearing "budgie smugglers" and a pair of thongs. So I'd have an all over tan. I've built make-shift scaffolding out of plastic milk crates. Stood in the bucket of a front-end loader, hitching a ride to the gold room. The horror stories don't end there. It was just how we did things back then. We didn't give it a second thought. Not like today.

With over forty years of mining and construction under my belt, I've experienced it all. From high flying seat-of-your-pants unrestrained working-at-heights, to kid-gloves and mollycoddling where you couldn't blow your nose without a permit. I've seen and had accidents—and I was underground when there was a fatality. Trust me, you never want to experience a fatality. Yet within days it was business as usual.

Accidents were a way of life back then. I'm talking '81.

I was born with sawdust in my veins. Dad was a "chippie" and so was my grandfather. So after mining for a couple of years, I landed an apprenticeship as a carpenter. I picked up more bad habits. We would modify our circular saws as soon as we bought them off the shelf. Removing the spring-back sawblade guard, then hacksawing half the guide plate off. There was no nook or cranny on a timber roof structure that I couldn't that my saw into. We didn't know any better, it was just what they taught us. When I was twenty-four, I put that sawblade right through my ankle. I nearly lost my foot. It was time to give up the tools and consider what I was going to do with my life. While recuperating from that accident, I went back to school and passed my builders ticket. Now as a registered builder, I landed construction manager roles back on mine sites. Building process plants, ore handling facilities and all sorts of mine infrastructure.

In 2002 I started a journey into personal development. I discovered that I had a knack for health and safety by accident (pun intended). You could say I developed projects until I discovered a passion for developing people. I've worked and lived at over forty mine sites across Australia and South East Asia and have worked on over 50 construction projects. And now—here I am. Author, facilitator, systems implementation lead and cultural change management consultant specialising in workplace transformations.

With a growing social awareness of workplace mental health issues, from the impact of fly in-fly out (FIFO) and remote site locations, my next focus is to understand how these issues affect families and relationships. When I'm asked to help companies with workplace mental health issues, I share with their work crew a common thread. I was raised in mining towns and have lived on remote sites all my life. Moving out of home and living in mining camps since I was sixteen. We never had FIFO back then. Your "donger" was your home. What they call R&R today, was me playing football and meeting friends at the local pub after work. So when I hear people's stories, I understand from personal experience. I've learned to appreciate every situation and not tar them with the same brush. Although things have changed a lot over the years, I realise we all want the same things in the end. Durable fulfilment and a sense of personal satisfaction.

The Mankind Project

Since 2002 I've been a community leader with a global personal development and empowerment network called the Mankind Project (MKP). I've conducted hundreds of weekly group meetings to support men and women in finding what's important to them and help them blend their values into the framework of family, lifestyle and work choices. I learned how to facilitate processes that allow people to breakthrough limiting self-beliefs. In 2004 I founded the West Australian MKP community, meeting once a week at the North Perth Tennis Club. It's still going today. We held Western Australia's inaugural New Warrior Training Adventure in 2006. The "NWTA" is MKP's premier training event. I've travelled to the US and facilitated NWTA's there too. With twenty years of personal development facilitation experience, it's very inspiring to combine these innovative life-skills and techniques with traditional workplace practices. I call it Personal Development for the workplace.

Dr John Demartini

I've studied with Dr John Demartini since 2006 and am a trained Demartini Method Facilitator. John's seminal personal empowerment program is called "The Breakthrough

Experience". It's taught me how to offer people the keys to their own empowerment. John is a world-renowned human behaviourist, researcher, author and global educator. He appears in the movies "The Secret" and "Oh My God" and travels the world three hundred and sixty days per year speaking and teaching to as many people he can approach.

John's work involves a multitude of powerful tools that can dramatically change people's lives. He has studied over thirty-thousand books across all defined academic disciplines which he shares to over sixty countries around the globe. His research on axiology (the study of human values) is very comprehensive and has greatly influenced my work. I have spent thirteen years attending his programs and studying over two hundred and fifty inspiring topics and disciplines with him. Ranging from ancient and modern philosophies, religions and sciences, human behaviour and the physical and metaphysical sciences. Much of what I have learned from John makes it into these pages. Particularly the chapter on Values.

It's About Mission of Service

Meeting the workforce where they are has revolutionised the way I approach change in the workplace. It's a different angle but one I'm having much success with. To put icing on the cake, in meeting global safety standards in a developing nation— Laos, I discovered it was much easier to introduce a safety culture where the workforce didn't have to "un-learn" embedded western workforce safety systems.

Also, I find that respecting individual values, providing strong engagement, a hands-on coach approach, working at the coalface and being part of the pre-shift briefing is far more effective than enforcing rules and procedures or running induction training programs from a classroom.

An interesting topic I'm pursuing further is the effect our

current work life and environment is having on mental health issues. This is an alarming trend for all the wrong reasons. If life and work are one and the same, where do you draw the line?

If someone claims to be having difficulties at work, do you attribute it to their private life or work life, or both? We have a propensity to attribute blame either way. It's part of our nature. But to try and pinpoint such a serious affliction to either environment raises the ugly issue of liability. I hope that common sense prevails, and it never gets to this. But my fear is that someone is going to miss out on the care they need because their ailment may be blamed on one environment more than the other, either work or home. I can't see that it is possible to distinguish the two. If I have problems at home and bottle it up at work, which environment is the source of my ailment? Is carrying it around bottled up, or the stress of the issue itself the source? Our follow up research in our next book will address this issue further. Let's not allow this to get out of hand. Let's nip it in the bud and offer real support, right here, right now. I'm sorry to say that "RU OK" days are not enough. These are 'What' based solutions in the absence of a solid 'Why'. Our next book will be as insightful as Get Real around this issue. Of course, I will be enlisting Theo. He has first-hand experience wrestling with the "black dog". I've only touched the tip of the iceberg as far as Theo's story really goes.

So what does this mean for the workforces that Theo and I engage with? Our experience tells us that consideration for an individual's own unique 'value' system will inspire them to take responsibility for their lifestyle and subsequent ownership of their workplace. The secret in maintaining production and safety goals for any company is not in workers aligning their values with that of the organisation, but the organisation aligning their values with that of the workforce. What this really means is that corporate value systems must include something of personal value to the worker for them to buy in to the company vision fully.

Apart from workers who have a personal stake in the shareholding of a company, values that boast shareholder profits is not going to inspire them to be safe. Even then, being a shareholder doesn't automatically create a connection and subsequent buy-in of its values either. Sometimes the founder of a company or a charismatic leader with high principles will espouse the values that workers find desirable. Otherwise it's the worker's values that will take precedence, if you want buy-in of course. This is the key to the future in our eyes. People matter most. There can be no other way.

The Reveley Agreement

A presentation for Theo is very intense. It takes a lot out of him. One of the most important things is his Psychic safety. Reliving the accident when he speaks, clearly has an effect and it takes him a while to recuperate afterwards. One day at the Reveley Bar, overlooking the beautiful Swan River in Perth, we made an agreement that he would never do a presentation without it always being in support of a greater cause or "mission". Anyone who is witness to Theo's presentation must always walk away with a deeper connection to his message, the 'Why'. The reason I mention this is to offer an insight into how agreements affect every aspect of our lives. This agreement is a personal one, made with Theo's overall wellbeing in mind. However, it is an example of how agreements work in the real world. So, I say let's try them at work too. I hope you agree.

"Good habits formed at youth
make all the difference."
—*Aristotle*

"No driver's license... no problem". My first job, 16yo. Boomali Gold Mine, Southern Cross, WA 1981. I reversed this Ute over the edge of an open-pit embankment (quarry). That's 200 metres down to my left. No windrows (barriers) in those days. Check out them legs!

Acknowledging the "Men of Service". On staff at an MKP training in Houston, Texas USA 2006. They called me the "Mission Man" when I presented my Hawthorn Vs. Geelong Grand Final mission process. Even though Americans don't understand AFL Football, they were thoroughly enthralled by the story. That's why I know this process works whether you like AFL football or not. It seems to have universal appeal.

Facilitating the Breakthrough Experience with Dr John Demartini. Melbourne Australia 2008. Inspiring people to reach for their dreams through mission and goal setting processes.

Diversity in action. Getting Real with other cultures. Facilitating a 2 Day Safety Summit for Phu Bia Mining in Laos S.E. Asia, 2014. Again, The Exploration Geology Team had no concept of the '89 Grand Final. But it had such a great impact. Below is the result of our Game Plan ('Why').

Mission
"We the Exploration team, run a Proactive, Efficient and Effective operation through Leadership, Initiative and Experience"

IN GRATITUDE

Ken: To my wife Pla, thanks for your loving support. Special thanks go to Theo, my friend, for putting up with my constant barrage of questions. Where you had to recall some terrible memories. Thanks to Anton Fouche for giving me a great opportunity and encouraging and supporting us throughout. Thanks to Peter Leaman for the advice and support, and to James Salmon for the edits. To my sons Lachlan and Jayden, who also work in the construction and mining industries. You've encouraged me throughout. Thanks to Bayley for being the beautiful person you are. And to the "old man", a veteran of the offshore oil industry—thank you Tom for all your support and anecdotes. Special thanks to Larry & Bronnie for seeing something special in me when there was a time (long ago) that I didn't. In loving memory to my mum. An author, teacher and healer in her own right. You gave me the gift of being real 'ma'—at all costs.

Theo: To my children Ruan, Pierre and Rene, your unconditional love and friendship continue to sustain me daily. In loving memory of my father, Willie—my rock. To mother who groomed me from a young age to recite poetry in public. How did you know I would need those skills one day? Thank you to Garry Chard who persuaded me to speak to a small work crew the first time. Did you ever imagine I'd eventually speak to hundreds of thousands of people? To the angel physiotherapists, and to Hahn Nguyen who patched me up and put me back together. Physically, mentally and spiritually. Thanks Ken for never giving up until we finished. Even though I never want to revisit those memories again, it was worth it. And to Brandon, how could we forget you?

ENDNOTES

[1] Zwetsloot, G.I.J.M., Aaltonen, M., Wybo, J.L., Saari, J., Kines, P., Beek, R., 2013. The case for research into the zero accident vision. Saf. Sci. 58, 41–48.

[2] Donaldson, C. (2013, March). Zero harm: Infallible or ineffectual? OHS Professional, P. 22-27.

[3] Dekker, S. (2014, August). Employees: A problem to control or resource to harness? Professional Safety Journal. Griffith Research Online, P. 32.

[4] Jennifer Bowers, Johnny Lo, Peta Miller, Daveena Mawren, Brooklyn Jones. (May 14, 2018). Psychological distress in remote mining and construction workers in Australia.

[5] Reason, James. (1997). Managing the Risks of Organizational Accidents, p. 9, (The 'Swiss Cheese' model of defences).

[6] Hopkins, Andrew. (2005). Safety, culture and risk: the organisational causes of disasters, p. 5.

[7] Carroll, R. L. 1988. Vertebrate paleontology and evolution. W.H. Freeman and Company, New York.

[8] Sharot, Tali (2011-12-06). "The optimism bias". Current Biology. 21 (23): R941–R945. doi:10.1016/j.cub.2011.10.030. ISSN 0960-9822. PMID 22153158.

[9] Schultz, Wolfram (23 April 2010). Behavioral and Brain Function. Dopamine signals for reward value and risk: basic and recent data: https://doi.org/10.1186/1744-9081-6-24.

[10] Berridge KC, Kringelbach ML (May 2015). "Pleasure systems in the brain". Neuron. 86 (3): 646–664. doi:10.1016/j.neuron.2015.02.018. PMC 4425246. PMID 25950633.

[11] LeDoux, Joseph. (6 June 2018) On Fear, Emotions, and Memory: An Interview with Dr. Joseph LeDoux. Page 2 of 2 "Brain World" https://brainworldmagazine.com/on-fear-emotions-and-memory-an-interview-with-dr-joseph-ledoux/2/

[12] Damasio, Antonio. Descartes' Error: Emotion, Reason, and the Human Brain, Putnam, 1994; revised Penguin edition, 2005

[13] Intrinsic motivation. (2017, October 31). Wiktionary, The Free Dictionary. Retrieved 12:44, December 18, 2018 - https://en.wiktionary.org/w/index.php?title=intrinsic_motivation&oldid=47935851.

[14] Sinek, Simon. Start With Why: How Great Leaders Inspire Everyone To Take Action, p. 38.

[15] The study performed under an international collaboration between UCL, NICT (Japan) and Western University (Canada) by Nobuhiro Hagura, Patrick Haggard and Jörn Diedrichsen. Perceptual decisions are biased by the cost to act, Research Article Feb 21, 2017.

[16] MacLean, P. (1990). The triune brain in evolution, p. 453.

[17] Prechter Jr., Robert R.. The Wave Principle of Human Social Behavior and the New Science of Socionomics (Kindle Locations 2294-2295).

[18] Prechter Jr., Robert R.. The Wave Principle of Human Social Behavior and the New Science of Socionomics (Kindle Location 6165).

[19] Duhigg, C. (2012). The Power of Habit. Why We Do What We Do, and How to Change, p. 17.

[20] MacLean, P. (1990). The triune brain in evolution, p. 247.

[21] Wikipedia contributors. (2019, January 28). First law of thermodynamics. In Wikipedia, The Free Encyclopedia. Retrieved 05:14, February 8, 2019, from https://en.wikipedia.org/w/index.php?title=First_law_of_thermodynamics&oldid=880590475

[22] Yager LM, Garcia AF, Wunsch AM, Ferguson SM (August 2015). "The ins and outs of the striatum: Role in drug addiction". Neuroscience. 301: 529–541. doi:10.1016/j.neuroscience.2015.06.033. PMC 4523218. PMID 26116518.

[23] Harari, Y. N., Harari, Y. N., Purcell, J., & Watzman, H. (2015). Sapiens: A brief history of humankind.

[24] Wikipedia contributors. (2019, May 18). Pain and pleasure. In Wikipedia, The Free Encyclopedia. Retrieved 01:52, July 13, 2019, from https://en.wikipedia.org/w/index.php?title=Pain_and_pleasure&oldid=897714276

[25] Duhigg, C. (2012). The Power of Habit. Why We Do What We Do, and How to Change, p. 46.

[26] Duhigg, C. (2012). The Power of Habit. Why We Do What We Do, and How to Change, p. 17.

[27] Graybiel, Ann M. (2008) Habits, Rituals, and the Evaluative Brain. P. 361. Annu. Rev. Neurosci. 2008. 31:359–87 The Annual Review of

Neuroscience.

[28] Brittish Safety Council. (10 July 2018) NEWS: Fatalities at work rise against backdrop of Brexit and government cuts. ttps://www.britsafe.org/publications/safety-management-magazine/safety-management-magazine/2018/news-fatalities-at-work-rise-against-backdrop-of-brexit-and-government-cuts/

[29] Health and Safety Executive, Great Britain, 2018. (http://www.hse.gov.uk/statistics/fatals.htm). [Similar trends can be seen globally].

[30] Keen, Lucille. (Feb 4, 2016). Psychological Workers Comp Claims To Rise. Financial Review article. https://www.afr.com/news/policy/industrial-relations/psychological-wokers-comp-claims-to-rise-20160204-gmlisc.

[31] Berkowitz, Leonard (2000). Causes and consequences of feelings. West Nyack, N.Y.: Cambridge University Press. pp. 67–95.

[32] Schacter, D.L., Gilbert, D.T., Wegner, D.M., & Hood, B.M. (2011). Psychology (European ed.). Basingstoke: Palgrave Macmillan.

[33] Caskeya, J. Bugra Ozelb N. (2016). Earnings expectations and employee safety. Research Article: Journal of Accounting and Economics Volume 63, Issue 1, February 2017, Pages 121-141.

[34] Decide from Latin -cide, -cidium, both from caedere 'kill', infinitive of dēcīdō ("cut off, decide"), from dē ("down from") + caedō ("cut"). Oxford English Dictionary.

[35] Gretchen A. Mosher. (2013). Trust, Safety, and Employee Decision-Making: A Review of Research and Discussion of Future Directions. The Journal of Technology, Management, and Applied Eng., Vol 29, No. 2. Abstract, p. 2.

[36] Nobuhiro Hagura, Patrick Haggard, Jörn Diedrichsen, (2017). Perceptual decisions are biased by the cost to act. Research Article Feb 21, 2017.

[37] Packer, C., Pusey, A. E. (May 1983). "Adaptations of female lions to infanticide by incoming males". American Naturalist. 121 (5): 716–28.

[38] MacLean, P. (1990). The triune brain in evolution, p. 247.

[39] Wikipedia contributors. (2018, December 21). Self-concept. In Wikipedia, The Free Encyclopedia. Retrieved 06:36, February 11, 2019, fromhttps://en.wikipedia.org/w/index.php?title=Self-concept&oldid=874842402.

[40] Donaldson, C. (2013, March). Zero harm: Infallible or ineffectual? OHS Professional, P. 22-27.

41 Dekker, S. (2014, August). Employees: A problem to control or resource to harness? Professional Safety Journal. Griffith Research Online, P. 32.

42 Dreamworld: Four people killed on Thunder River Rapids ride at Gold Coast theme park". ABC News. Australian Broadcasting Corporation. 25 October 2016.

43 Duhigg, C. (2012). The Power of Habit. Why We Do What We Do, and How to Change, p. 97. Keystone Habits or the Ballad of Paul O'Neill.

44 Wikipedia contributors. (2019, February 7). Maslow's hierarchy of needs. In *Wikipedia, The Free Encyclopedia*. Retrieved 12:57, February 15, 2019, from https://en.wikipedia.org/w/index.php?title= Maslow%27s_hierarchy_of_needs&oldid=882261315.

45 Mental illness: key area handbook. (1993) The health of the nation. London, UK Department of Health. p.11-24.

46 Gus Worland. (2016). Man-Up, ABC TV. Episodes 1-3. From https://www.abc.net.au/tv/programs/man-up/

47 National Alliance for the Mentally Ill (NAMI). Fact sheet. Facts about mental illness and work. August 1999 (www.nami.org). (NAMI is a United States non-profit self-help advocacy organization.)

48 Gretchen A. Mosher. (2013). Trust, Safety, and Employee Decision-Making: A Review of Research and Discussion of Future Directions. The Journal of Technology, Management, and Applied Engineering, Volume 29, Number 2. Defining Trust, p. 4. From Web. 21 December 2018. lib.dr.iastate.edu/cgi/viewcontent.cgi?ar+**ticle=1602&context=abe_eng _pubs.

49 John Kotter and Lorne Whitehead, Buy-In: Saving Your Good Idea From Getting Shot Down (Harvard Business Review Press, Boston, Massachusetts, 2010).

50 Wikipedia contributors. (2018, Dec 9). Carl Rogers. (Incongruence). In Wikipedia, The Free Encyclopedia. Retrieved December 18, 2018, from https://en.wikipedia.org/w/index.php?title=Carl_Rogers&oldid= 872775900.

51 Brian Thorne, Pete Sanders. (2013) Carl Rogers. P. 31.

52 Dr. John Demartini. (2002). The Breakthrough Experience, p. 106-108.

53 Wikipedia contributors. (2018, November 10). Oskar Schindler. In Wikipedia, The Free Encyclopedia. Retrieved 10:54, December 18, 2018, from https://en.wikipedia.org/w/index.php?title=Oskar_Schindler&oldid =868102552.

54 Frankl, V. (1959,1962,1984). Man's search for meaning, p. 97.

[55] The Guardian. (2018, December 28th). Great Pyramid tombs unearth 'proof' workers were not slaves.https://www.theguardian.com/world/2010/jan/11/great-pyramid-tombs-slaves-egypt.

[56] Stewardship. Merriam-Webster Dictionary. Retrieved 18:08, December 19 2018 from https://www.merriam-webster.com/dictionary/stewardship.

[57] Jocko Willink, Leif Babin. (2015). Extreme Ownership, p. 12.

[58] The Editors of Encyclopaedia Britannica. (July 04, 2018). Hyman G. Rickover. Retrieved December 19, 2018 from https://www.britannica.com/biography/ Hyman-G-Rickover.

[59] Major Edwin L. Kennedy Jr. (re-published 1991, Pickle Partner Publishing). Australian Light Horse: A Study Of The Evolution Of Tactical And Operational Maneuver, p. 15.

[60] Paulus, P. "Groups, teams, and creativity: the creative potential of idea-generating groups". Applied psychology. 49 (2): 237–262.

[61] Jocko Willink, Leif Babin. (2015). Extreme Ownership, p. 12.

[62] Kofman, F. (2018). The Meaning Revolution: Leading with the Power of Purpose, chapter 8 Response-Ability. United Kingdom: Ebury Publishing.

[63] Kofman, F. (2006). Conscious business: How to build value through values, p 46. Boulder, CO: Sounds True.

[64] Wikipedia contributors. (2018, October 27). Meaningful life. In *Wikipedia, The Free Encyclopedia*. Retrieved 11:06, December 20, 2018, from https://en.wikipedia.org/w/index.php?title=Meaningful_life&oldid=865917994

www.ingramcontent.com/pod-product-compliance
Lightning Source LLC
Chambersburg PA
CBHW072054020426
42334CB00017B/1503